I Am Aztlán:
The Personal Essay in Chicano Studies

Edited by
Chon A. Noriega and Wendy Belcher

UCLA Chicano Studies Research Center Press
Los Angeles

193 Haines Hall
Los Angeles, California 90095–1544 USA

E-mail: press@chicano.ucla.edu
Tel: 310-825-2642
Fax: 310-206-1784
Web: www.chicano.ucla.edu

UCLA Chicano Studies Research Center Press.
© 2004 by the Regents of the University of California
All rights reserved. Printed in the United States of America.

Essays reprinted from *Aztlán: A Journal of Chicano Studies*, except the introduction and article by Jerry Garcia, which are original to the edition.

Cover image reprinted by permission of Jerry Garcia © 1995

Library of Congress Cataloging-in-Publication Data

I am Aztlán : the personal essay in Chicano studies / Chon A. Noriega and
Wendy Belcher, editors.

  p. cm.

  Most articles previously published in Aztlán : a journal of Chicano studies,
between 1997 and 2003.

  "Bibliography of Chicana/o Autobiography and Personal Essays in Spanish &
English": p.

  Includes bibliographical references and index.

  ISBN 0-89551-099-5

  1. Mexican Americans--Ethnic identity. 2. Mexican American--Biography. 3.
Mexican Americans--Intellectual life--20th century. 4. Mexican Americans--
Social conditions--20th century. I. Noriega, Chon A., 1961- II. Belcher,
Wendy Laura. III. Aztlán.

  E184.M5I15 2004

                              2004048035

CONTENTS

Autobiography Without Apology
CHON A. NORIEGA AND WENDY BELCHER   V

Exile and Going Home

Subterranean Homesick Blues
MAX BENAVIDEZ   1

Phantoms in Urban Exile
HARRY GAMBOA JR.   11

The Maguey: Coming Home
SANTA C. BARRAZA   19

Home / Work

Research Note
CHON A. NORIEGA   25

Beyond the Cinema of the Other, or Toward Another Cinema
FRANCES NEGRÓN-MUNTANER   33

Entre Familia

Heroes and Orphans of the Hacienda: Narratives of a Mexican
American Family
VINCENT PÉREZ   41

The Measure of a Cock: Mexican Cockfighting, Culture, and
Masculinity
JERRY GARCIA   109

Testifying

Activist Latina Lesbian Publishing:
esto no tiene nombre and conmoción
TATIANA DE LA TIERRA   141

Silencing Our Lady: La Respuesta de Alma
ALMA LOPEZ   177

Breaking Down Glass Walls
RUBEN Ochoa   195

Field Reports

Turning Sunshine into Noir and Fantasy into Reality: Los Angeles in
the Classroom
ALVINA E. QUINTANA   201

Ethnicity, Fieldwork, and the Cultural Capital that Gets Us There:
Reflections from U.S. Hispanic Marketing
ARLENE DÁVILA   211

Bibliography of Chicana/o Autobiography & Personal Essays in Spanish & English

Primary Literature   231
    Books
    Anthologies
    Personal Essays
Secondary Literature

Index   249

Autobiography Without Apology

Chon A. Noriega and Wendy Belcher

In Rudolfo A. Anaya's novel *Heart of Aztlán* (1976), the protagonist leaves the barrio of Barelas in Albuquerque to search in the mountains for Aztlán, the mythical homeland of the Aztecs:

> Time stood still, and in that enduring moment he felt the rhythm of the heart of Aztlán beat to the measure of his own heart. Dreams and visions became reality, and reality was but the thin substance of myth and legends. A joyful power coursed from the dark womb-heart of the earth into his soul and he cried out I AM AZTLÁN! (131)

We take this cry as the starting point for this anthology. Anaya's protagonist had been looking for a myth of origins by returning to the sacred lands he had been forced to leave in order to seek employment in the city. But he finds, instead, himself—a "plural self" (Sommer 1988, 130), a singularity that nevertheless embodies a collective experience and call to action. Anaya's novel—published in the latter years of the Chicano civil rights movement—weaves together the communal and the personal through a narrative about labor relations, social protest, ethnic identity, and pre-Colombian spirituality. Indeed, the protagonist first learns about Aztlán at a meeting of striking union members!

We focus on the process of self-naming—the ubiquitous "I am . . ."—because it is found not just in early Chicano literary, performing, and visual arts, but in Chicano scholarship as well. Consider, for example, *Aztlán: A Journal of Chicano Studies*, which was founded in 1969 by a group of graduate and undergraduate students associated with the UCLA Chicano Studies Research Center. As the first issue announced, the center's publications "were created to provide responsible and reliable sources for materials on Chicanos" (1970, vi). The journal in particular was seen as "a forum for scholarly writings" and as the first university-sponsored serial publication on the Chicano population. Given this academic orientation, then, it is of note that the first text to appear in the new journal is an excerpt from "El Plan Espiritual de Aztlán," which ends by explicitly linking its political agenda with self-naming. "We are AZTLAN" it declares(1970, iv).

In so beginning, the editorial staff—which included Juan Gómez-Quiñones (history), Roberto Sifuentes (Spanish), Reynaldo Flores Macias (education), Andres Chávez (political science), and Deluvina Hernández (sociology)—not only challenged the earlier scholarly literature on Chicanos for its biases and prejudices, but also opened up a space for a "Chicano voice" within academic publishing. That is, by using the first person ("I" and "we") as part of a larger social and academic project, the editorial staff articulated a worldview and set of collective experiences that had been excluded from higher education, public policy, and popular discourse within the United States.

To be autobiographical, then, often represented an applied dimension within a scholarly article. By using "I," the Chicano scholar made particular claims within a field of study or discipline, often in sharp contrast to the general and more stereotypical arguments put forth by some non-Chicano scholars. But by drawing upon personal experience and self-reflection, the Chicano scholar also provided an arena within which these ideas could be tested, put to use, and improved. Thus, in the second issue of *Aztlán*, Gilbert Benito Córdova wrote a brief memoir on his experiences teaching, which started with a very atypical academic essay opening:

> During the summer of 1969 I was in charge of Head Start at
> my little community—Abiquiú, New Mexico. For the first time
> I was on my own professionally! Now I could try out all I had
> learned at college about child education. (103)

Arriving at the school, Córdova was quickly struck by the inappropriateness of both the English and Castilian Spanish storybooks provided to the children and invited local elders to the school to tell the children stories. This worked marvelously well: "The children fell in love with their storytellers and stories" (104). The article includes a transcription of a unique folktale by Steven Suazo, one of the elders, for use by other teachers of Chicana and Chicano schoolchildren.

Córdova did not offer a close reading or analysis, but neither was he content to just reproduce the tale. Instead, he expressed concern about the general approach to Chicano children as "underprivileged children, underachievers, underdeveloped children, culturally deprived, and so on" (104). After citing some scientific sources on the topic, Córdova wrote

> It seems to me that if any of these experts would stop for just a
> minute and think, it might occur to them that there is no
> such thing as a culturally deprived child. Either a child has a
> culture or he does not have a culture; and if the child does not
> have a culture, then he is not a human being. He is some
> other form of animal than human. As for the other terms,
> how about underprivileged children? Would its counterpart
> be overprivileged children? (105)

Córdova's use of the "I" in this brief, four-page essay is not only moving, but important. From it, we get insights into the motivations and efforts of early Chicano scholars and their intertwined educational and
political struggle. It encapsulates the commitment of so many Chicano
scholars who have sought to return their own advantages in education to
the community, but who have also approached their community as a resource in its own right and not as a "disadvantaged" place.

Since Córdova's article, many scholars have commented on the necessity of expressing the self and "drawing from our own specific racial and
cultural experience" to contribute to public knowledge and overcome the
strictures of the dominant culture (Herrera-Sobek and Viramontes 1988).
Yvonne Yarbro-Bejarno points out that in the context of oppression, to
focus on the self is not a selfish act: "The Chicana writer finds that the self
she seeks to define and love is not merely an individual self but a collective
one" (141). Indeed, "individual subjectivity [emerges] … through the ar-
ticulation of collective experience and identity" (143-44).

And yet, as a recent book observes, "At no point in the evolution of
higher education was the autobiographical or personal as a mode of learning or genre of writing considered valid" (Freedman and Frey 2004, 2). As
such, there has always been a defensive tendency among those who champion autobiography as a literary or scholarly form. The traditional disciplines reject our work! But in looking at Chicano studies, which has always
been interdisciplinary, we see something different: autobiography without
apology. This phrase is an allusion to Edén E. Torres's *Chicana Without
Apology* (2003), itself an excellent example of the critical self in cultural
studies. But such an approach is not new. Consider Ernesto Galarza's *Barrio
Boy* (1971), written as an anecdotal response to the "psychologists, psy-
chiatrists, social anthropologists and other manner of 'shrinks' [that] have
spread the rumor that these Mexican immigrants and their offspring have
lost their 'self-image'" (2). In contrast to this scientific "rumor," Galarza
wryly notes, "I can't remember a time I didn't know who I was. . . . It

seemed to me unlikely that out of six or seven million Mexicans in the United States I was the only one who felt this way" (2). What is of special interest here is that *Barrio Boy* is not *just* an autobiography. It was written and published as part of the United States–Mexico Border Studies Project at the University of Notre Dame and sponsored by a grant from the Ford Foundation. In other words, not unlike Torres's more recent book, Galarza's memoir was positioned *institutionally* as a scholarly contribution to the emerging field of Chicano studies. Ramón Saldívar, echoing Renato Rosaldo, situates the text in this broader context: "Replacing the political or philosophical essay, his autobiography is a personal document where historical self-explanation, philosophical self-analysis, and poetic self-expression merge to tell with irony and humor a social story: an individual's participation in one of the grandest migrations of modern times—the influx of Mexicans into the American Southwest" (168).

In this volume, we bring together several important personal essays published in Aztlán under our editorship since 1997. We also include one new essay that had been submitted to the journal and successfully peer-reviewed but that we felt rounded out the selections in this volume. The contributors are Chicana and Chicano, but also Puerto Rican and Cuban American; and they include scholars as well as writers and artists. The common thread involves their contribution to a Chicano studies journal and its thirty-five-year mission of creating "a forum for scholarly writings" related to the Chicano community. In these essays, the authors ask not so much the traditional autobiographical questions of "Who am I?" or "How did I become who I am?" but "How did we live and think?" They focus on where their lives intersect history writ large and small. In other words, the presence of the self is a given within the text. It is done without apology, which is not to say without being self-critical.

In the first section, "Exile and Going Home," three writers/artists reflect on exile and the process of going home as an integral aspect of the creative process. Max Benavidez writes about internal exile and displacement as a Mexican Angeleno. He writes lyrically about constructing his own identity through the process of recollection. He remembers learning English, listening to his great-grandmother's stories, reading Don Quixote, seeing the bruises on a beautiful bride, and following a Hopi Indian painter. Through the human drama of family, we absorb, struggle and grow up. And having created an identity through home, we must learn to tell those stories. Harry Gamboa Jr. documents and interprets the contemporary urban Chicano experience through almost a dozen electronic communications first circulated on

CHICLE, an electronic discussion list. He deconstructs the freeway, perceptual pollution, stereotypes, fine dining, call-in shows, anti-representatives, solipsistic conversations, and the death of self. Santa C. Barraza, the painter, remembers her journey home, after a twenty-five-year absence, to the Texas town where she was born. Reflecting on what she has learned in the interim, she offers that her artistic vision has been shaped by the land of South Texas and in particular the maguey, the symbol of home and identity.

In the second section, "Home / Work," two scholars examine their work and find some notion of "home" informing their intellectual inquiries. Chon A. Noriega writes about the influence of his father, the man "who inspired my ongoing intellectual quest." After discovering that his sister has saved all of their father's Mexican LPs, Noriega uses his skills as a historian and critic to examine the albums and come to a "more compassionate understanding of my father" and his career as a journalist, and thereby gain insights into his own career as a scholar. Frances Negrón-Muntaner, an award-winning filmmaker, writer, and cultural critic, asks how we can move beyond the supplemental status of the "cinema of the other" in order to produce "another cinema"? Originally presented at a panel, the essay went unpublished as too controversial. Negrón-Muntaner addresses the idea of home as an unresolved and politically charged problem to which film gives witness.

In the third section, "Entre Familia," two scholars critically challenge the code of silence about "internal" matters within the Chicano community signaled by the phrase *entre familia*. To identify an issue, such as sexism or homosexuality, as *entre familia*, was to say that it could not be talked about in public, and, hence, not at all, since doing so was believed to betray or undermine the Chicano community in its political struggles. Jerry Garcia, with one of the most provocative opening paragraphs in academic discourse, addresses the role of cocks in his father's life. Playing with ideas of masculinity and machismo, he describes the illegal cock fighting that the men in his family, Mexican immigrants, participated in. Garcia considers how cockfighting shapes familial relationships and its role in the daily life of his family. Vincent Pérez engages with both the literary tradition and the critical scholarship on Mexican American autobiography in telling the story of his grandfather. Through anecdotes, secrets, and personal memories he brings personal and national history together in telling us about Francisco Robles Perez and the secret rape that shaped his family history. Any biography has a complicated relationship to the truth; he examines testimonial memory as a form of repression and resistance.

In the fourth section, "Testifying," three writers/artists address the creation of public works of art and politics. Here the authors recount or reflect on their roles within public history. Alma Lopez, a visual and public artist, creates digital artwork of fantastically surreal images that recontextualize major cultural icons, bringing issues of race, gender, and sexuality into relationship with transnationalist myth and the urban environment. She reports from the field on recent censorship attempts against her work in New Mexico. Her response is a modern day *respuesta* to the Catholic Church, among others; and it provides an inspiring model for challenging institutional policies. Next, tatiana de la tierra offers a fascinating and thoughtful account of two Latina lesbian journals she co-founded and co-edited in the early 1990s. In addition to this important history, her essay offers a model for a self-critical account of Latino and Latina publications and their role within cultural and intellectual production. Last but not least, artist Ruben Ochoa responds to the glass walls and ceilings that have limited Chicano access to social and cultural institutions with … a glass zoot suit! In the fine tradition of Chicano conceptual art—for example, Asco's *Spray Paint LACMA, 1972*—Ochoa turns his own body into a cutting commentary on the exclusionary "white cube" of the American museum.

In the fifth section, "Field Reports," two scholars offer personal reflections on their pedagogy and research methodology. While in some ways less "personal" that the other essays in this collection, these also hit closer to home in terms of how we work in the academy. Alvina E. Quintana considers her experiences as a native Californian and a Chicana professor teaching East Coast students about Los Angeles. As the University of Delaware's resident multiculturalist, Quintana gives us a slice-of-academic life in the post-diversity moment. Her thoughts on multicultural pedagogies, particularly the responses of her mostly white students to course readings on ethnicity and social change, are illuminating. Arlene Dávila draws upon her recent ethnographic research on U.S. Hispanic marketing in order to raise questions about methodology and to offer a larger critique of the challenges posed to fieldwork and ethnography in the age of globalization. She argues that there is much to be learned from the predicaments of fieldwork and how researcher's ethnic backgrounds intersect with their research. In particular, she describes how her access to marketing agencies and employees were mediated by their perceptions of her. Dávila's concerns and insights echo those found in the first issues of *Aztlán*, for they speak to the necessary presence of the Chicano and Latino scholar within the very world he or she would study and thereby change.

We hope that these essays will prove useful not only to scholars of Chicano studies but also to students just embarking on their academic careers. The scholars—from history, anthropology, cultural studies, and literature—demonstrate the diverse ways in which personal voice and experience can inform both disciplinary and interdisciplinary research. The writers and artists demonstrate the continued importance of the arts within Chicano studies—not just as an object of study, but as a form of historical and analytical thinking central to the field's larger social mission.

Acknowledgment

This book was made possible in part by a generous grant from the University of California Institute for Mexico and the United States (UC MEXUS).

Works Cited

Anaya, Rudolfo A. 1976. *The Heart of Aztlán*. Berkeley: Editorial Justa Publications, Inc.

Córdova, Gilbert Benito. 1970. A Hispano Tale from Abiquiú, New Mexico. *Aztlán: A Journal of Chicano Studies* 1, no. 2 (fall): 103-110.

Galarza, Ernesto. 1971. *Barrio Boy*. Notre Dame: Notre Dame University Press.

Freedman, Diane P., and Olivia Frey. 2004. *Autobiographical Writing Across the Disciplines: A Reader*. Durham, NC: Duke University Press.

Herrera-Sobek, Maria, and Helena María Viramontes, eds. 1988. *Chicana Creativity and Criticism: New Frontiers in American Literature*. Albuquerque: University of New Mexico Press.

Saldívar, Ramón. 1990. *Chicano Narrative: The Dialectics of Difference*. Madison: University of Wisconsin Press.

Sommer, Doris. 1988. "Not Just a Personal Story": Women's *Testimonios* and the Plural Self. In *Life/Lines: Theorizing Women's Autobiography*, ed. Bella Brodzki and Celeste Schenck . Ithaca: Cornell University Press.

Torres, Edén E. 2003. *Chicana Without Apology: The New Chicana Cultural Studies*. New York: Routledge.

Yarbro-Bejarno, Yvonne. 1988. Chicano Literature from a Chicana Feminist Perspective. In *Chicana Creativity and Criticism: New Frontiers in American Literature*, ed. Maria Herrera-Sobek and Helena María Viramontes. Albuquerque: University of New Mexico Press.

Exile and Going Home

Subterranean Homesick Blues

Max Benavidez

> We are the river of Heraclitus, who said that the person of yesterday is not the person of today, who will not be the person of tomorrow. We change incessantly.
>
> Jorge Luis Borges, *Seven Nights*

I was born in Los Angeles, the quintessential temple of dreams. It is a megalopolis—willed out of a smoky desert—where mythmaking and illusion arise on a grand scale: a perfect setting for creating a defiant vision. Like every other place on earth, Los Angeles breeds its own aesthetic sense; it creates its own aesthetic moments. Here its basis is impersonal freeways, visual clutter, vast economic disparities, and a restless cultural eccentricity surrounded by disorder and fragmentation.

For a Mexican born in Los Angeles, it is a also a city of internal exile and displacement. The late twentieth-century Mexican Angeleno is often seen as part of a sub-working class with little formal education, scant resources, and no viable future. In a city founded by Mexican settlers, the Mexican floats within and around a highly stratified urban social structure. Not Native American, yet of the Indian. Not Spanish, yet of Europe. Not even Mexican in the strictest sense of the term. And the U.S.-born Mexican is rarely, if ever, considered "American."

As many have said, "History is hysterical." And U.S. Mexicans have experienced more than their share of racial and cultural hysteria.

I myself have lived such a life. I have lived through and survived hysterical cultural imperialism. Yes, I have also devoured the dominant culture. I learned to speak English without a Spanish accent. I read all the Western classics. Watched the great Hollywood movies and European art films. Consumed Coke. Went to Disneyland. I even owned a Chevrolet once upon a time.

1

Quixote in Durango

Above all, I was influenced by the English language. Ironic, really, since I come from a family where Spanish was in the air, woven into the texture of my aural life, a sotto voce soundtrack of the mind. I recall my maternal great-grandmother sitting in a rocking chair rolling her own cigarettes by hand, an ink-stained copy of *Don Quixote* in the original Spanish sitting on a table by her side, while she watched flickering black-and-white images of Mexican movies on the local Spanish-language television station. From time to time, she would talk to herself in Spanish. Years later, I memorialized her in a poem called "Durango."

> Grandmother
> Great grandmother
>
> I see your old trunk
> the one you brought
> from Mexico in 1913
>
> Wood, painted flowers
> cracked
> leather straps
>
> the tarot cards
> wrapped
> in black velvet
>
> whose fortune did you tell?
> yours? Mexico's?
>
> Grandmother
> great grandmother
> you read *Don Quixote*
> I touched your book
> I read the passages
> marked by your hand
> in thick India ink
>
> I remember
> you liked old movies
> They said you loved
> "The Hunchback of Notre Dame,"
> the 1939 version

In writing the poem, I recollected my memory. And, that process of recollection is one example of how I discovered and constructed my sense of cultural identity. I realized I was of Mexico in a very real sense through the traces of my great-grandmother's DNA that pulsed within me, along with her brave actions and eccentric predilections. When I touched her trunk, the one she had dragged all the way from Durango, Mexico, to Los Angeles, California, I touched a vestige of the dust roads and harsh tribulations of an actual refugee from the crimes and glories of the Mexican Revolution. When I read her copy of *Don Quixote*, I read a book she had handled with her two hands for many, many years. Those pages were infused with her energies and her essence.

In reading that particular book, I experienced a strange sort of empathy. Perhaps just as she entered into the work of art created by Miguel de Cervantes, I entered or "felt into" the book and through it, both in a tactile and intellectual sense, into her life. That feeling can be compared to the Theory of *Einfuhlung* where the spectator (or reader in this case) feels an instantaneous emotional identification with the work of art. I felt an intense identification with her, the book, and the author, and a commingling of all three in my mind.

Don Quixote became a building block of my personal literary cultural history. This cinematic Spanish novel that comments about a major historical transformation with great irony, humor, and literary creativity is a touchstone for me that "says" Mexico, culture, grandmother, Spanish, revolution, duality, and art all at once. Whether reading Vladimir Nabokov's lectures on *Don Quixote* or Borges's "Pierre Menard, Author of the Quixote," I was always reminded of the old woman who sat in my living room watching faded prints of old Mexican movies on Spanish-language television. In essence, my cultural sensibility was formed at an early age. As time went on and new cultural experiences entered my consciousness, I had already learned how to process them and even place them on a cultural list of priorities.

As Nabokov said, "The key to the problem of reestablishing the past turns out to be the key of art." In the same way, the key to the problem of establishing a cultural identity turns out to be the key of art. Just as in a novel, for example, there is a narrator who is created by the author, in cultural identity there is the consciousness that makes choices and takes bits and pieces from various life experiences to create a specific sense of self.

Stealing Beauty

I remember a very beautiful young woman from my childhood. She was my mother's cousin, Chata. At her wedding, as she walked down the aisle, her beauty seemed to stun everyone into speechless awe. And her groom, who looked like a bronze Elvis Presley, fell back with his hand raised in mild shock. It was as though he were saying, "She's too beautiful for me."

The wedding reception was a happy mélange of Mexican music, food, and dancing. I will never forget the green chile enchiladas or the perfection of the flan. For one moment in time, life seemed golden.

A few weeks after the wedding, my mother began getting mysterious phone calls from the bride. My mother would often take them in her bedroom and whisper in hushed Spanglish. I instinctively wanted to protect Chata.

Then, one night, very late, she showed up at our house with a suitcase. She was distraught. My mother told me to go to bed. I could hear crying in the living room. It was the bride sobbing.

My mother then took Chata into her bedroom. I had to see what was going on. With great stealth I tiptoed down the dark hallway and toward my parents' bedroom door. It was open just a crack. In the low light I could see my mother helping the bride undress. Chata stood still in a black silk slip, large purple bruises and welts on her arms and thighs. She took off her slip and showed my mother dark bruises on her firm brown breasts.

Her husband had been beating her for weeks. Every night he whipped her and then raped her.

I went back to my bed with a strange mixture of arousal and rage. I felt liquid. It was as though I was melting into the bed, into the floor, down into the earth. I realized I was crying.

I learned that night that beauty can be destroyed. I realized that there are destroyers. That a Cortés can come into a place, into a family, and destroy everything. It dawned on me that not just physical beauty can be destroyed but also our insides. The bruises could heal and disappear. The welts would fade away. Although Chata didn't see Francisco again, she was never the same.

Years later, we heard that she had died in a car crash. We all went to the wake. Her face looked so tired. They said it had to be reconstructed. Everything was all wrong. I remembered then that the actor Montgomery Clift had lived that way for many years, with one side of his face reconstructed. Like a fallen angel. Beauty can be lost or stolen, just like anything else. Like a movie star, Chata was the beautiful celebrity of our family and the object of our dreams and desires. And like a Marilyn Monroe or a Montgomery Clift, she could be broken into pieces; she could fall from grace.

Chata lay on the white pillow inside the coffin. She was dead but I think she really had died long before the car accident. She was already dead inside when she came to our house that night. It seemed to me then that some people were too fragile for life.

Years later, when I was reading *Pedro Paramo* by Juan Rulfo, I was reminded of Chata's husband, Francisco. Paramo and Francisco were the same: brutal bullies who enjoyed destroying beauty. They were the fascists. But I was also reminded of Chata when I came to the section in the book where two people converse inside their common grave.

One asks the other, "And your soul? Where do you think it's gone?" The other says her soul is wandering on earth, that it hated her and wanted her to keep living, but finally she just sat down to die.

"'This is the end,' I told it. 'I can't go any farther.' I opened my mouth so it could leave, and it left. I felt something fall into my hands. It was the little thread of blood that tied it to my heart."

That was Chata to me. She was tired of living her life. The man she adored, hated her. One day she simply could not stand it any longer. So she told her soul to leave and the next thing we knew she was dead in a car accident.

A Mexican Daedalus

All through my childhood there were people in my life such as Chata. While I was absorbing pop culture, continental literature, and foreign films, I was also observing the human dramas that were playing themselves out in my family. Since my family was Mexican on my mother's side and New Mexican on my father's side, drama, conflict, and the centrality of death were always close and laced with the Spanish language. *Muerto. Chismes. La familia.* Etc.

I also struggled with the undercurrent of prejudice that seemed to swirl around me as I was growing up. I remember going into a department store to buy some clothes and asking my mother if I could give the clerk the money. As I handed the money to the clerk she instinctively pulled back at the sight of my little brown hand. Her mouth tightened as she forced herself to take the money from me and then toss the change back into my waiting palm. I would never forget that little exchange because it made me realize that there were people who saw me as something to be avoided and looked down upon, an outcast.

Although English was the main language of my natal home, Spanish was the magical tongue. That dichotomy was the beginning of my consciousness about the power of language and the nature of duality. I remember being aware that I was involved in a life-and-death struggle. My intuition told me to master English. Study it. Dissect it like a scientist in a sociolinguistic laboratory.

Years later I read the self-exiled Irish writer, James Joyce, and realized he was a kindred soul. He, too, lived under cultural domination. He, too, knew what it was like to hear English spoken by its owners. Even more, he wrote down what it was like to bear linguistic and cultural dislocation. He wrote:

> The language we are speaking is his before it is mine. How different are the words *home*, *Christ*, *master*, on his lips and on mine! I cannot speak or write these words without unrest of the spirit. His language so familiar and so foreign, will always be for me an acquired speech. I have not made or accepted its words. My voice holds them at bay. My soul frets in the shadow of his language.

There it is. The "acquired speech." Something "foreign," like an invisible microbe, that insinuates its way deep into one's consciousness until every intimate thought is in English. This living, ever-present juxtaposed consciousness of something strange yet "familiar" made Joyce's soul fret "in the shadow." Like Joyce I vowed to be a shadow warrior. Unlike him, I wanted to find an island of tranquility in my troubled psychic landscape.

I searched for maps that could show me the way beyond bitterness and self-loathing. One map or path I found was Dante, the Italian poet and author of the *Divine Comedy*.

He was someone who started out with many difficulties and conflicts in his nature and yet he was able to turn them into something positive. I knew that in one way or the other, I had to create. That in the process of creation, in the process of transformation, there was salvation. Dante shows us in the *Divine Comedy*, in his epic of descent into the abyss, the journey of an individual from a state of confusion to a state of self-actualization. By studying Dante and his work, I was able to see that one can overcome conflict and produce something worthwhile out of that conflict.

Spider Woman's Son Spins Stories

Another path was shown to me by a Hopi Indian painter and poet whom I had met while on a magazine assignment. He helped show me the connection between creativity and spirituality. I spent a lot of time on the Hopi Reservation with him. In some strange way, he was the indigenous reflection of my roots. He and his father, a famous artist who had painted Hopi-inspired murals on walls of the U.S. embassy in India during the Franklin Roosevelt Administration, were extensions of my paternal roots in the pueblos of New Mexico.

Once he wanted to show me some ruins. A place called Awatovi. It was an old Hopi village that had been destroyed by the Hopi themselves in a conflicted mad rage in the 1600s because the village had converted to Catholicism. He wanted to show me some murals that still remained on the walls of crumbling kivas. He said they were his inspiration.

He borrowed his father's old pickup and we took off—to Awatovi. Out near Antelope Mesa. About halfway there it started to snow.

The snow fell in a white blur. We were on a dirt road filled with gashes, holes, and bumps, bouncing around inside the truck. I remember looking over to my right and seeing a group of wild horses. There must have been fifteen or twenty. I think they saw us just as we saw them. You know how horses can be: out of the blue they started to run with us.

We were heading south along this road with the snow driving down. The horses galloped right alongside us. We could see their breath steaming in the cold air, fuming out of their flared nostrils as they strained to keep abreast.

It was a like a dream.

At that point he told me he was a member of the Snow/Water clan and the snow meant that his dead relatives were watching out for us. And then he said, "In Hopi you are identified as a cloud when you die. Clouds bring rain and snow. They bring life. When I die I hope to return as a cloud."

In the midst of the wild horses, the steady snowfall, and the closeness of ancient, forbidden ruins (you needed a special permit to visit Awatovi)— he began to talk about one of his paintings. It was called, "Coming to Pick Up the Dead, or Entering into the Spirit World." In that painting, *kachinas*, the Hopi's masked gods, carry off a dead body.

He said, "The cloud spirits carry us into the cloud world."

We arrived at the ruins, the site of a massacre. The snow began to let up as we wandered around the old village, destroyed one night over three hundred years ago because it had converted to another religion, my birth religion.

We studied the faded paintings, peered down into abandoned kivas. The horses stood nearby, as if they were guardians sent by watchful gods to protect us from the toxic vapors of hate and destruction that subtly permeated the ruins.

That evening we sat in his mother's house. She lived in the old village of Shuongpovi on Second Mesa. It was pitch dark outside. A deathly quiet surrounded us. It was as if we were engulfed by a great, deafening silence.

He told me that the Hopi were still practicing their ancient ceremonies, that they live by a ceremonial calendar. I didn't have the nerve to tell him that I had been raised Catholic but no longer practiced.

The next morning I awoke before dawn. I went outside and saw waves of gray clouds rolling above the mesas from the east, rushing toward me at a great speed. I didn't believe it then. I couldn't believe it. But the clouds were people who had died during the night. And above me, in the form of fleeting clouds, the dead were being carried off into the spirit world.

From this Hopi painter I learned that I had to go back to my home and my culture and tell the world about the stories that I found there.

Notes from the Underground

So I came back to Los Angeles and began telling the stories of Chicano artists in Los Angeles. I was especially attracted to ASCO (Spanish for nausea or repulsion), the underground art group from East L.A. To me they were the Beatles of the Chicano art scene. Before they broke up, they epitomized life in Los Angeles as a Mexican. Their work captured the essence of the times, the harsh yet ironic truth hidden behind the ideological and cultural facade of Chicano fundamentalism.

The Chicano art that has come to occupy my attention is about alienation and estrangement. It is about the duality of presence and invisibility: about the coexistence of pride and self-loathing; about moral corruption and cultural redemption. Taking my cue from the fictional antiheroes of nineteenth-century gothic literature, who were aware of their duality and torment, I attempted to outline Chicano gothic art.

Such art brings us images of tormented and heightened self-consciousness laced with grim cynicism. One aspect of this antithetical or double identity is self-abhorrence.

All my life I have never felt hatred or bitterness toward "white" or Anglo people. Hatred and racism are my enemies and I never wear their masks because I find these twin sins disfiguring.

But there was a period in my life when I simulated whiteness in response to my experiences of prejudice and discrimination. It was not assimilation because I still retained a secret sense of my Mexican self and what that meant in this society. However, it was simulation. I couldn't change the color of my skin but I could act white, speak white, even pretend to think white. Simulation is to assume a false appearance. This simulation of a plastic whiteness was a pretense, a false front that I presented to the world, even to myself. I was very good at it. In a sense, it was my first performance art.

So self-abhorrence can come in many forms. Some Chicanos loathe the created "white" self as well as the Mexican self who allowed the creation of the simulated, masked persona. While it is an act of creation, this manufactured self can be a monster, not a beautiful creation but a horrible one.

Like the tormented creature in Mary Shelley's "ghost story," *Frankenstein*, the self-aware Chicano knows what it's like to be maligned, misunderstood, caught in the tangle of an anxious but romantic terror of hyper self-consciousness and, as Harold Bloom put it, living as "the antithetical halves of a single being." As artists and individuals, we Chicanos survive racism and its malignant growths by taking the real, if somewhat abstract, torment of our metaphysical desires and transforming them into a calculated and often subtle assault on the cultural status quo.

As the new millennium unfolds, the circumstances we find ourselves in have an eerie resemblance to those encountered by the creators of gothic fiction. The early nineteenth-century, as in the late twentieth-century, was a time of great turbulence: political, social, economic, cultural, and existential. The Chicano has lived with this type of turbulent upheaval throughout history. Ironically, it is this very awareness that gives Chicano art, especially the art made in Los Angeles, a spectacular resonance with our times. It also seems that the rest of American society has caught up with the ironic disillusion born of barrio-influenced life.

If there is one painting that represents our historical moment for me, it is Gronk's signature piece for his "Hotel Senator" exhibition. With that one painting, he reached a gothic height. The blue creature, whose head is on fire, functions as a signifier for the whole series.

I noted in an essay at the time: "This thing has intuited Auschwitz, Chernobyl, Soweto and San Salvador—not by reading the international news but through the banal experience of life's incessant brutality. . . . this being has been emotionally lobotomized by incremental violations of the spirit." It could be about accursed humanity at any point in history, anywhere. It could be the L.A. riots. The Oklahoma City bombing. That power to "read" the raw depravity of humanity gives "Hotel Senator" a mythic edge. What I saw was the impermanence and horror of life elevated to a supernatural level where the two become that thing that art and high religious ritual can be: witness to our being.

"For one translucent moment," I wrote, "within the confines of our brief existence we are totally transfixed by our reflection. That's when we experience what someone once called the 'ecstasy of catastrophe.' The depravity and ungraspable forces we see in 'Hotel Senator' are frightening not because they exist somewhere downtown but because they exist within us."

What many Chicano artists in Los Angeles have accomplished is to present us with images that come out of a long line of defiant questioning and self-questioning, not only of our own position in this society but our very circumstance as human beings. Because of our acute awareness of our bicultural reality, of our divided selves, many of us have reached excessive levels of self-consciousness. Like the Romantic writers such as Mary Shelley, we have tried to overcome this through the use of our imaginations. Although our cultural and social heritage cannot be divorced from our very existence, there is in our work a potential opening that amplifies our experience and illustrates the parallels between our specific cultural condition and the existential reality we all face.

Keeping the Demons Out

When Frankenstein's creature asks, "Who was I? What was I? Whence did I come? What was my destination?" he is unable to find an answer.

But there is an answer; there is an escape route. Liberation comes with the knowledge of who we are, what we are, where we came from, where we are going.

A. I. Becker, in an essay on the *wayang kulit*, the Bali shadow puppet theater, asked a master puppeteer how the *wayang* controls power gone amuck, demons, disease, or stupidity? Sources of chain-reacting linear power? The closest answer to his question: "'The music and shadow play move round and round and keep the demons out.' Then the puppet master paused, laughed heartily, and added, 'Demons think in straight lines.'"

The answer for those of us still in the ever-constant process of creating a cultural identity is to move round and round. To recognize the wisdom in coincidence. To realize that paradox is a form of logic. As the puppeteer also said, "Demons and people possessed go in straight lines." It is time for us to curve around each other. To not talk straight and to keep the demons out.

Phantoms in Urban Exile

Harry Gamboa Jr.

Man under the Asphalt

I've heard rumors that the freeways in L.A. are the concrete ribbons of a package that will never be opened before exodus. The asphalt coating of billions of square feet is the icing on the multiple social layers of a dysfunctional environment. I speed along at 70 mph, attempting to tie a perfect knot of the Pasadena Freeway, the Golden State Freeway, and the Ronald Reagan Freeway. Miles accumulate as I repeat the round trips, week after week, until finally a metallic implosion—compounded by leaking oil, burnt rubber, and bent plastic—causes my '88 Ford Festiva to succumb to 192,006 miles of abuse. I walk across an urban desert in search of an oasis. My cup of sand runneth over. I am crawling under the oppressive smog and heat until my bones are bleached white near the anonymous necropolis of stranded motorists. Within a few days, a new coating of asphalt decorates the urbanscape with an opaque black facade. I cannot see or hear the traffic that speeds by as I rest in peace and silence.

Amnesia in the Air

Faces, places, and names are all a blur as I run to the nearest pay phone. I dial numbers at random until my fingers are bloodied. The operator demands to know what this is all about. I can't explain but it is extremely urgent that I get through to someone who can make sense of what I've just witnessed. The victims are sprawled across the hoods of cars, across parking lots, sidewalks, public spaces, private homes, and freeways. The worst of it is that they have no idea of what has happened to them. They are

11

vanishing like aimless ants descending into the catacombs of self-nullification. The buzzing of the phone harmonizes with the sad melody of the victims who whistle while nothing works. The concrete tumbleweeds stampede against the one-way street like anonymous heads that roll in disbelief. I continue to dial until I reach you, hoping that no explanation will suffice, and that the sound of a hissing noise will provide a lost memory of adequate human communication.

No Tears in Dystopia

The brutal marks have disappeared via erase relations. The beautiful smile, awkward glance, flick of the wrist as the knife heads toward its victim, all of the images vanish when exposed to the hypnotic toxic whitewash. The Santa Ana winds have kicked up the dust and for a brief moment the veneer of normalcy is exposed as an artificial portrait of decay. The actual surface of experience is stretched beyond transparency. Awareness bursts as the tip of the blade finds its mark at the societal jugular. Nothing bleeds because it is all a hoax. The collapse of memory is contagious and we are all lost on our own turf. Zombies execute poor judgment but we are nevertheless under the law and order of the walking dead. I have irradiated dust in my eyes and everything appears to be glowing and eternal. The mirage of personal perspective persists even when the lights are out. My iris is in crisis. My cries against perceptual pollution are manifested by the evaporation of tears that are scattered as lost angel dust by the violent winds.

The Sky Has Fallen

The shattered glass takes on the form of a distended chandelier that encompasses my field of vision. The buildings continue to shake as the windows are propelled beyond the horizon. I am dancing on the high wire as the domino effect causes a perpetual wave of social collapse. There are no survivors as the pattern of collective shock eliminates perceptual stability. The wire becomes increasingly taut with each step as the distance between the rumba, cha cha, the twist, and the disaster below is exaggerated by a tremendous height. The harsh winds make coexistence with erratic cyclones a fact of life. Glass particles penetrate the solitude of the dead. I look forward and see that the wire heads skyward into nothingness. Each step requires a certain tap of the shoe, a particular realignment of the toe, and a major pivotal response. In order to counter imbalance, I must present an assertive attitude that rejects the forces of gravity and aerodynamics. The rubble and rotting flesh blends easily with the scintillating facade that was once a valid environment. Altitude and direction become increasingly irrelevant as a dark fog settles in. I continue to dance to the beat of fundamental forces that are beyond awareness. Intuition takes the lead as I follow.

Eating my Own Memory

MENU: When the crash course is the main course, no tip is required. There isn't time to digest the images or to discuss the issue of disgust. A quick byte leads to perceptual deprivation.

WAITER: I recommend the atomic burrito special. Not too spicy and there are plenty of hot neutrons wrapped in a wonderful blanket of lead tortillas.

CUSTOMER: I'll have the number 5. Can you replace my tacos with something less invasive?

WAITER: You can have plutonium in your guacamole as a substitution but you'll have to pay in advance and in cash.

CUSTOMER: Is that the normal policy of this restaurant or have you just been through too many unexpected detonations in your time?

WAITER: I've seen it all and I promised never to be stiffed by someone who doesn't intend to be around for too long anyway.

CUSTOMER: Let me talk to the manager. Your attitude stinks.

WAITER: So does the food. It's the manager's day off. I settle all complaints. What's the problem?

CUSTOMER: You're the problem. All I wanted was a slight change in my order and I wanted to put it on my green charge card.

WAITER: That's impossible. No exceptions. I reserve the right to refuse service to anyone and since you're just "anyone," get the hell out of here.

CUSTOMER: O.K. Here's $20.00 and a promise not to complain. I'm very hungry and desperate for the chain reaction of anonymous beans. Keep the change.

WAITER: The customer is always right.

MENU: Not responsible for lost or stolen stereotypes.

Refried Has-Been

RADIO: WE MUST REMEMBER THAT EACH EFFECT HAS A CAUSE BUT THAT NOT EVERY CAUSE IS EFFECTIVE.

LISTENER: Racist brainwasher. Give me a jingle not jingoistic poetry.

RADIO: THE COUNTRY SUPPORTS OUR POSITION. SHOOT EVERYONE ON SITE IF THEY DON'T HAVE WHITE IN THEIR "I."

LISTENER: Is this AM, FM, or Exterminate 'em?

RADIO: OUR BORDERS NEED TO BE BLOCKADED. OUR SCHOOLS NEED TO BE DESIGNED FOR CULTURAL DRAINAGE. OUR PRISONS MUST BE POPULATED TO SUPPORT THE NEW MIDDLE CLASS OF SECURITY PERSONNEL.

LISTENER: This isn't a voice, it's a hypnotic mantra. Shut up.

RADIO: THEY EVEN HAVE THE AUDACITY TO PENETRATE SUBURBIA. THEY SHOULD GO BACK TO THEIR URBAN HELLHOLES. I DON'T WANT THEM IN MY NEIGHBORHOOD.

LISTENER: I prefer to listen to music, not dangerouis static. Maybe if I push a button . . .

RADIO: GOT A RUSH FROM THE BLOOD THAT GUSH FROM YOUR HEAD
ON MY WAY FOR THAT HAPPY MEAL
NOT MUCH OF A LAST SUPPER

JACKING EVERYTHING IN SIGHT
I KNOW IT AIN'T RIGHT
FEELING GOOD
MUNCHING ON FAKE FOOD

AIN'T GOT THE CHANGE
BUT THE GLOCK IS AS GOOD AS GOLD
GIVE ME SOME FRIES AND A COKE
PUT SOME 9 MM PEPPER ON YOU

LISTENER: I shouldn't believe everything I hear. Sometimes the noise just keeps me company.

Defy the Reign

Dear Anti-Representative,

I am writing to you out of concern for the safety of my culture, my children, my job, my health, my air, my water, my skin, and my existence/coexistence/subsistence. Your veiled hatred has holes in it. Are you gasping for that final breath or are you spewing venom? Your public persona comes in crisp and clear whether the TV is on or off. You have made a mess of things with surgical precision. How did you manage to produce such a plague of self-hatred? Certainly mass hypnosis is a trick.

The rabid rabbit in your hat has been gnawing on everything that generates positive self-esteem. The lucky rabbit's foot you've been passing around spreads the germ of doubt, paranoia, violence, and unnatural disaster. There are many of your nonconstituents who have voted to cure our environment of your infectious waste. With the help of the many concerned citizens and noncitizens who have incurred your wrath, please be advised that an antidote is forthcoming. No thanx for your lack of concern.

Siempre,

Anonymous Anomaly

(This message has been rubber stamped onto the foreheads of unassuming party members, party crashers, and part-time employees who work for the overthrow of exploiters in blue suits or starched skirts.)

No Magic in Realism

There is a card trick in which all of the aces are burned, the hearts are broken, the diamonds are lost, the joker is rabid, the clubs and spades are buried up the sleeves of quick-talking dealers who manage to read your mind as they empty your pockets. A similar game can be played with exploding dice, poisoned dominoes, and 9 mm roulette. The game of NO CHANCE is as popular as ever.

Round and around it goes, where it stops nobody knows. Life and death are on the same coin.

People vanish but they never reappear. Is that a trick?

Mass hypnosis vs. mass hysteria, is that a question or a trick with mirrors?

Tossing knives into the air and running out into the rain, is that a trick?

Never any answers to the important questions. Pick a number, spin the wheel, and let it ride. Bet it all.

Premonition of a Déja Vu

MYSELF: I knew I would have been there before but the opportunity was lost before it had ever begun.

YOURSELF: You're losing it. Get a grip. Make sense.

MYSELF: I didn't feel it would happen so suddenly. Everyone is gone. I can't recognize anyone anymore. There really isn't much difference between inorganic and organic matter.

YOURSELF: In your case that is quite obvious. I could carbon date your brain and wind up with a date somewhere near July of next year.

MYSELF: Everything looks like it will be so familiar tomorrow. But what am I supposed to do about today?

YOURSELF: Masturbation is out of the question. You've got no sense of passion or privacy.

MYSELF: My watch is permanently set to high noon. It is OK to be correct at least twice a day.

YOURSELF: I liked it better when you were in a coma.

MYSELF: Every time I blink I am convinced that I'm dying.

YOURSELF: Do caffeine I.V.

MYSELF: My awareness is mainlined to eternity but it's boring.

YOURSELF: Close your eyes and count backwards from one billion.

MYSELF: Zzzzzzzzzzzzzzzzzzzzzzzzzzzzzzzzzzzzzzzzzzzzzzzzzzz.

Tiptoe through the Aftermath

(A man/woman is walking in his/her neighborhood without the aid of a gun. Toes are exposed through torn socks/stockings. His/her shoes were blown off by an unexpected burst of energy. He/she is looking for meaning in the charred ruins. Fragments of objects jut out from the ground to form a random path of chaotic swirls. The man/woman is amused by an endless landscape of smoke and ash. He/she steps into the first of many paths to come. Each step leads closer to the end. He/she entertains himself/herself by singing a song to the mysterious shadows, which remain eternally motionless. The unintentional melancholy and melody become a subtle memory of disaster.)

He/she: You stick your right foot out,
               You stick your left foot in,
               There's never a partner when you need to
               Overdosey dose.

               C'mon baby,
               Let's do the twist,
               C'mon honey,
               It's a nuclear mist,
               'Round and around we go,
               In a brilliant cloud like this,
               Let's do the twist,
               Let's do the fission twist.

(He/she suddenly slips into an abyss of redundancy as the swirling path runs into itself causing a frightening array of high voltage sparks and violent chemical reactions. He/she is vaporized into a sour note that no one hears.)

Note

Phantoms in Urban Exile (1995–1997) were an original series of email communications first distributed via The Chicle electronic discussion list hosted at The University of New Mexico. To learn more about Gamboa's work, please see www.harrygamboajr.com.

The Maguey: Coming Home

Santa C. Barraza

In the hot, humid summer of 1996, after twenty-five years of absence from Kingsville and the South Texas soil where I was born, I am driving home. I am moving back. I am traveling on a surreal, blacktop highway, straight and flat as can be found only in South Texas. I was born in a flat place, a place of marshlands and prairie grass, where you can see for miles and where the intensity of the heat rises as vapor on the horizon. You can see it rising as steam and escaping into the sky. I begin to reflect back on a time when my ancestors occupied that land. I loosely combine those thoughts with what I have learned while I have been away from my birthplace. . . .

My artistic vision comes from this timeless land. It comes from looking at the South Texas horizon line and observing the land melting into the sky—the two merging together in infinity. I am entranced by the combination of these opposing forces—the earth and the sky, the physical and the immaterial ethereal, blending and becoming one. This perspective inspires creativity and moves me to question why—to question the unknown, to ponder the unconscious. The creative forces come forth from this source, from this land. And I am moved to wonder about those who came before us—our *antepadres* and *antemadres*. What did they do? Did they feel the same way about nature, about the sky, about the cosmos? Because it is so powerful, so overwhelming, this harsh, sometimes unforgiving land, whose history Gloria Anzaldúa describes as "una herida abierta" (open wound) (1987, 3), inspires creation. I have learned that this land centers me. It envelops, teaches, and compels me to become one with it—to create, to bring forth those ideas, those forces.

As I drive down the monotonous blacktop, the undulating hum of the tires against the road reminds me that I have embarked upon a journey. Leaving Chicago, upon reaching the outskirts of the windy city, I found abundant cornfields lining the highway on either side. Those beautiful, bountiful fields lined the charcoal road, creating an opening, a gateway. They formed a passageway leading me back to Texas. ...

As I continue to drive deeper into Texas, I see a large maguey slightly ahead of me, on my right. I stop the car. The maguey—or, more specifically, its image—has become an icon for me. Because it is indigenous to this area, it is a symbol of home and identity. My mother, Frances Contreras, always told us, "Plant a maguey in front of your house, in your front yard; it brings good luck to the house." Thus she planted a maguey in front of our house. When you think about home, you think about your mother. She was creative—she conceived you and gave you life. Like the maguey, woman is life sustaining. As the plant renews and sustains life, woman procreates and maintains. The maguey is the symbol of home, of *hogar*.

I would use the maguey in my own work because I could relate to it—because of the legends, myths, history, folklore, and spirituality affiliated with it, and because it is tied directly to my mother. I remember her stories about the maguey, and then I recall her dissatisfaction with my using it as a symbol in my artwork. Her worries stemmed from a local story about soldiers in the Mexican Revolution who would copulate with the maguey in the battlefields. Its leaves then would produce ghost images of a fetus. She felt that it was bordering on witchcraft to use the plant in my artwork.

To fully appreciate the importance and symbolism associated with the maguey, one needs to consider the plant's origin. According to myth, the young goddess Mayahuel was stolen by Ehecatl-Quetzalcoatl. She was chased by the feared star demons, Tzitzimime, who destroyed her. Ehecatl-Quetzalcoatl buried her body. The first maguey plant sprouted over her grave (Miller and Taube 1993, 112). Consequently, Mayahuel is represented emerging from this particular plant, symbolic of vegetation-fertility.

It is not surprising that, similar to the maguey goddess, the Virgin of Guadalupe appeared above a maguey. In 1531, ten years after the conquest, the Lady appeared at the hill of Tepeyac, the same site where the earth goddess Tonantzin was worshipped. She left her imprint on maguey fiber—on the *tilma* of Juan Diego.

In pre-Columbian times, the actual maguey plant also was the temple of worship for the Aztecs. The victim was sacrificed over the plant; and the human heart—the life force of the body—was offered to Huitzilopochtli, their supreme deity of war, and placed over it. Thus, through the process of sacrificing and offering the victim, life, death, and spirituality were combined and integrated into this plant. Metaphorically, the plant then became a significant point of departure from which the soul of the sacrificed victim carried his or her message from the immediate community to the gods. A mythico-religious concept of the central force of life and death of this entity—of life and death, resurrection, rebirth, and regeneration—was embodied in the image of the maguey. This is how, personally, the cactus has become an important symbol of the incarnation of the forces of nature and humanity.

In the summer of 1996, my journey is coming to an end as I ponder all these things during the fifteen-hundred-mile drive from the Midwest to South Texas. I contemplate my decision, at age forty-five, to return to Kingsville to begin another *etapa* (stage) in my lifelong struggle to reclaim my own Chicana identity. I've done much of my work elsewhere, outside *Tejas*, especially in Pennsylvania and Chicago. But now I am returning home, to the place that it hardest of all to live in—the disputed, often violent space of South Texas, the Borderlands. I am returning to the contradictions, dualities, and daily resistance to the historical obliteration of our female selves—as *nativas*, *indígenas*, *mestizas*, Chicanas, Mexica-Tejanas. Gloria Anzaldúa, Chicana *patlache* feminist theorist and writer, as well as author Pat Mora, uses the concept of *Nepantla* to describe the in-between spaces that Chicanas always have occupied, the spaces within which we have constructed ourselves and our history. This concept articulates the structure of the artwork I have been doing all my life.

Yet I do not feel that I am "at home" until I notice water standing in the highway. This optical illusion is caused by the intense heat of this area rising from the roadway into the surrounding dry air. The movement distorts the vision and creates wavy images that appear to be situated directly above a roadway with water lying on it. Since the terrain is so flat, I can see for miles ahead of me as I drive. The entire horizon begins to shimmer. This is a South Texas mirage. I am being welcomed by the topography and climatology.

Within a couple of days, I have seen the land slowly transformed from an urban Chicago scene into a South Texas landscape—a unique experience. It is a hot, humid, arid place, but it is home. Finally I am home again.

Note

Excerpted from "Santa C. Barraza: An Autobiography," *Santa Barraza: Artist of the Borderlands*, edited by María Herrera-Sobek. Number 5, Rio Grande/Río Bravo Series. College Station, Texas: Texas A & M University Press, 2001. Used with permission. To order, call toll-free 1-800-826-8911.

Works Cited

Anzaldúa, Gloria. 1987. *Borderlands/La Frontera: The New Mestiza*. San Francisco: Aunt Lute Books.

Miller, Mary Ellen, and Karl Taube. 1993. *The Gods and Symbols of Ancient Mexico and the Maya: An Illustrated Dictionary of MesoAmerican Religion*. New York: Thames and Hudson.

Home / Work

Research Note

Chon A. Noriega

Men should sing with their heads thrown back, with their mouths wide open and their eyes shut. Fill your lungs, so they can hear you at the pasture's farther end.

> Américo Paredes, *"With His Pistol in His Hand"*:
> *A Border Ballad and Its Hero*

Perhaps don Américo was wrong, men should *not* sing with their heads thrown back, with their mouths wide open, and their eyes shut. In the pasture's farther end, another story echoes. ...

> Chon A. Noriega, *Shot in America: Television, the State, and the Rise of*
> *Chicano Cinema*

On a recent trip to Chicago, I encountered a most unusual set of artifacts that challenges my own challenge from the quotation above. I will write about these artifacts momentarily, but first I want to provide some context. In my book about the rise of Chicano cinema, I had sought "the irony of knowing more than your own story" in order to render a more complicated account of how minorities first gained access to film and television. To me, that history was filled with paradox, irony, and ambivalence, whereas Américo Paredes presented the archetypal study of Chicano resistance through a masculine expressive form, the corrido. Paredes was none other than the father of Chicano studies, and what he had to say about the corrido—and resistance more generally—seemed to be all about my own father. I knew that story all too well, and so I looked elsewhere. Besides, as I confessed in the acknowledgments, I could not sing. . . .

While I stand by my original research, and my challenge of Paredes, I have begun to wonder if perhaps I was wrong, too. In other words, if the history I wrote was filled with paradox, irony, and ambivalence, then the same must be true of the historian himself. In fact, as I noted at several points in my book, it was often difficult to draw clear boundaries between historian and history: there were certain events I simply could not narrate as a historian and so on these points I remained silent. And I acknowledged this. These silences were self-conscious attempts to honor and yet contain my participation as an advocate and activist within the historical narrative I was telling. I would have to write about this part of my intellectual life in another context.

But there was another, more profound silence within my book that spoke to a relationship outside the book's subject matter. This relationship had to do with the person who inspired my ongoing intellectual quest: my father. He did so in a way that drove me to approach all things as a life-and-death struggle. But he also wrote poetry. And how he could sing, throwing his head back and filling his lungs, so that he could be heard at the neighborhood's farther end … much to the horror of my sister. In Miami, where we grew up, corridos and rancheras stood out, calling attention to our difference from the Cuban and Anglo neighbors.

In January 2002 I discovered a new archive in Chicago: my sister Reni's collection of our father's Mexican LPs. As a child, I had fixated on the album covers, the most intriguing of which showed Antonio Aguilar kneeling over his dead horse, pistol raised, and head thrown back, singing a corrido, of course (see fig. 1). My father, who listened to these albums every weekend, informed me somewhat tongue-in-cheek that in Mexico all songs were love songs, and the objects of these songs were either horses or women, but mostly horses. He taught himself to play guitar and sing his favorite love songs, and when he played, I would always request that he sing my favorite song of all, "Cucurrucucú Paloma." Most summers our family returned to his hometown of Alamogordo, New Mexico, where my father would sing a corrido to and about his own father, Gavino Noriega. I now suspect he had modified another corrido, "Gabino Barrera," from the Aguilar album with the dead horse.

While I have carried the image of these albums with me to this day, I had long since let go of them as objects. So it was a surprise to find them in my sister's living room, especially since she never quite identified with our

CORRIDOS : ANTONIO AGUILAR

GABINO BARRERA
Y 11 EXITOS MAS

153

musart

Fig. 1. Album cover of Gabino Barrera y 11 Exitos Más by Antonio Aguilar.

Mexican patrimony. Nevertheless, she had made a point of preserving these albums, even if she never listened to them, could not understand them, and had even forgotten she had taken possession of them. My sister shared my own commitment to the archive, where one collects first and asks questions later. Now, with the objects in my hands again, we began asking questions about our father that ended up providing some answers about ourselves.

The albums can be divided into two periods. The first group was purchased in the early 1960s, apparently in the two years between my birth and that of my sister. The singers are male and exemplify postrevolutionary masculine ideals in Mexico: Jorge Negrete, Pedro Infante, Antonio Aguilar, Javier Solis, and Los Tres Ases. Solis clearly served as the model for my father's singing voice. I imagine my father felt considerable cultural dislocation and isolation in Miami and that these singers provided a connection with his sense of self as a "Mexican." If so, that connection was an ironic one on at least two levels. First, from what I can gather, my father's taste in music during the 1950s ran much more toward country and western and rock 'n roll. Indeed, he loved to sing Hank Williams and Johnny Cash songs and he wore heavy black-rimmed glasses that affected a "Buddy Holly" look. Second, the imprints for these albums came from Miami-based companies; the very place that created a sense of cultural isolation also served as a gateway for the music that eased that isolation.

At the time, my father was a reporter covering the Latin American beat for the Associated Press. But after a few close calls during the Cuban Missile Crisis, he realized that the political upheaval in Latin America was too dangerous for a new father. And so he left journalism for a career in public relations (see fig. 2). He also left behind his Hemingway-esque aspirations to become a writer. But he clung to love songs that helped define what it meant to be Mexican after the revolution.

Former Sports Editor Takes PR Position

Saturnino Noriega, f o r m e r Florida state radio-tv editor for the Associated Press, has been named senior account executive of the Gerald Schwartz Agency, Miami Beach public relations firm.

Noriega, who was with the AP for two and one-half years, was sports editor of the Alamogordo Daily News prior to serving in the United States Army for two years.

He has traveled extensively in Mexico and the Caribbean and will direct the Latin American division o f the Schwartz Agency.

SATURNINO NOREIGA

Fig. 2. Article from *Alamogordo Daily News* (New Mexico) c. 1963.

In 1972 my father was promoted and transferred to the regional office in Chicago of a trade association. We entered the middle class in a dramatic fashion, moving into Hemingway's suburban hometown, Oak Park. The second group of albums was purchased in 1978 and 1979, a period during which my parents divorced, my father lost his job, and I left home. The singers are female and are fewer in number: Lola Beltrán and Maria de Lourdes. Sometimes the songs are the same, songs about a person who would rather suffer, accept blame, and even be lied to than be alone. Only now that person was a woman, at least in song. In this period, my father and I attended a performance by Antonio Aguilar at a sports arena in Chicago. Aguilar rode his horse from one end of the arena to the other, singing corridos about crossing the border to a new and uncertain life. It was as if the album cover had come to life in the heroic moments just before the horse would be shot. In such moments, sombrero in hand and head thrown back, a man could survive anything. My father, who endured and struggled against rather explicit racism from his employers before losing his job altogether, slowly built his own business over the next two decades. I was one of his first employees. He also rebuilt his life, as did my mother. Last year, he retired and returned to Alamogordo, building his own house, although his second wife drove the tractor.

The value of the archive is not always what one would expect. I remember everything. And I have pictures, too. But these artifacts have challenged such certainties, bringing a nuanced and more compassionate understanding of my father and his impact on my life. Sitting in my sister's living room, we listened to each of these albums, some nearly forty years old, while I translated the lyrics. Our father's spirit was in the room—in us—whereas before it had been the room, the neighborhood, the universe. His history was now ours, too, rather than being the thing that had created and stood between us in our need for each other.

After we had listened to the albums, and my sister promised to burn them into CDs for me, we put on a formative album from our youth—a collection of disco hits—and spent the next hour dancing with Reni's five-year-old daughter, Anna. My nephew Martin, two years older than his sister, peered in from the hallway, embarrassed by our dancing. Decades from now Anna and Martin may re-encounter that album and reclaim a bit of the past in each other. They need each other, and someday they will need to understand why (see figs. 3 and 4).

This essay is a research note because it signals a profound and still-emerging change in my scholarship. I wanted to write about the personal

Fig. 3. Chon and Reni, around ages 7 and 5. Photo by Saturnino Noriega.

basis for that change insofar as it relates to my object of study and the historical method. For the past decade, my personal history has functioned as a structuring subtext or as an allegory informing my research. As such, the archive allowed me to confront my past as an object—or as a set of artifacts—that I could isolate, understand, narrate, and thereby master. That is one reason why I remained silent when I encountered myself as a political actor within my own historical narrative. I seemed to be all over

Fig. 4. Anna and Martin, ages 5 and 7. Photo by Reni Celeste.

the place: writer, allegory, and actor. This conundrum of our place within our own work and the world is the intellectual's dark side. We cannot bring light to this place—the fantasy of enlightenment being that the mind can free itself from the body and its past—but we can bring understanding and compassion to the darkness. This editor's commentary is a note—a tone, a sounding, a key of an instrument—that serves as one way in which I can sing for my father.

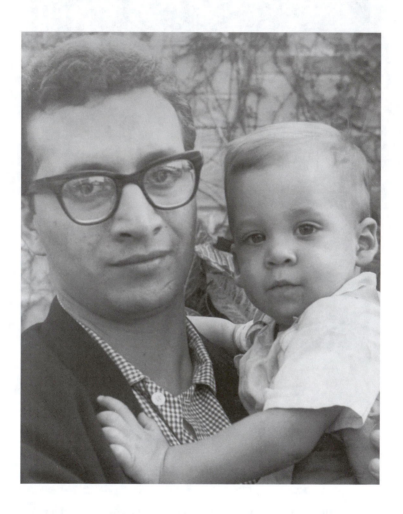

Beyond the Cinema of the Other, or Toward Another Cinema

Frances Negrón-Muntaner

For the past three years, "Beyond the Cinema of the Other or toward Another Cinema" has been fittingly nomadic. Several journals and anthologies have almost published it, but a last minute act of God or censorship has allowed the original text to survive only as spoken words on half-forgetful ears. And perhaps the only two reasons to disrupt this state of affairs by its publication is the puzzling impact of such unthreatening words on certain gatekeepers, and the quiet testimony this simple address provides about the mutability of purpose and truth.

The text was originally written in Spanish as part of a panel presentation organized by filmmaker Ana María García at the San Juan CinemaFest, during October of 1995. The panel opened up the discussion for "Made in the U.S.A.," a sampling of works by Puerto Rican U.S.-based filmmakers.

At the time of enunciation, these words were greeted with some bewilderment and a degree of apprehension, in part because I accompanied them with images of previous films, culminating in a three minute clip of *Brincando el charco*, representing several female couples in different phases of a sex tease. At the time, the moderator broke the silence by asking, *"Están en shock, ¿no?"* The audience responded with laughter. Unfortunately, reason bars us from packaging a multimedia presentation for current readers; hence here are the words, not surprisingly, translated into English.

Homecomings

During the seven years spanning my first professional film, *AIDS in the Barrio* (1989), to my last, *Homeless Diaries* (1995), I have been invited on multiple occasions to recount the process through which I have become a Puerto

Rican filmmaker in the United States. A mouthful, no doubt, and not something you are born into. The "answer" to this inquiry has mutated, transformed, and resignified itself so many times, that it has become a story. Like all stories that are repeated in different places and for diverse audiences, the story can't always be, nor mean, the same thing. Due to the increasing tediousness of the biographical on occasions like this, I would prefer to speak to you today about a proposed film practice, not as a function of identity, but as a space of possibility. Possibilities that may not always be realizable, not even agreeable to everyone, but perhaps simply available to some spectators, or one person's life. Cinema has often been a plane ticket to places that I never wanted to go, but that is the only true risk of this proposal.

Given my continuous transit between diverse geographic, sexual, and creative localities, the cinematic space can enact a resignification of home, and partially serve as its witness. The house-space of cinema certainly comes with twisted porches, doors leading to pleasure or hell, lots of people, lots of noise, and also with a deafening silence (perhaps that is my room of nightmares), but ultimately stands as people are free to wander from room to room. For the house of cinema is an invitation to occupy (un)common seats, regardless of where one physically rests at any given moment. Because film is nothing if not a provocation to travel, and hence, a possibility for encounters, displacements, seductions not real. Because those of us who continuously go through it have the maddening habit of carrying many keys, although most do not correspond to any doors in particular, and even if they did, we wouldn't use them since safety is another house of cinematic illusion.

The house trope emerges from the critical response to *Brincando el charco: Portrait of a Puerto Rican*, and the subsequent videos, *Puerto Rican ID* (a meditation on one Puerto Rican's relationship with American TV), and *Homeless Diaries* (a dialogue with several homeless advocates from north Philadelphia). The trope comes to life after arriving in Puerto Rico to show *Brincando el charco*, and one of my first exchanges with a local journalist ends in the following way: "Welcome home, if we can talk about home after seeing your film." A comment that triggered another memory, where a spectator in an academic screening in New England proposed that in *Brincando el charco*, home is an unresolved, fundamental, and politically charged problem because the film does not articulate a clear position regarding the political as a national project. But this is not so much a problem, as an alternative proposition. In *Brincando el charco*, home is closer to what Caribbean and Afro-American writer Audre Lorde called "the very house of difference" than a political metanarrative. In this sense, my cinematic proposition is one that tends toward questions and critical ambiguities, where objectivity is constituted through and within a debate among different positions, and not in the authority of a single version.

Challenging home—that heterogeneity not contained in the categories of nation, race, class, ethnicity, and identity—is part of creating communities where both dialogue and cacophony are possible. Particularly, when one must acknowledge that the notion of home itself is not easily discardable for subjects whose positions as daughters, lovers, lesbians, colonized, and migrants, have precisely resulted in the potentially productive trauma of being forced to move away from home. Just as for the anorexic, her only obsession is to eat; for those who feel that they have no home, there is no other desire but to find one, even when it has been in the process of inhabiting the chronotope of homelessness, that a more inclusive and democratic notion of community has been produced, lived, and enjoyed.

Contradictorily, the fact that one may become obsessed with reaching home does not entail that the traveler actually wants to, or can, reach it. One can fall in love with the pain that offers symbolic centrality, however fleeting, thus avoiding more healing possibilities. From this, the nomad's tent, the ancestral cave, the letter's ink postscript, the open spaces, the borders, become enticing tropes to think about divergent notions of community, as well as divergent ways of seeing and seeking pleasures. But also, these tropes can have devastating results when instead of symbolic, empowering strategies, these constitute policies imposed by some groups over others. This last observation was my most important lesson in videotaping *Homeless Diaries*. For the activists featured in this video diary, many of whom were literally homeless, facing the cold and the rats—real and symbolic—the most transgressive trope is not their condition, but their potential becoming as owners of a concrete house: a house hopefully made out of solid materials, in a clean and drug-free neighborhood with running water, gas, and electricity.

In *Brincando el charco*, the problematization of home stems from the exclusion of at least four communities from the island's nationalist imagination: Afro-Puerto Ricans, homosexuals, lesbians, and U.S.-born Puerto Ricans. In the insistence of representing those voices and bodies, I proposed a continuous questioning of the construction of home as the everyday practice of tolerance, and a rupture with dominant cinematic practices by Puerto Rican filmmakers. But mostly, cinema became a symbolic attempt to return "home" after a period of engaging in a filmmaking practice rooted in the "other." A practice motivated by a political desire of finding a place as an ethnic subject in the United States. This last conceptualization was an alternative to understanding my stay in the United States as a form of exile—the condition in which the present is mortgaged to a future that will never be the past one yearns for—and to imagine new solidarities with multiple communities. The ethnification of my political location, which is nothing but a way of seeing and inhabiting the world as a decentered participant rather than as a protagonist, has been a crucial part of my critical position challenging totalizing discourses. However, due to my class and ethnic background, the cinema of the other became a cinema about certain Puerto Ricans in the United States. Puerto Ricans tendentiously concentrated in poor neighborhoods, and whose cultural practices are often coopted as symbols of resistance by writers, filmmakers, and academics, whom, however, enjoy a privileged distance from the everyday lives of the people who live in these communities.

Although the above-mentioned proposal can help create class alliances to contest authoritarian apparatuses of representation, it is no less true that it could also have politically problematic effects, particularly if these interventions don't have a degree of reflexivity in their structure. The fact that middle class Puerto Ricans and Islanders are the ones usually interpolated to represent the "other" Puerto Ricans has resulted, with few exceptions, in a cinema where "Puerto Ricanness" is equivalent with "otherness" itself. Ironically, this is a cinema that locates those who practice it in a position of power as spokespeople of communities that ultimately continue to have limited access to self-representation. The strong nationalist inflection of this work also constitutes a silencing of many Puerto Ricans whose cultural practices, pleasures, and perspectives are neither represented nor acknowledged, except as pathologies. In a broader context, this tendency also works by displacing the relatively privileged position of the filmmaker (even if symbolically peripheral), to that of the economically marginal of the represented subject. This discursive operation does very little to transform the positioning of the represented subject, or even facilitate a critical reflection about the differences and hierarchies involved in any context where Puerto Ricans meet.

In critiquing the Puerto Rican cinema of the Other, which is fundamentally also a self-criticism, I do not want to suggest that this type of intervention may not have an important strategic value. *AIDS in the Barrio*, for example, was the first independent film with Puerto Rican producers and directors that proposed an antihomophobic discourse in relation to the AIDS epidemic. It also cleared a few frames for the representation of gay Puerto Rican voices and bodies. In this sense, this kind of intervention is part of creating spaces where the challenge is not simply the representation of subaltern subjects, but of proposing other narrative modes for representing these subjects.

Responding to the problematic aspects of *AIDS in the Barrio*, especially on the realist premise of representation of the "other" Puerto Rican, *Brincando el charco* constructs a lesbian character, distant from the island, residing in a body intersected by contradictory discourses. Many have read this as a transparently autobiographical gesture, attempting to suggest that the film is eccentric, and therefore, an easily discardable provocation. The only truly autobiographical aspect in the film, however, relates to my shared desire with the protagonist of multiplying the travel routes, the various ways one can come and go, without being forced to exclusively dwell within the house of the national. A conceptualization that, I believe, tends to subvert the multiple possibilities of the "Puerto Rican" sign.

Without doubt, I wanted *Brincando el charco* to provoke some type of polemic. At the same time, although the film invites the spectator to a dialogue, it also fears it. In the last instance, I expected the film to answer the question of whether it is possible to return home, or at least to return to some houses in common. The answer is that, without doubt, it is possible to travel home through film, not as a cinema of the other but another cinema. A film practice that unceremoniously sends the nostalgia of a paternalistic, racist, and classist nineteenth century to a mausoleum (or museum), and destroys the notion that every Puerto Rican's life should be a duel to death with the evils forces of colonialism (as if these were exterior to our own practice). Ultimately, a radically contemporary cinema capable of addressing those radical needs and desires that we hear today shouting in a whisper, but that before long will come down shattering all the wine glasses, even those kept under lock and key.

Once I abandoned the paternal home, the possibilities of dwelling multiplied, even as nostalgia has clearly overtaken me. Because of this, I will leave you with the possibility of yet another cinema: a surprising one. To define it more, from the authority that the podium and the university confers, would no doubt constitute a violent act.

Epilogue

Since facing the not necessarily hostile, yet silent, University of Puerto Rico classroom in 1995, I have been engaged in productions that elastically expand or even bypass the question of home. Moving to South Florida in 1997 took care of much of my physical alienation: no more English only, cold winters, pale faces, or Quaker restraint. Two plane hours from Puerto Rico and three from the Big Apple, the island of Miami Beach could well be the center of one universe.

But there is something more. Photographing *The Splendid Little War*, a two-hour film on the context and impact of the Spanish-American War (1895-1917), I traveled to the Philippines, Puerto Rico, and Guam looking for a broader community, and found it, alas, no more friendly or familiar than New York, Los Angeles, or Miami. In some cases, I traveled more than nine thousand miles to search for alternative images to those solemnly preserved at the Library of Congress, only to find a ripped-out copy of *Harper's History of the Spanish-American War*. In some ways, searching for the authenticity of place seemed to be an excuse for the lack of imagination at home. Seeking what is lacking here in the United States brought me face to face to what is here already, what one hundred years of colonialism and massive displacement from and to the U.S. has created. In other words, there is part of here there, and here part of there, but in the transit that is time, their coming together on one plane is fortuitous.

Entre Familia

Heroes and Orphans of the Hacienda: Narratives of a Mexican American Family

Vincent Pérez

> To remember is not only the act of not forgetting but the act of not being forgotten, just as remembering the past as utopian cultural terrain reveals the very conditions of cultural dislocation that made a necessity of retrospective communitarian idealization.
>
> —Genaro M. Padilla, My History, Not Yours

> I came to Comala because I was told that my father, a certain Pedro Páramo, was living there. My mother told me so, and I promised her I would come to see him as soon as she died. . . . She told me, "Don't ask him for anything that isn't ours. Just for what he should have given me and didn't. Make him pay for the way he forgot us."
>
> —Juan Rulfo, Pedro Páramo

Chicano literary and historical studies have increasingly focused attention on Mexican American autobiography. Since 1988, when a special issue of *The Americas Review* entitled "United States Hispanic Autobiography" appeared, commentators have examined its status as a distinct genre, and explored the socioideological and cultural dimensions of its nineteenth- and twentieth-century texts.[1] Since many of Chicano literature's foundational narratives are autobiographies, or fictions in large measure autobiographical, critics of Mexican American writing have always had to wrestle with the nature of autobiographical texts.[2] At the same time, Luis Leal's pathbreaking work in Chicano literary criticism has directed his successors toward the archaeological endeavor of recovering that vast catalog of Mexican American autobiographical narratives that have remained unpublished or unavailable to a wide audience.[3] Genaro Padilla's *My History, Not Yours* follows both critical paths. Not only does he proclaim the need for "the archival recovery, editing, translation, and publication of this body of foundational literary discourse," which in his own case revolves around that set of Mexican American texts, most still unpublished, collected during the 1870s by the California historian Hubert H. Bancroft, but Padilla also demands, from himself and others, "critical and interpretive activity that shall establish the discursive genealogy (its continuities as well as discontinuities) of our literary traditions" (1993, 7).

Drawing on the work of Padilla and other scholars of historical and autobiographical works, I would like to examine Francisco Róbles Pérez's "Memorias," an unpublished journal of personal reminiscences, written between 1990 and 1992, by a Mexican American immigrant.[4] Born in 1908 in the state of Zacatecas, Mexico, Pérez is a former farm laborer. He is also my paternal grandfather. The 250-page manuscript, seventy pages of which have been transcribed from the original handwriting and translated from the Spanish, recounts his childhood on a hacienda in Mexico, his emigration at the age of thirteen to the United States, and his youth as a farm worker in Southern California (see figs. 1 and 2). I would like to amplify Padilla's work by examining not only the nostalgic cast of my grandfather's account, but also a second family narrative that "Memorias" effectively suppresses—a narrative that foregrounds class and gender conflicts in turn-of-the-century Mexican hacienda society.

My interest in this project developed in a rather unorthodox fashion. While transcribing my grandfather's manuscript, quite by chance I became involved in a clash between two branches of my family (see figs. 3 and 4), which took place at the funeral of my "Aunt" Isabel "Chavela" Róbles.[5] The source of the conflict was a second version of Pérez history offered by the Róbleses, a group of relatives whose genealogy from the later nineteenth century to the present is closely interwoven with the Pérez family line. Largely suppressed in my family until comments at Chavela's funeral dramatically brought it to light, the Róbles narrative led me to question the ideological contradictions, rhetorical strategies, and sociohistorical particularities of "Memorias." In this essay I will first show how certain counterhegemonic socioideological articulations embedded in nostalgic memory make "Memorias" a perfect example of Padilla's model. My second and broader objective, however, is to show that as Padilla carries out

Fig. 1. Francisco Róbles Pérez acquired this document from the Mexican Consulate in Los Angeles in 1929 at age twenty-one, having lived in the United States as an undocumented alien for eight years. He used it in lieu of a birth certificate or United States visa to apply for residency status. Although the document states that he emigrated in September 1922, according to "Memorias" he arrived in 1921 at age thirteen.

Fig. 2. Francisco Róbles Pérez at age twenty-three with his two eldest children, Esther and Juan, at Long Beach, California, in 1931.

43

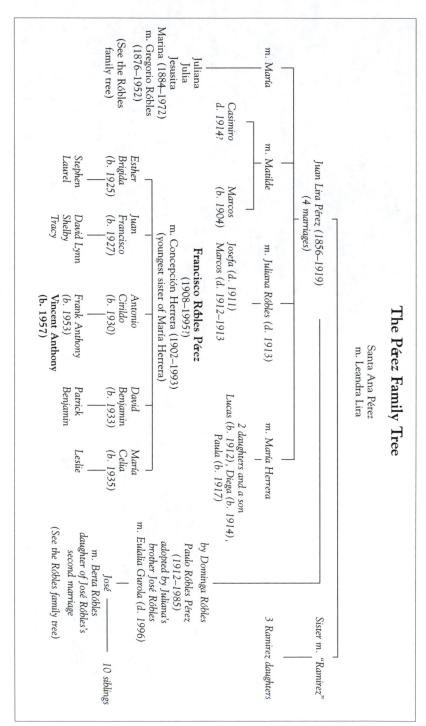

Fig. 3. The Pérez Family Tree

his project to restore the dignity and integrity of the lives of early Mexican American autobiographers, and to extend the Chicano literary canon into the nineteenth century, he almost inevitably resuppresses underlying class and gender contradictions in California (Mexican) hacienda society—a suppression most notable in his account of the Mexican American politician, rancher, and author, Mariano Guadalupe Vallejo.

Padilla proposes a sociohistorical reading of autobiographies that refuses to treat reductively that range of cultural and ideological meanings that his groundbreaking study displays in these texts. *My History, Not Yours* urges contemporary Chicano critics not to dismiss nineteenth-century Mexican American autobiographies simply because, as the products of a social elite dispossessed by Anglo American conquest and colonialism, their authors often nostalgically embrace early Mexican hacienda society instead of providing examples of "heroic narrative resistance" (1993, 39). Padilla argues that when colonized by the United States after the United States-Mexican War of 1846–1848, Mexicans "immediately gave utterance to the threat of social erasure" at the hands of a foreign culture and imposed political system (4). Critics dealing with narratives of that era must "examine the various ways in which autobiographical expression emerged from social rupture and was formed within a matrix of dislocation, fear, and uncertainty" (10). Calling their works "narratives of dispossession," Padilla convincingly suggests that "nostalgia for an earlier world produced not a non-critical reaction to loss, but an oppositional response to displacement, albeit a response often deeply mediated by a language of accommodation" (x).

My History, Not Yours thus uncovers a "retrospective narrative habit" in nineteenth-century Mexican American autobiographies that "goes beyond reconstructing an individual life." Instead, such a life "is measured within a communitarian configuration and against the disruption of identity as identity and is situated within an imagined cultural community of the past" (232). For the Vallejo family, for example, the wealthiest and most powerful in pre-1848 "alta California," U.S. annexation of Mexico's northern region meant economic dispossession and disenfranchisement. This economic and political disempowerment under Anglo American hegemony brought rapid cultural fragmentation and displacement for the entire Mexican American population. As Padilla remarks about Vallejo's five-volume historical narrative, "Recuerdos históricos y personales tocante a la alta California" (Personal and historical remembrances of alta California) (1875), "the autobiographical act, therefore, becomes a

The Róbles Family Tree

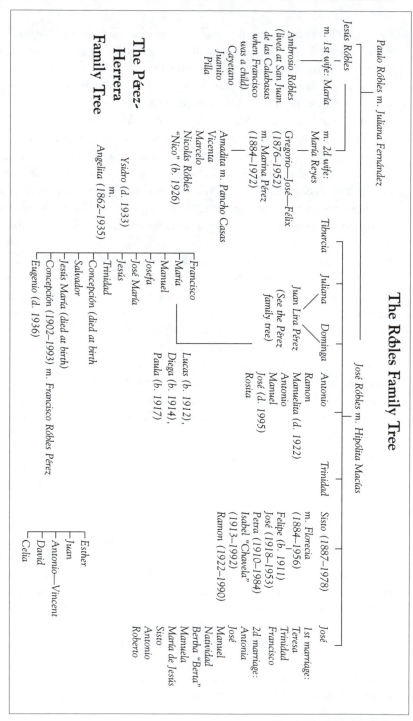

Fig. 4. The Róbles Family Tree

tense ritual of gathering and sorting the relics of the communal past, narratively reifying the cultural legacy while rearranging the national one, proclaiming a desire to become an American but doing so in a language and discourse of opposition" (89).

Following Padilla's paradigm, I attend first to my grandfather's nostalgic idealization of hacienda life in prerevolutionary Mexico. Rather than mark this aspect of the text with an ideological label, however, I will, as Padilla's nuanced readings of Mexican American autobiographies propose, measure the utopian aspects of my grandfather's account against 1) his dislocation and dispossession as a child, buffeted by the social upheaval of the Mexican Revolution, and 2) the economic exploitation and sociocultural fragmentation he experienced as a Mexican immigrant laborer in the United States. As in many Mexican immigrant narratives and nineteenth-century Mexican American autobiographies, nostalgia for an "idealized and unobtainable" past serves a fundamental oppositional function in "Memorias," certainly enacting an imaginative communion with the narrator's lost family and community, but also articulating "resistance to cultural evisceration" in the United States. Or as Padilla puts it, nostalgia serves "the reintegrative psychic and social need for sustaining an idea of the past and for fixing a version of history within a cultural text that would mark historical presence in the face of erasure" (16).

My next level of analysis, however, responds to my accidental encounter with the Róbles narrative to show that while correct in defending early Mexican American autobiographies from the charge of indulging in the "hacienda syndrome,"[6] Padilla's model obscures social contradictions in those foundational life stories by male and/or upper-class members of pre-1848 California (Mexican) society. Within my own family, the Róbles's oral narrative turned my grandfather's text into a terrain of intense contestation, challenging his nostalgic memory in ways that cannot be contained or elaborated by Padilla's theoretical framework. As I evaluate Padilla's usefulness for understanding my grandfather's complex deployment of nostalgia, the recovered Róbles counterhistory, which foregrounds women's narratives and declares my great-grandfather's role as a hacienda manager in the repressive Porfirian hacienda economy, inevitably moves to the foreground. Recovering the suppressed, antinostalgic counterversion of Dominga Róbles's—who according to her family narrative was raped by her brother-in-law (my grandfather's father), Juan Lira Pérez, in 1912—not only rehistoricizes my grandfather's representation of his father's life, but like Rosaura Sánchez's recent analysis of class and gender discourses in the California testimonios, challenges Padilla's "close" readings of early Mexican American autobiographies.

My interest in these foundational narratives obviously constitutes part of a larger genealogical project to uncover an unclear family and community history. But further, though my own family's narrative is no more representative of the Mexican American past than any other Chicano family's, I have found that investigating my own background has helped me better negotiate the history of Mexican American society as a whole. My essay in this way seeks to bridge Mexican American oral narratives and historical literary scholarship. Peeling back the layers of my family's Chicano and Mexicano history has, for instance, strongly convinced me that whether narrated by my grandfather, by other Mexican American grandparents and families, by Chicano fiction writers, or by Mexican American historians, the recovery of our past remains incomplete, often suppressed, and untranscribed. Like members of the Buendía clan, who struggle for more than a century to read and translate Melquíades's encoded parchments in Gabriel García Márquez's *One Hundred Years of Solitude* (1967), we have only begun to decipher our history and escape the labyrinthine "city of mirrors." Though such contemporary works as Alejandro Morales's historical novels, Ernesto Galarza's autobiography *Barrio Boy* (1971), and Chicana writings that deconstruct and historicize Chicano/Mexicano patriarchy stand as exceptions,[7] too many of our writers seem unengaged by the conflictive power relations to be found in our not so distant Mexican (hacienda) social history. As we have searched for our historical origins, our Mexican cultural legacy that has been objectified, denigrated, or destroyed by a hegemonic United States culture ever since the annexation of northern Mexico in 1848, too often we have read our *abuelos'* (grandparents) stories uncritically or failed to pursue these histories wherever they may lead. Just as so many autobiographies by our nineteenth-century ancestors reify a pre-American communal religiocultural inheritance in the face of cultural rupture and dispossession, so too, in the interest of recovering our history, have some of our most informed writers and critics placed their faith in a utopian vision of a harmonious Mexican cultural and spiritual homeland.[8] Even Padilla, though he foregrounds the constructed, even fictional, character of all Mexican American autobiography, himself evades but cannot help but evoke the profound ideological contradictions, arising from nostalgic desire, in these nineteenth-century texts.

My History, Not Yours shows that while Mexican history has been reified in these autobiographical accounts, they nevertheless represent an honorable Mexican American historical and cultural legacy preserved for, and available to, later generations. What is missing from his model is an explanation of how and why, in sociohistorical terms, key aspects of our history were mythologized or suppressed. Having recovered a part of the encoded "parchments" and embraced it as our own, we must now decipher, interpret, and historicize the remainder of the text. By looking at my grandfather's "Memorias" and the family clash that called them into question—set in the imaginative space of the Mexican hacienda—I hope to begin carrying out this task.

Nostalgia and Resistance

My father had three nieces, named Ramirez, who were distinguished, older women in their forties, all unmarried. They were couturiers. They owned a fashion shop in the commercial zone downtown, where they sold expensive, custom-made dresses for young women and suits for men. Jerez was the [commercial] center for the entire outlying hacienda community, and so their shop was the only one of its kind for thirty kilometers or more around the town. These women belonged to high society . . . and lived in a mansion—surrounded by bougainvillea—with electricity, a garden with beautiful plants, and a swimming pool. You'll probably ask how they had a pool in the center of town, but I'm one step ahead of you. In that part of Jerez, there was a stream called the Rio Chiquito, which passed close to their mansion, and two kilometers away was the Rio Grande. But let's return for a moment to the house. My father and I were often invited to go and dine with these sisters. You see, my family had all of the same luxuries as they had during the 1890–1912 period. The Ramirez sisters were one of the illustrious families [of Jerez] that have now passed into history, but I remember them as a part of my own family, of whom I am very, very proud. . . .

   The disturbers of the peace, that is, the revolutionaries, wouldn't leave my father alone. They wanted to assassinate him. Many times he escaped by the skin of his teeth. Other times he hid in wells . . . we finally escaped from Jerez under the cover of night by burro—one for each of us—so that our loyal Mexican "brethren," who one day were our employees and we the employers, could not detect us. . . . So departed a citizen of Jerez who was at one time a descendant of the most prosperous and landed hacendados in the entire valley of Zacatecas. . . . We left all of our property behind; it was many, many years before I slept in a bed again.

—Francisco Róbles Pérez, "Memorias"

> Domination and suppression, the reality of the group's material and so-
> cial condition, is often narratively occluded, or transformed into a life
> in an imaginary pre-American past through which aristocratic pretense,
> genealogical invention, and political self-deceit articulate resistance in
> language often ideologically deaf to itself.
>
> —Genaro M. Padilla, *My History, Not Yours*

I began to delve into my family's history when, as an undergraduate, I
went to Mexico for two years to study Latin American literature. Prior to
my visit, I had recognized that I could not reveal certain legends about my
Mexican ancestors to my Chicano university friends without risking un-
dermining my own cultural authenticity as a working-class Chicano. I often secretly questioned the genealogical lore narrated by some of my
Chicano college friends—not the humble origins of their *antepasados* (ancestors) nor their families' suffering as immigrants and laborers in the United
States, but the romantic representation of their ancestors' role in the Mexican Revolution (1910–20), invariably as peasant combatants. I understood
that many of my Mexican American friends were, like my own family,
descended from *los de abajo* (people of the lower classes)—to use the title
of Mariano Azuela's novel of the Mexican Revolution. But after I began to
read modern Mexican literature and to develop a clearer understanding of
the hacienda—the foundational socioeconomic institution in Mexican
history—I felt that we had, as a group, become alienated from our history.[9]
When speaking with my Chicano friends or family members, I either held
my peace about my grandfather's obscure past, or revised my history. Rather
than acknowledge my grandparents' unspoken pain and profound ambivalence about the revolution and its aftermath, I portrayed my paternal grandfather, who emigrated from Mexico in 1921, as an impoverished *campesino*
(farm worker) whose family had sympathized with Pancho Villa's revolutionary insurrectionists.[10]

This romantic narrative of origins was not entirely a fabrication; like
most Mexicans of his generation, my grandfather embraced the romantic
Villa legend and idolized Francisco Madero, the liberal Constitutionalist
political leader who helped topple the regime of Porfirio Díaz in 1911. But
my omissions marked the unconscious ideological content of my family's
genealogy, omissions also found in some of the Chicano literary and historical studies I had read up to that time. These, like many recent works, desig-
nated the inception of Mexican American history as either the "great
migration" to the United States during the 1900–30 period or the military

defeat of Mexico in 1848 (for Texas, 1836).[11] Privileging the modern Mexican American social experience, they rarely delved into the Mexican period in the Southwest—when a semi-feudal and patriarchal hacienda (rancho) system dominated the region—or the prerevolutionary nineteenth-century hacienda era in Mexico. Rather than imagining links between Mexican historical models and the Mexican American experience, or applying the borderlands paradigm to the realm of history, many instead constructed boundaries between the early period and the modern.[12] This contradiction became more apparent when I visited Mexico to attend classes at UNAM (Autonomous National University of Mexico). While studying there, I first read the fictions of such modern Mexican authors as Juan Rulfo (*Pedro Páramo*, 1955) and José Revueltas (*El luto humano* [Human Mourning], 1943). Long before the poets and writers of the Chicano movement began their project to recover, revitalize, and embrace our Mexican cultural origins, these earlier writers had deconstructed the Mexican national mythologies and ideologies surrounding both the revolution and the prerevolutionary (hacienda) period. The narratives and myths I had sought out as a Mexican American college student participating in the struggle to contest and expand mainstream U.S. histories had been rigorously interrogated by Mexican writers, artists, and scholars. Rulfo, for example, carried out a definitive critique of the Mexican myth of origins, demonstrating how the hacienda, as a founding nineteenth-century institution and particularly its identification with a tradition of *caciquismo*, determined the direction and outcome of the Mexican Revolution. Revueltas's earlier novel debunked the mythology of the revolution itself, portraying it as a peasant movement ultimately betrayed by state bureaucrats in thrall to conservative political and business interests. Rather than discovering a stable originary "homeland," which, when I was in my twenties, I still believed was possible, I found in Mexico a society marked by contradictions and almost unfathomable complexity—one still struggling to come to terms with its own history and "lost" origins. Speaking of the development of Latin American history, Carlos Fuentes remarked that "[t]he Utopia of foundation was exploited, degraded, and finally assassinated by the epic of history, activity, commerce, and crime,"[13] a sentiment that my readings at that time underscored. The engagement with the past by Mexican and other Latin American writers achieved its apotheosis in Rulfo's fiction and García Márquez's *One Hundred Years of Solitude* (1967), the latter work indebted to both Rulfo and Revueltas, and thus one that speaks to Mexican and Chicano history as well as to the more general Spanish American past.

Though García Márquez, Rulfo, Revueltas, Fuentes, or even Faulkner did not hesitate to delve into the labyrinthine convolutions of historical memory—where Rulfo and Faulkner felt the most at home—I have encountered in some Chicano literary and historical narratives a reluctance to embark on critical genealogical inquiry into the early Mexican (American) past. Our historical condition as an oppressed minority demands that we document and analyze the contemporary period, yet these circumstances can also limit our historical and imaginative vision. Even in my own research I find myself drawing back from certain investigative paths, denying myself the critical freedom needed to approach the "truths" about history. (In an earlier version of this very essay I unintentionally (re)suppressed the story of the rape of Dominga Róbles, and thus downplayed my great-grandfather's role in the hacienda economy.) And as "Memorias" implicitly demonstrates, many members of my family, and particularly my grandparents, have been displeased to find me using my education, which they made possible, to retrieve and expose long-buried secrets.

Chicano writers and historians have not only (un)consciously suppressed and nostalgically mythologized distant Mexican American history, but also marginalized it in their attempt to address urgent contemporary cultural and political issues. In a remarkable interview, one of our most accomplished fiction writers, Tomás Rivera, dismisses the need to conceptualize, let alone interrogate, a Mexican American historical consciousness rooted in an earlier Mexican period:

> I don't really feel that I have a strong relationship with [Mexican culture]. . . . I read the Mexican classics . . . [and] I felt a strong affinity to [them]. When I visited Mexico, it reinforced that feeling. Then I began to realize that I'm not a Mexican. All of these feelings are a result of learning, not of growing up in Mexico with all *its* problems, *its* history, *its* beauty, and all *its* affinities. I thought, "It's not really mine. I know [Mexico] as mine, now, because I've learned it. I don't actually have it, nor have I lived it." After that I had to come back and say this is reality right here. . . . The fact is that if I had not gotten a college education I would know very little about Mexico (Bruce-Novoa 1980, 152–53).

These remarks, which capture the fundamental historical and cultural paradox that Mexican Americans as a group have lived, at one level recall Richard Rodriguez's well-known renunciation of the "private" Mexican side of his cultural identity in his *Hunger of Memory: The Education of Richard Rodriguez* (1984). Even though in much of his writing Rivera mounts a sustained materialist critique of hegemonic ideology, while Rodriguez embraces a middle-class assimilationist ethic, I would suggest that both writers arrive at a similar *cultural* impasse precisely because they do not retrieve and draw upon the multiple and contending (suppressed) histories that make up the Mexican American historical consciousness. Though Rivera's cultural politics are antithetical to Rodriguez's, both authors seek to establish rigid cultural, as well as chronological, boundaries between Mexico and the United States, rather than imagining Chicano history and subjectivity as spaces marked by the pervasive presence of contradiction and discontinuity. Rivera's novel *And the Earth Did Not Devour Him* (1971) does recover a communal farm worker cultural memory, but neither he nor Rodriguez thematizes Mexican (American) origins and ancestry.

My genealogical research attempts just such a recuperative project, and in fact, my grandfather's memoirs are themselves the result of the investigation into my family's history I began fifteen years ago while studying in Mexico. While a graduate student in the late 1980s, I began a series of taped interviews with my grandfather, which over the course of six years developed into a full-length written autobiography. Though I had not imagined, nor do I believe today, that as an assimilated Mexican American child growing up in a working-class suburb of Los Angeles I had lost part of my history or culture, these lengthy interviews were my opportunity to explore my family's Mexican past as well as to establish a closer relationship with my grandfather in the language of his forebears. I could not have known how the conflicted genealogy they would bring to light would continue to weigh on the lives and consciences of family members.

A critic of Faulkner once remarked that all of the author's major characters "enter the fiction trailing behind them clouds of familial and regional qualifiers . . . the grandparents, parents, and siblings, the hill country or bottom land or tidewater, whose cumulative significance is the indispensable background of identity" (Karl 1988, 133–34). Similarly, I found that certain (over)determining historical qualifiers—which in *Absalom, Absalom!* reach back into distant family and community memory—also determine contemporary Mexican American subjectivity and culture. Juan Preciado, the Mexican campesino in Rulfo's *Pedro Páramo*, returns to the rural village where his mother grew up to search for his father and lost origins; Quentin Compson, tormented and obsessed with the past, attempts to recover the history of the United States South in Faulkner's novel. In the same fashion, Mexican Americans today carry on our shoulders and in our conscience the sum of the "combined memories" of our families and communities. For the same holds true in Mexican American society as Faulkner observed in the south: "there is no such thing as *was*. ... time [history] is not a fixed condition, time [history] is in a way the sum of the combined intelligences of all men who breathe at that moment" (1932, 179). Yet, for Mexican Americans, the collective memory of our communities is rooted not only in a twentieth-century urban or rural United States context, but inevitably in the hacienda and rancho social economy of prerevolutionary Mexico and the nineteenth-century Southwest.

Since I could only visit my grandfather twice a year, on one occasion I asked him to begin writing down the stories of his life in Mexico and as an immigrant. Thirty-five notebooks, filled with Spanish prose written in the stilted style of a child and carefully numbered to avoid chronological confusion, have been the result. Noting that his education "was only three years in primary school" (3), my grandfather repeatedly apologizes for his "poor orthography and grammar." And yet he is proud of his acquired knowledge, drawn from his lifelong experience in the real world in Mexico and later in the United States. "My philosophy is my own—I didn't go to any university," he states early in the narrative. "What I'm saying I've compiled from a long and bumpy journey over the face of our mother Earth" (26). Although I have estimated that the edited manuscript will be 250 pages, the final version may be longer. I have not translated many of the post-1936 era notebooks, nor have I determined precisely how the hours of tape-recorded interviews—which complement the written account—will be integrated into the text.

I also recorded hours of interviews with my paternal grandmother, Concepción Herrera Pérez—which I am incorporating into a written family narrative—who, in keeping with her reputation for shrewd family diplomacy and unlike my grandfather, measured each word that she spoke with the painstaking care of a politician. (I later learned the reasons for her reticence, see below.) In what initially struck me as a deliberate refusal to grant me entry into the vaults of family history, she skirted events that I suspected were crucial to our family's narrative of origins. I felt like an ethnographer trying to wrest critical anthropological information from an unwilling or suspicious interlocutor. The analogy of an outsider may seem an odd one to apply to my relationship with my grandmother, but illustrates my ignorance, ten years ago, of my family's history and particularly the women's stories in our narrative of origins. By retrieving one woman's account from a longstanding patriarchal tradition of family legend and lore, I hope in this essay to begin filling in some of the tradition's gaps and omissions. For all of my grandfather's candor in narrating his childhood experience of hacienda society, it displaced more effectively than my grandmother's reticence a side of our early history that Chavela's funeral would only coincidentally bring to light. Since the patriarchal myth is rooted in sociohistorical reality, it must be examined for what it can tell us not only about the Mexican American historical consciousness, but about the role of the hacienda in the formation of this consciousness.

Though I first encouraged my grandfather to write his story, and I now serve as its translator and editor, the journal itself is entirely my grandfather's work.[14] It begins with his childhood in the prerevolutionary period, which he portrays as a pastoral and idyllic life in the hacienda communities outside of Jerez, where his father worked. Though born in 1908, my grandfather nostalgically reconstructs the Porfirian hacienda period of the late-nineteenth century. The text ends with the account of his attempt to rear five young children on farm worker wages during the United States depression. "Memorias" thus spans roughly thirty years of Mexican and Mexican American history.

My grandfather, Francisco, was the son of a bookkeeper named Juan Lira Pérez, a business associate from the 1880s until 1913 of a group of landowning *hacendados* (ranchers and landowners) near the city of Zacatecas in central Mexico. Though born into relative privilege in an era of socioeconomic polarization that set the *hacendado* elite apart from the masses of campesinos and laborers, my grandfather's comfortable early circumstances were shortlived. Orphaned at eleven, he was forced to fend for himself during a time of social and economic upheaval.[15] Emigrating to Southern California in 1921, he worked for more than fifty years as a ranch laborer and field hand. Forty-two years were spent at Rancho Sespe, a 6,000-acre citrus ranch owned by the Spalding sports equipment manufacturing family in Ventura County. My grandfather had a number of agricultural occupations at this ranch:

> I picked fruit for twenty years, then, as a gardener, planted vegetables and flowers and trees. . . . I once helped dynamite a mountain on which the owner built a cabin; and for two years I worked with an agronomy engineer to build a nine-hole golf course, which Mister Keith Spalding had ordered. (40)

My grandfather and his wife reared a family in the ranch's workers' camp, Sespe Village, where 150 Mexican families lived.[16] Unable to return to

Mexico and reclaim his father's land and status because of the civil war
and its economic aftermath, my grandfather remained within the ranks
of agricultural laborers in a country where Mexicans were not only cultural outsiders, but exploited as laborers and excluded as racial others.
His family's fall from the Mexican upper class due to the war's disruption
of the hacienda economy left my grandfather with a dual class identity.
He could thus sing the praises of the revolutionary leader Villa, yet also
revile him as a bandit who had disenfranchised Lira Pérez and forced
young Francisco to leave his homeland for good. Similarly, he could nostalgically recount the heroics of the martyred Constitutionalist leader
Madero, yet with pride list the modernizing accomplishments of the dictator Díaz whom Madero toppled.

In the early sections of "Memorias," my grandfather imaginatively reconstructs the life of that fifty-seven-year-old established businessman and
accountant who was his father. In these early passages and elsewhere, my
grandfather harks back to life in a "harmonious" rural community in a
prerevolutionary and "colonial" Mexico.[17] He was born in 1908, on the
eve of the civil war, to "Don Juan Lira Pérez and Doña Juliana Róbles de
Pérez," in the "beautiful small town of Jerez, in the state of Zacatecas" (1).
"Direct descendants of the seventeenth-century Spanish pioneers and
founders of Jerez," both his parents had deep roots in that region. My grandfather remembers his father saying once that his own "father, Santa Ana
Pérez, and uncles were descended from the original founders and settlers of
the town" (2). "Memorias" thus forges a genealogical link between Lira
Pérez and the Spanish colonial settlers of Mexico. Assuming that the
locality's first settlers had been "conquistadors," my grandfather concludes,
despite a vast chronological discrepancy, that his own "grandfather" must
have come from Spain. He points out that the town's name may have been
"inspired by the town of Jerez de la Frontera in southern Spain" (2).[18] This
Spanish link reappears at the time of my uncles' and my father's births, for
these light-haired infants are cited as proof that the blood "from my Mexican ancestors, descendants of the [Spanish] *gachupines*, continues" (32).

On the surface, these passages seem to reflect little more than those
contradictory racial and class biases rooted in the Spanish conquest and
colonial domination of Mexico's indigenous peoples that are still widespread in Mexico to this day. Rather than acknowledging his *mestizo*
(Spanish/Indian) cultural and ethnic heritage, my grandfather, steeped
in his father's Hispano-centric nineteenth-century mores, which deni-
grate indigenous origins, claims his descent from the "racially pure"

Spanish conquerors.[19] As Jesús Flores Olague points out, although in the sixteenth century "[t]he presence of diverse racial groups was one characteristic of the [Zacatecan] mining centers, . . . the permanent relationship established between these groups . . . exhibited the presence of one dominant group: the *mestizo*" (1996, 83). Even without taking into account the various groups of Chichimeca Indians in that region conquered by the Spanish, "numerous groups of indigenous Mexicans, Tarascans, and Tlaxcaltecans—who accompanied the Spaniards in their expeditions and participated in the pacification of the Indians who inhabited the region—formed part of the new settler population around the Zacatecan mines" (89–90). However indirectly, my grandfather acknowledges this Indian and mestizo history through his use of the word *gachupin*, a term for Spaniard that can be used pejoratively. Its use in the above quote suggests the narrator's (un)conscious desire for cultural distinction from the Spanish conquerors as well as his identification with the region's Indian and *mestizo* population.

Other sociocultural motivations and forces contribute to this problematical aspect of my grandfather's autobiography. His nostalgia for a legendary Mexican (Spanish) world, and more specifically his construction through memory of a childhood and youth spent within this "mythic" hacienda past, are examples of what Padilla has called the author's "epistemological ground of subjectivity" (1993, 158). Like other early Mexican American autobiographers, my grandfather sets this pre-American cultural and social originary ground of being and memory against the nightmare of Mexican life under the Anglo American sociocultural regime.

Let me briefly explain how my grandfather's effort to reclaim his origins leads me to Padilla's theoretical model. Coming six years after the death of his mother, Juliana Róbles Pérez, and definitively marking the end of his hacienda childhood and the start of his hardscrabble existence as a *descalzo* (barefoot waif), the death of his father is the defining moment of my grandfather's life. Nostalgic desire is thus interwoven with retrospective longing. As a boy orphaned at an early age and forced to support himself at various jobs before making his way the United States, my grandfather wished to embrace a father and a community that he knew only in childhood. By retrieving his father's myth from the social and familial ruins of the revolutionary period, my grandfather's testimonial remembrance reenacts the short-lived relationship that his father's unexpected death in 1919 abruptly ended. But, if we accept orphanhood as a figuration embodying deeper sociohistorical and cultural forces, the death of Lira Pérez can also stand as that traumatic moment of social and cultural rupture that Padilla identifies as key to understanding the Mexican American autobiographical and historical consciousness. In the figure of the descalzo, my grandfather alluded to his suddenly precarious socioeconomic status:

> The person writing this [account] was a descalzo, because the first shoes that I owned were bought sometime in 1910. Since my feet grew fast, I couldn't use them for very long. I didn't own another pair until I crossed the United States border in 1921. Someone bought me a secondhand pair there for twenty-five cents, but they were too big for me. When I put them on without socks and walked, my feet sweated and slipped. The noise they made when I crossed the border at Juárez made me think that someone was following me. When I recall this event, it now seems both curious and fitting to me that I write it down, so that you know where Don Francisco came from. (15)

My grandfather used *descalzo* not only to capture his desperate situation when he crossed the border at El Paso, but also the many sociocultural and class-bound "ideological" transitions he was forced to make since then."[20] The first shift was from membership in the "high" society of the Mexican rancher class to the status of a homeless orphan at the height of the revolution. The second took him from his life as a servant for a wealthy Mexican family in the city of Torreón to that of an impoverished, displaced immigrant laborer in a foreign country.

But, as the above passage suggests, for my grandfather descalzo also had a tragicomic and picaresque quality to it, for unlike most Mexican immigrant autobiographies, my grandfather shared with early-nineteenth-century Mexican American writers the distant remembrance of an actual "upper class" hacienda past. According to family history, Lira Pérez had by the late-nineteenth century become a relatively successful accountant, managing the affairs and finances of several local haciendas: large cattle and livestock ranches owned by the elite of central Zacatecas. Though not a hacendado himself, by the turn of the century he had apparently prospered enough to be closely identified with this privileged class. Orphanhood thus functions in my grandfather's account at two discursive levels. On the one hand, it represents his abrupt separation from his father's financially secure world, and soon after from the Mexican culture of his ancestors. The descalzo is, therefore, a prince in disguise. (Though he had only a third-grade education, my grandfather sometimes set his "high" cultural status against the lower-class background of the farm laborers with whom he worked at Rancho Sespe. The community in turn acknowledged this background respectfully, selecting him to several local public positions.) On the other hand, "Memorias" is obviously an immigrant narrative as well, which charts the narrator's struggles as a destitute Mexican laborer in what he increasingly came to view as a materialistic society overtly hostile to Mexicans. At this level, orphanhood signifies his cultural and socioeconomic alienation as a marginalized and exploited immigrant in the United States. He will thus always be a descalzo.

The contestatory Róbles narrative will expose certain sociohistorical deceptions in this notion of orphanhood as well as in the construction of Porfirian hacienda society in "Memorias." For the moment, though, let us consider the usefulness of Padilla's paradigm for understanding this figure, and "Memorias" in total. Padilla has established that early Mexican American autobiographies and modern Mexican immigrant autobiographical narratives exhibit a "consciousness split by contending sociocultural regimes" (1993, 51). Much like W. E. B. Dubois's concept of the double "self," this "double-consciousness" originates in that moment when the Mexican American author's pre-American religiocultural identity comes under the dominating influence of an Anglo American sociocultural regime. For the nineteenth-century Mexicans living in what was once northern Mexico and is now the Southwest United States, this moment came violently with the 1848 American military victory over Mexico and the annexation of its northern region. As my grandfather's memoir and other narratives of Mexican emigration show, an equally sharp cultural break has taken place among twentieth-century Mexican immigrants. Symbolized by the border crossing, this modern rupture results from both the forced emigration from the "homeland" and the inevitable cultural accommodation that Mexican immigrants have had to make in a country with fundamentally different sociocultural traditions.

All of the many studies examining Mexican immigration to the United States agree that a huge number of immigrants arrived during this century's first three decades. Mario Barrera, for example, cites an estimate that by 1928 more than one-tenth of Mexico's population had moved to the United States (1979, 68). More recently, David G. Gutiérrez writes that "[a]lthough immigration and demographic statistics for [the] era are notoriously inaccurate, most scholars concur that at least one million, and possibly as many as a million and a half Mexican immigrants entered the United States between 1890 and 1929 (1995, 40). In accounting for this large-scale migration, Barrera notes that while the political upheavals created by the Mexican Revolution caused a great many to emigrate—particularly "those who happened to be on the losing side at a given moment"—economic and social factors were perhaps more significant, for "[a] large number of agricultural workers during this time were displaced from the land as the process of [Porfirian] modernization was ruthlessly pursued" (1979, 68). Furthermore, between 1875 and 1910, the Mexican population increased by approximately 50 percent. As Friedrich Katz explains, "the number of laborers available to central Mexican haciendas greatly increased . . . as the massive expropriations . . . created a new landless proletariat, which the limited industry in most parts of central Mexico could not absorb" (Katz as quoted in Barrera 1979, 68).

In *My History, Not Yours*, Padilla examines the dramatic break in sociocultural self-consciousness portrayed in late-nineteenth-century Mexican American autobiographies—one typically represented in twentieth-century Mexican immigrant autobiographical narratives by the border crossing. Refusing to dismiss early California "Hispano" texts as politically and ideologically self-deceiving, he views their nostalgic impulse as a complex narrative strategy with a hidden counterdiscursive objective. As we shall see in my grandfather's narrative, though admittedly shot through with ideological, cultural, and historiographic contradictions, this strategy sustains the Mexican American autobiographer's pre-American and communitarian cultural identity in the face of threats from Anglo American social institutions. Viewed in this light, my grandfather's efforts to link himself to Spanish colonial forebears invokes the powerful cultural presence of his Mexican ancestors. Such a legacy grants my grandfather, and his largely assimilated Mexican American children, grandchildren, and great-grandchildren, a cultural identity in the face of "orphanhood" in Mexico and the United States.

Like the nineteenth-century Mexican American California autobiographers who measure the past according to their "present" socioeconomic and cultural dilemmas, my grandfather foregrounded his struggles with poverty, displacement, and "slavelike" experiences as an immigrant farm worker. Without seeking pity and in an understated tone, he relates the brutal, inhuman work, and his own felt status in the United States as a victim, a commodity, and a deracinated and alienated figure apparently without hope or future. "Memorias" identifies three forces of rigid exclusion and severe abuse during the 1930s: the exploitation of Mexican agricultural laborers by American ranchers, the suppression of Mexican efforts to organize a union, and the racial segregation that farm workers endured at every level of society.[21] Taken together, these forces constitute my grandfather's depression-era economic, sociocultural, and personal plight.

Grandfather's account of his participation in a labor union strike in Placentia in 1936 epitomizes this precarious and alienated condition—as well as his efforts to lift himself and those around him above the impoverished status of farm workers:

> I joined a society of united Mexican workers and started to work on its behalf. We fought to defend the human, civic, and economic rights of Mexican agricultural workers. But we were a small group, perhaps forty in number, and none of us was educated nor had funds to sustain the organization. We asked ten cents in dues from each worker's paycheck. We eventually called a strike to try to improve our lives, but it was in vain. We lost after two months. Many of the strikers were thrown in jail and others were physically abused on the picket line. In one confrontation, the police used tear gas against us. In this struggle, [the ranchers] had no respect for women or children. Our only recourse was the Mexican Consulate in Los Angeles, but [the ranchers] later blocked our communication with this office. (33)

In her history of the Southern California communities of San Juan Capistrano and Santa Ana, Lisabeth Haas provides an account of this 1936 strike. Haas's reconstruction of the violent response by ranchers and police closely parallels my grandfather's remembrance of events. As she puts it, "[a]ttacks on the barrio . . . [reflected] the way in which race politics fortified coercive labor structures. Vigilantes attacked participants in the nightly strike meetings in each barrio, sometimes using tear gas. On July 7 during a meeting of 115 Mexican men, women, and children in Placentia, 'one hundred ranchers drove up . . . each . . . armed with a new axe handle' " (208). My grandfather's oral story, as told to me during an interview, of his narrow escape from armed attackers who broke up a union meeting in Placentia supports the following description in Haas's book:

> On the single evening of July 10, vigilantes smashed the windows of a meeting place in Anaheim while the meeting was in progress, disrupted a large meeting in La Habra, and broke up a smaller one in Placentia, where they hurled twenty tear gas bombs into the room and wielded clubs against those who ran out. Barrio residents said they could not sleep because the tear gas filled their homes. The sheriff had already issued a "shoot to kill" order against the strikers, thus implicitly giving license to vigilante activity. (208)

My grandfather's activism reflects the widespread labor unrest during the 1930s among Mexican and Mexican American workers in

California. During that time, a series of strikes and labor-related protests by Mexican and Mexican American laborers ravaged the state's agriculture industry (Gutiérrez 1995, 102, 106). "[W]ell over 160 major strikes occurred between 1933 and 1937 alone" (101). As Rodolfo Acuña notes, "[g]iven the industrialization of agriculture, the exploitation of Mexican labor, and the abuses of the contract labor system, conflict would have occurred without the depression; the events of 1929 merely intensified the struggle" (1988, 209).

My grandfather's account endorses the view that Mexican and Mexican American labor strife during this period "often took the form of organized race conflict" (Gutiérrez 1995, 100). Because of his role as a union activist, my grandfather and other Mexican organizers were blacklisted by Orange County ranchers. Forced to move his family to Ventura County, some fifty-five miles away, he was soon hired to pick grapefruit, for twenty-eight cents an hour, near the town of Fillmore. (He contacted Gregorio Róbles, his brother-in-law, who, along with other Róbles family members, had made his way to Fillmore several years earlier.) Grandfather recalled that the foreman at Rancho Sespe asked him where he had moved from. When he said Orange County, the foreman asked if he was a striker. My grandfather, of course, said no: "If I had said yes, they wouldn't have given me work . . . and at that time I had four children to support and feed, all of school age with the exception of the youngest, who was three" (42).

During the 1960s, when the United Farm Workers began organizing workers at Rancho Sespe, my grandfather voiced support but refused to join the new union. Not only had his youthful experience as an organizer—as well as his concern for the livelihood of his wife and five children—made him cautious, but in 1941 he had narrowly managed to keep his job and (company) home during a mass firing and eviction of striking farm workers at Sespe. In that strike, at least 80 percent of the Mexican and Mexican American families in the village were left homeless; ranch owners removed their possessions and left them on the side of the highway one mile away. My father, who was eleven at the time, recalled seeing these displaced families, whose children were his friends, waiting with their few possessions on the road as it rained. The strike occurred throughout Ventura County, and eventually over 6,000 workers and their families were evicted from company housing (Menchaca 1995, 87).

Martha Menchaca provides an account of the events of 1941 in her study of Mexican Americans in Santa Paula, a town located five miles from Rancho Sespe. As she explains, "the coalition of [Ventura County agricultural] unions . . . crippled the county's lemon industry because the walkout prevented the harvesting, packing, and distribution of all citrus. In essence, there was a complete work stoppage because the harvesters, packers, and canners were all on strike" (84). After threatening to evict the strikers if the strikers did not return to work, "the growers carried out their [threat] . . . a devastating experience for the workers especially since many of them had resided on the ranches for two or three generations" (87). As my father recollected, though some of the strikers made their way back to Sespe, the mass eviction transformed the small workers' community in Fillmore—particularly with the arrival of many "Okie" agricultural workers to replace the strikers.

A second encounter after my grandfather's arrival in Sespe in 1936 underscored for him that, although his location had changed, his social position as a Mexican remained the same:

> After we settled into our little house in the workers' camp at Rancho Sespe—the last great hacienda in California—I met an American rancher and foreman whose property bordered the camp. He introduced himself, then said to me, "I hope that your family, especially your children, respect my property and don't trespass beyond that wire fence." He added these humiliating words: "Any individual who doesn't own a piece of land, or at least, a home in which to live, is not worthy of being a citizen of any country." We were thus eating the bitter bread of the exiled. (35)

For my grandfather, these two exchanges with American ranchers captured something crucial about his life. "Why was man born?" he asked. "To struggle, just as birds were born to fly." To remain steadfast in the face of unjust suffering formed a defining component of Francisco's existence as a farm worker during the 1930s. His description of himself at twenty-seven as "ambitious, genial, self-confident, humorous, and above all, hardworking" (34) makes it clear that my grandfather felt more than up to that struggle.

And yet, as Esther Pérez Doran, Francisco's daughter and eldest child, and my aunt, wrote in 1965 for a college class, life in Sespe Village continually tested the Pérez family's strength, spirit, and resilience. According to Esther, the village community lived under a "feudal system" completely dominated by the ranch owner, Keith Spalding. Esther juxtaposes this North American hacendado first to her own family's impoverished status and meager living conditions in the farm worker camp and then to her father's brutal work as a laborer:

Once a month the lord and master, the owner of Rancho Sespe, would make his rounds on horseback and look down at his "peasants." An "edict" would first go out to the village stating when Mr. Spalding would arrive so that we could prepare by watering our beautiful yards and by putting on our best Sunday clothes. But I made it a point never to appear to show any interest in this event, in this wealthy man who was the giver of all things in Sespe. I already knew better; I had seen my father, black with dust and soaked with perspiration, come home from picking lemons and oranges after a hot day. For this backbreaking work he was paid the great sum of a couple of dollars a day and allowed to rent a three-room house without heat, without indoor water, and without indoor plumbing (the homes were very cold and damp; in fact, I am still trying to get warm after all those cold years). My mother worked in the ranch's packing house at Sespe, where the pay was worse; later, my brothers also worked picking fruit. At Sespe, the Mexican community had a life without any hope for the future. I hated the people who were responsible for this, who made my father and mother work so hard for a crust of bread and a dried tortilla. But my father showed that while a man's body may be economically bound, his spirit is not; although he had only a third-grade education, he read avidly and passed this habit along to his children.[22]

For the white community of Fillmore, education translated into opportunity and hope. Within the racialized space of the Spalding hacienda for Mexican Americans, however, a high school education did little to change one's status and circumstances. Esther relates her own efforts, after finishing high school, to obtain an office position as a clerk at the rancho:

I had gotten straight A's as a student, which helped me realize my dream of going to nursing school. In high school I had also taken courses in typing, bookkeeping, and shorthand. I did very well in these classes, and my bookkeeping teacher recommended me to work in Rancho Sespe's payroll office. I interviewed and was not accepted. Later, I learned that a white girl who had not finished high school was given the job. My family was very upset by this rejection. . . . Several years later, I was visiting my family in Sespe after graduating from nursing school. The same man who had refused me the job came by to see my father. He saw me carrying my new uniforms. He was surprised, and congratulated me on graduating. He remarked, "Now you can take care of me when I get sick." Although I said it to myself, my response was, "You can drop dead!"

My grandfather's idealization of a mythic Mexican homeland founded on the imagined pastoral terrain of rural Zacatecas, therefore, not only represents a spiritual solidarity with the farm worker immigrant community sharing his origins, but also stands as a defense against the perpetual "threat of social erasure" by colonizing United States sociocultural and economic institutions (Padilla 1993, 6). His imaginative return to the pre-American pastoral environment of his *abuelos* (grandparents) and his ancestor's hacienda society must be understood in relation to Esther's descriptions, the earlier comments like the rancher's, and the accounts of the 1936 and 1941 strikes. This nostalgic recuperation reaffirms cultural and genealogical continuity in the face of my grandfather's forced separation from that world as a child, and his continued alienation from both Mexican and American society as an adult. It thus forms the foundation of his children's Mexican American cultural identity within the racially hostile environment described above.

Just as his orphanhood may be read as a figuration for the cultural fragmentation of all Mexican immigrants in the United States, the reconstituted topography of rural Zacatecas stands as the originary "epistemological ground" of his cultural subjectivity. Situated "exactly in the center of the Mexican Republic" (2), the Zacatecas region where he was born is for my grandfather the geographic and cultural "heartland" of the nation. As descendants of its Spanish settlers, he and his father are thus "native sons" of a region which, according to popular sentiment in Mexico to this day, embodies the Mexican national character. When recalling his visit to the city of Zacatecas shortly after his family was forced to leave Jerez in early 1914, my grandfather asks the reader's patience as he not only "describes the topography of that great capital," but also strategically conflates this topography with Mexico's Spanish colonial history. "The city was founded in 1600 after the Spaniards discovered silver there," he explained. "It is situated in a small valley surrounded by mountains. The most prominent is the 'Bufa' mountain, which contains the richest silver mine ever discovered on the American continent" (5). Accounts of early Zacatecas illuminate the origins of the city as a mining center. As Enrique Semo explains, "[o]n September 8, [1546], a small detachment of Spanish soldiers, headed by Juan Tolosa, discovered the deposits of what has since been known as Cerro de la Bufa (Zacatecas.) The exploitation of these deposits, carried out under very difficult conditions . . . quickly fulfilled all expectations" (1993, 73). King Philip II granted the mining town of Zacatecas the title of "city" on October 17, 1585. Three years later, the king and the Council of the Indies added to this official title the words "noble and loyal," and granted the city a coat of arms. As stated in the royal enactment, the inhabitants of Zacatecas had "served [the King] with faithfulness and care, and defended the city from the Chichimeca Indians . . . as well as [serving] through the benefits accorded by the silver mines on its outskirts, from which have been, and continue to be, derived much wealth" (Flores 1996, 90). By the turn of the century, Zacatecas [became] the third largest city in the country." A description from 1620 mentions "more than 1,000 European families, and a total of 40,000 inhabitants; the city [also] had 25 large *haciendas de beneficio* (livestock hacienda)" (Semo 1993, 73).

What my grandfather did not identify was the actual status of these great mines—symbolized by the prominent Bufa Mountain in the center of the city of Zacatecas—at the end of the Porfirian period. In their study of economic dependency, Fernando Enrique Cardoso and Enzo Faletto (1979) illustrate how the Mexican mining industry exemplified the late nineteenth-century dilemmas of underdevelopment throughout Latin America. While acknowledging that during the thirty-five-year reign of Díaz (1876–1911), "Mexico recovered much of its economic dynamism thanks chiefly to renewed exploitation of its silver wealth," Cardoso also notes that by 1914, when my grandfather saw the Bufa for the first time, three-quarters of Mexico's mines "belonged to foreigners" (105). My grandfather's mythic, pastoral, and communal vision of Zacatecas shows no sign of the enormous concentration of property in the hands of politicians, foreign speculators, and surveying companies, which Cardoso finds characteristic of the time (106).[23] Nor did he mention here the conflictive nature of the earlier colonial period. As Semo writes, "[t]he handful of Basques who embarked on the risky exploitation of the Bufa mine represented the beginnings of a silver aristocracy who appropriated virtually all of the North's resources. Within a few years [after the founding of the mines], they owned large agricultural and cattle properties and commercial and mining enterprises, and they financed, with their own means, expeditions of discovery and conquest" (1993, 74).

Similarly, the complex early history of the hacienda in Zacatecas does not find a place in my grandfather's account. During the eighteenth century the hacienda system in Zacatecas went through a period of consolidation. In the late-seventeenth century, property owners took advantage of new laws passed by the Crown to acquire lands that belonged to Indians. These laws "were a means of justifying the growth and development of large areas of land, confining Indians to smaller and smaller space, and controlling [Indians] economically and socially—along with castes and mestizos—so that they would not be able to acquire more land" (Flores 1996, 88). The Indian population became "condemned to dependency on the agrarian structure determined by the hacienda [system], which as it grew increasingly stronger converted them into peons, renters, and later, tenant farmers and salaried laborers" (88–89). By justifying abuses against Indians and lower-class mestizos, and particularly the illegal occupation and plunder of lands, the laws thus contributed to the formation of the feudalistic hacienda system, which lasted into the twentieth century.

For my grandfather, his Spanish ancestors, the Mexican "heartland," and the outlying terrain of his mining and hacienda society together established a heroic, legendary, and prosperous Mexican past, rather than a photograph of disjuncture and exploitation. Other references to prerevolutionary Jerez added to his portrait of a land populated by descendants of illustrious Spanish founders. Especially powerful were his memories of his father, the principal inhabitant of that "colonial" and late-nineteenth-century world. Since my grandfather left the hacienda community at age six, stopped regularly attending school at seven, and became orphaned at eleven, his memories of the "prerevolutionary" period probably derived from stories heard as a child from his father. My interviews with my grandfather and the text of "Memorias" suggest that his knowledge of early Mexican history came primarily, though not exclusively, from the same source. Not surprisingly, then, his memories of his father were inseparable from his romantic representation of the outlying hacienda terrain of Jerez—a town situated forty miles from the capital.

Nor did his father simply embody familial origins; in fact, as Pérez patriarch his overshadowing figure participated in that genealogical and sociocultural rootedness in Mexico that my grandfather traces back to its Mexican (Spanish) colonial "founders." Though my grandfather enjoyed reading imaginative writing, I do not think he had ever read Juan Rulfo or any of the other modern or nineteenth-century Latin American historical novelists. And though detective fiction and the science fiction of Jules Verne delighted him, he did not seem fond of sweeping historical or epic narrative (he once told me that Don Quixote had not impressed him because he considered it "fantasy"). Nevertheless, my grandfather often described hacienda society in a manner reminiscent of Juan Rulfo's mythic rendering. At the opening of Rulfo's novel *Pedro Páramo*, for example, when asked which lands near a central Mexican rural town belong to a local hacendado, a peasant answers with a series of admonitory questions: "See that mountain, the one that looks like a pig's bladder? Good, now look over there. See the ridge of that mountain? Now look over here. See that mountain way off there? Well, all that's the Media Luna, everything you see. And it all belongs to Pedro Páramo" (1955, 4). The mountain described is Cerro de la Bufa itself, said by some to resemble a bloated animal bladder, which is located near Rulfo's native community in the bordering state of Jalisco. In much the same way as Rulfo's novel, my grandfather noted that in "colonial" times "people of property didn't measure their property in hectares, parcels, or plots, but rather by how far their vision reached; once these men began to dedicate themselves to the raising of sheep and other livestock, within the course of years, they counted herds in the thousands, if not millions" (2). Here, and in many other places as well, my grandfather grants a larger-than-life quality to that Mexican colonial history that Rulfo both refracts and deconstructs. And yet, these renderings of the mythic dimensions of the founding Zacatecan haciendas find support in historical accounts. Semo cites a 1579 report by the *alcalde* mayor of Zacatecas, Hernando Vargas, which states that in the Valley of Aguascalientes, the granary of the Zacatecan mining industry, "more than 100,000 cows and 200,000 sheep and 10,000 mares grazed between the town of San Juan [del Río] and Querétaro, which are seven leagues apart" (1993, 73). In keeping with this portrait of a bountiful hacienda landscape, San Juan de las Calabasas, the hacienda community where my grandfather spent much of his childhood, was his "beloved native village," a place where "everything was the color of roses and all of the food was sweet" (14). The imaginary geocultural terrain of central Mexico stands in sharp opposition to my grandfather's later cultural uprootedness, permanent forced exile, and "slavelike" experience as a farm laborer. Hacienda life in Jerez was a carefree "vacation" or "adventure," the rural landscape symbolizing the innocence and expansive freedom of childhood.

And in the center of this pastoral landscape stand the boy and his father, whose close relationship, rooted irrevocably in the nineteenth-century hacienda world, is conveyed through brief and poignant remembrances of childhood. Early in "Memorias" my grandfather remembers

> asking my father, when I was four or five, the following question: "Tell me how many tortillas I have eaten in my entire life." My father answered, "I'd say about a hundred." Wouldn't you agree that such childish questions, though silly, are at the same time philosophical? (5)

In this way, the landscape of the hacienda contains within it not only communitarian rootedness, but familial intimacy between father and son. Of course, other relatives inhabit this world as well, providing background on the maternal side of my grandfather's family, and complementing the emphasis in "Memorias" on patriarchal lineage. His maternal grandparents, ghostly presences in the narrative, lived in a hacienda village near Jerez and took care of him while his father worked. By proudly providing elaborate nineteenth-century names of these abuelos, Don Ambrosio Róbles (who in fact was his grandfather Don José Róbles's nephew) and Doña Hipólita Macías Róbles (his grandmother), he reasserts cultural continuity and familial pride in the face of their total erasure from the United States historical ledger. He insists on carrying such a name forward himself, often referring to himself in "Memorias" as "Don" Francisco, the title his father always affectionately used and thus a constant reminder of his father's love and perhaps even of the writer's "upper class" hacienda ancestors.

As for his own mother Juliana, daughter of Don José Róbles and Doña Hipólita, my grandfather says that he doesn't remember her at all. She died in 1913, soon after giving birth to her third child; thus the only "mother" my grandfather knew was Doña Hipólita. (In the following section I will address the central roles Juliana and her younger sister Dominga play in "Memorias.") As if to claim for his mother and her parents the same nobility he posited for his father's ancestors, my grandfather asserts that Doña Hipólita and the Róbleses "were from a proud family with deep roots in Zacatecas, and though I never knew my mother, I use her family name as a part of my own" (30).[24]

Mexican customs, traditions, and events such as weddings and funerals are also set within the hacienda's retrospective geographic space. Like the landscape, these practices affirm as well the communitarian and familial qualities of my grandfather's pre-American cultural environment. Hacienda weddings, for instance, were "grand events" in which "all families and friends in the community cooperated" (28). The food preparations were highly communal. Some families

> would prepare a cow for the celebration's meal, others two lambs, three pigs, and a few goats—this, of course, doesn't include the dozens of chickens. As for tortillas, no fewer than ten women were grinding corn and making tortillas before and during the celebration. Not only family members came, but the whole community, without any need for invitations. A second party took place the day after, a *tornaboda*, with music and more music and dancing. (28)

This communal and nostalgic vision of Mexican hacienda society is closely linked to that self-contradictory "rupture" of crossing the U.S.–Mexican border. In a telling passage about listening to a record by his favorite opera singer, Mario Lanza, my grandfather reflected on his ancestral Mexican hacienda community and its Spanish colonial past:

> I feel content in my journey through this life that I did something for my family and that I continue being the "trunk" of the future family tree, [following] those Spanish pioneers who one day gave us a language and a religion—even though, as Bernal Díaz del Castillo said [in his account of the Spanish conquest of Mexico], they came with the cross and the sword. (37)

Although the last line momentarily acknowledges that buried, contradictory historical reality of the Mexican (Spanish) colonial mythos, which the Róbles counternarrative will foreground, "Memorias" elsewhere elides prerevolutionary social conflict. Dwelling on the work's ahistorical projection of an impossibly harmonious communal past, however, is less fruitful than placing it within the wider context of my grandfather's life as a deracinated Mexican who, after seventy years in the "belly of the monster," to use Jose Martí's description of life as an Hispanic in the United States, still viewed himself and his American-born descendants as displaced "migrants" and "orphans" regrettably alienated from Mexican culture and history. Recording his Mexican (Spanish) colonial heritage was his way of bequeathing to his immediate family and Chicano descendants a connection to a heroic and noble past.

Not simply aristocratic pretense or genealogical self-invention, then, my grandfather's nostalgic desire for a mythic Spanish colonial world was a socially empowering reassertion of cultural continuity and pride, in the face of deeply felt cultural displacement and fragmentation. "With my hand on my chest, Don Francisco is writing this history," he announces early in the narrative, "the descalzo who one day crossed the Río Grande somewhere near El Paso with his rags on his head—and I am not at all ashamed to say this, because it is the truth" (3). Rejecting the shame that U.S. cultural and economic formations seek to force upon his Mexican American descendants and community, he implicitly urges his Mexican American readers to follow him in shedding their internalized "American" habits. More important, by juxtaposing his status as an orphaned descalzo with his action as Don Francisco, writing the "history" of the family, my grandfather assures that his "nostalgic" narrative must be read in the light of his later U.S. experience of alienation and exploitation.

While specific memories of his father were interwoven throughout my grandfather's vision of hacienda society, other pre-American passages placed his father within the more mundane world of day-to-day affairs. Though described throughout the narrative as a businessman who worked most of his life as an accountant for hacendados, Lira Pérez in fact operated several other businesses after his departure from Jerez. At one point he bought and sold animal bones, a product he acquired from the livestock haciendas of central Mexico. (Wool, hides, tallow, horsehair, and bones—along with meat—were standard products of livestock haciendas.) Grandfather remembered accompanying his father more than once to examine train cars filled with bones, which his father was selling or purchasing. After leaving Jerez, for a time Lira Pérez also owned a butcher shop.

As "the only trained business administrator in that region," before his displacement from Jerez, Lira Pérez had apparently prospered in the hacienda economy: "He was educated at the university in the state capital in business administration, [and] since he was fifty-two-years old when I was born, I imagine that he must have already practiced his profession for more than thirty years by then" (6). Following this chronology, Lira Pérez would therefore have begun his career in 1878, two years after the rise of Porfirio Díaz, the dictator whose name is synonymous with the period of the "modern" hacienda, and with the widespread socioeconomic injustices and repressions this quasifeudalistic economy brought about. Although Díaz met opposition throughout the 1880s in Zacatecas, "[t]he consolidation of the Porfirista regime, which was initiated with the assassination [in 1886] of the last dissident [General Trinidad García de la Cadena], . . . culminated [in the state] in 1888, when Jesús Aréchiga became governor" (Flores 1996, 139). Díaz's thirty-five year reign is a complicated period. He has been credited with "industrializing" the hacienda system and thus bringing modern capitalism to a predominantly rural society. In his analysis of early twentieth-century Mexican emigration to the United States, Acuña explains that Díaz's policies "encouraged the industrialization of agriculture, mining, and transportation, which led to the uprooting of the Mexican peasants, many of whom moved northward" (1988, 147). Modernization under Díaz, in short, led to the demise of the communal village and commercialization of the hacienda. And yet, as Cardoso points out, for Díaz "the old hacienda system remained the most effective means of keeping the peasants submissive," therefore he "needed its support" (1979, 107). Lira Pérez's career thus spanned the Díaz period of hacienda dominance from 1880 to 1911.[25]

Or as my grandfather proudly announced, in his father's youth "the great haciendas and latifundios began to be formed . . . and that was exactly where my father first began to practice his profession" (11).

The single extant photograph of Lira Pérez was taken in September 1912, during Independence Day celebrations in Jerez (see fig. 5). He was fifty-six, a tall, well-dressed, gaunt man who appears to be of higher socio-economic status than the townsfolk around him. While the aged campesino at the extreme left, and most of the others in the photograph wear sombreros made of straw, my great-grandfather's sombrero appears to be made of felt and displays embroidery on its rim. Dark and weatherworn, his expression stern, he stands in front of what appears to be a patriotic parade, grasping the reins of a wagon drawn by three white horses and decorated with Mexican banners and flags. Though actually well to the right, Lira Pérez seems to be at the center of this photograph of his community's most important public celebration, while the man in the middle of the photo may be the son (or perhaps a relative or foreman) of Don Jacinto Carlos, a hacendado who employed Lira Pérez. The lower-class folk in the audience behind these two men seem to squeeze into the photograph's frame. At the picture's extreme right stand Lira Pérez's two young sons. My grandfather Francisco, age four or five and dressed in the white clothes of Mexican campesinos, holds his hand before his face. Marcos, his older half-brother, stares like his father directly into the camera.

Fig. 5. *Juan Lira Pérez (standing at right in dark sombrero) with two of his sons, from far right, Francisco and Marcos in Jerez, Mexico, on Independence Day, September 1912.*

I have often imagined how this photograph survived the events of the ten years that followed—not only the chaos of the revolution itself, but the family's forced departure from Jerez in early 1914, their journey during the civil war, the death of Lira Pérez in 1919, and the subsequent orphanhood and emigration of Francisco. Since my grandfather could not have carried the photograph with him when he emigrated in 1921, a Herrera or perhaps Róbles relative from Jerez must have transported it when those families also emigrated (see family tree).

By writing his memoirs, my grandfather tried to grant "textual permanence" to his father's life and his own (Padilla 1993, 4), thus bequeathing to his Mexican American descendants the foundational narrative of their familial and cultural origins. At another level, though, he struggled with the need to resist those material and economic forces that had led to his fragmented cultural condition in the United States Though often eliding the social conflicts of the pre-American past, "Memorias" therefore participates, however deeply mediated by a language of nostalgic reflection, in that critical discourse that Ramón Saldívar has identified in modern Chicano narratives. Notwithstanding its suppressions, if judged first as an immigrant narrative, my grandfather's autobiography joins with other oppositional autobiographical works, such as Ernesto Galarza's *Barrio Boy* (1971), to explore what Ramón Saldívar has termed the "imaginary ways in which historical men and women live out their lives in a class society, and how the values, concepts, and ideas purveyed by the mainstream, American culture that tie them to their social functions seek to prevent them from a true knowledge of society as a whole" (1990, 6). But another layer of the palimpsest of history in "Memorias" remains to be peeled back. As the Róbles family narrative will reveal, my grandfather's representation of Mexican hacienda society both records and obscures its underlying socioeconomic and cultural formations.

Chavela's Funeral

> It's just incredible. It just does not explain. Or perhaps that's it: they don't explain and we are not supposed to know. We have a few old mouth-to-mouth tales; we exhume from old trunks and boxes and drawers letters without salutation or signature, in which men and women who once lived and breathed are now merely initials or nicknames. . . . [The people] are there, yet something is missing; they are like a chemical formula exhumed along with the letters from that forgotten chest,

carefully, the paper old and faded and falling to pieces, the writing faded, almost indecipherable, yet meaningful, familiar in shape and sense, the name and presence of volatile and sentient forces . . .

—William Faulkner, *Absalom, Absalom!*

Fictions and the fiction-making process are a central constituent of the truth of any life as it is lived and of any art devoted to the presentation of that life.

—Paul John Eakin, *Fictions in Autobiography*

The genealogist needs history to dispel the chimeras of the origin, somewhat in the manner of the pious philosopher who needs a doctor to exorcise the shadow of his soul. He must be able to recognize the events of history, its jolts, its surprises, its unsteady victories and unpalatable defeats—the basis of all beginnings, atavisms, and heredities.

—Michel Foucault, "Nietzsche, Genealogy, History"

An incident that caused an unexpected shift in my recuperating and interpreting "Memorias" offers a cautionary reminder of what recent critics of autobiographical and historical narratives have termed the "impulse to self-invention" (Couser, 1989, 19).[26] Certainly, what happened at a relative's funeral underscores Padilla's emphasis on the "centrality of thick socio-historicized readings of formative Mexican American (autobiographical) narratives and the historical particularities of their production" (1993, xi). One could even see this event as an example of what Padilla calls "discontinuity" in the discursive genealogy of Chicano literary traditions (7). More important, though, the funeral encounter I will now discuss strongly suggests that readings—including Padilla's—of early Mexican American autobiographies must be self-critically aware of their own suppressions. As the Róbles family helped to reveal, my grandfather's nostalgic desire worked to conceal iniquities and social conflicts buried deep in his father's hacienda past. To insure that such powerful, shaping forces do not remain unexamined, scholars who recover and interpret autobiographical and historical narratives by individuals whose "voices have not merely been forgotten . . . but suppressed" (xi) must be constantly aware of the issue of fictionality in these texts, and must also delve critically into representations of pre-American history. The nostalgic impulse in Mexican American autobiographies is certainly the product of sociocultural rupture and fragmentation, but as Padilla himself has suggested, this impulse constructs a "master" narrative designed to suppress much of what does not conform to the author's idealized projection of the past. Nor does recognizing and retrieving such textual sublimations and contradictions necessarily undermine the obvious need to restore the dignity and integrity of these early autobiographers' lives. In fact, this restoration can be enhanced by foregrounding those submerged power relations so often inherent in the social manifestations of these lives.

At a time when I was beginning to transcribe my grandfather's manuscript, a strange occurrence at a cemetery revealed more about my grandfather's relation to his past and his sense of self-identity than I had to that point been prepared to grasp. When Aunt Chavela was laid to rest in July 1992, the myth of my grandfather's father, drawn in part from the Independence Day photograph, was figuratively exhumed. The funeral was held in Santa Paula, a rural community north of Los Angeles and not far from Fillmore, the town where my grandfather and his wife had reared their children. After attending the service, my parents and I followed the procession to the small cemetery where Chavela would be buried. Members of both sides of my grandfather's family, the Pérezes and Róbleses, were present, some Róbles relatives having come from as far away as central Mexico to pay their respect to a woman who had emigrated from their community some fifty years earlier. A priest read a prayer over the open grave, and my parents and I passed by Chavela's casket. After the prayer, we greeted members of both sides of my grandfather's family, some of whom were as unfamiliar to my father as to me. My father stopped to greet Nicolas Róbles (Nico) and his family—some other Róbleses, he later informed me, that he had not seen in twenty years. A younger couple, who introduced themselves as my father's cousins, but whom my father had never met, stopped for a short conversation.

While my father was engaged with them, I left to speak with other members of my family. When I returned a few minutes later, I was startled to find myself in the midst of an uncomfortably loud argument, one made all the more improbable by the circumstances and locale. My parents later told me that, after introducing herself, the woman launched into a tirade in Spanish against the Pérez family and especially against Juan Lira Pérez, who had been dead for eighty years. When I arrived, the woman was dramatically waving her finger in my father's face. That my father and his siblings, all American-born, neither knew their grandfather nor, with the exception of my Aunt Esther, took any interest in their dead ancestors, made this confrontation all the more baffling. Hearing the commotion, others gathered near us, watching in astonishment and dread: here was a person without shame, or any respect for family, their countenances seemed to say. Face-to-face with my father, our cousin attacked the moral character of the Pérez patriarch, and by association that of the four succeeding male generations, including my own. The spitefulness of the woman's colloquial Spanish cannot be captured in a literal translation. In effect, she called our long-deceased founding patriarch a "philandering criminal" who in prerevolutionary Zacatecas left a trail of hate and misery in his sinister wake. This, she claimed, was Lira Pérez's contribution to a trusting friendship between the two families that went back to the last century. Concluding her complaint with a string of curses, she informed her stunned audience that the Pérez family's cherished mythologized grandfather had at the age of fifty-six raped Dominga Róbles, his wife's older sister (who for a short period in 1912 had come to live with the couple while my great-grandmother Juliana was recovering from childbirth). Her accusations left everyone speechless. (Later I learned that the product of that crime, Paulo Róbles Pérez—half-brother and cousin to my grandfather—was adopted and reared by Dominga's brother, José.)

My grandfather, whose nostalgic and heartfelt remembrance of his father had created Lira Pérez's ennobling reputation and legend in our family, but whose stories make only passing reference to the Róbles complaint, had apparently been wary of just such a clash. Immediately after the cemetery service, he quietly left without speaking to any of the Róbleses. My father, like his four siblings, never knew his paternal grandfather. Though not likely to take insults without responding in kind, in deference to Chavela and others in attendance, my father listened to the woman's complaint without answering. Like many others at the funeral, he was dumbfounded by the curious spectacle, that, as we later learned, centered on a series of events that occurred in 1912 and 1913 in Jerez.

The forty-five-year-old woman before us, Berta Róbles, was José Róbles's daughter—but she was also a Róbles by *marriage*, having wed Paulo's son José Pérez (her second cousin).[27] Eighty-some years after Lira Pérez's transgression, on the occasion of the gathering of two branches of my grandfather's family, she now sought retribution. According to the Róbles account, as divulged by Berta and later supported by other Róbles relatives, the Róbles family hoped that the illegitimate Paulo would be legally recognized by his father, but the boy was spurned and he and his mother barred from claiming any inheritance upon the death of Lira Pérez.[28]

Growing up in the family of his mother, the child suffered the stigma of a confused identity as the bastard child of a man who was detested by those forced to rear the boy. Nor has my grandfather ever acknowledged the kinship. As if keenly aware of the Róbles's dispossession, in "Memorias" my grandfather proclaims his privileged status as "primogenitor," the legitimate firstborn son with inheritance rights to his father's property in Jerez (2).[29] My grandfather had even gone to a funeral in Santa Paula, California (where many Róbleses settled) also attended by his half-brother Paulo, but as one of my aunts later recalled, when directed to meet the elderly man, my grandfather answered, "I don't have any brother."

The figure of Don Juan Lira Pérez, though embodying honorable and even heroic "roots" in my own family's tales, served quite a different function in the Róbles family narrative. The legend of the rape and the father's repudiation of his child, passed down through several generations and carried to the United States when they emigrated, became a central metaphor and theme in the mythos of their family's historical origins. To this day, in their family narrative, Lira Pérez signifies not honor, origins, and ancestry, but rather those intangible historical and social forces, bound to the feudalistic hacienda economy, which contributed to the Róbles family's betrayal and suffering in Mexico, and later exodus to the United States.

Leaving us to gather ourselves at the edge of Chavela's grave, Berta and her husband then departed, but the story was not yet finished. Nico, another Róbles "cousin," who in the fifty years that he had lived and worked alongside the Pérez family had never spoken a word to any of us about our founding patriarch, then pulled my father aside. As if wishing to dispel any misplaced belief that Berta's remarks might simply be the unfounded "hysterics" of an angry *mujer*, he calmly told my father that the Róbles family had shown great self-restraint in dealing with the matter of the rape at that time. Though more discreet than Berta, Nico's final message was all the more startling for its brevity. Underscoring the historical injustice that Lira Pérez had, for them, clearly come to personify, he said, "your grandfather did something awful . . . y lo hubieran podido matar. . . . They [the Róbleses] could have killed him for what he did . . . they could have killed your grandfather for what he did to that girl"—words all the more chilling because Lira Pérez was Nico's grandfather .

Before I propose a resolution to the questions that arose from this incident, I should first briefly reconstruct those events occurring between 1912 and 1914 that my grandfather and Berta have so differently described.

I begin with the obvious: that part of the Róbles family has remained angry with the Pérez family for almost ninety years, as a result of events involving my grandfather's father two years prior to his departure from the town of his birth. In a manner different from my grandfather's usual sentimental bent, the account of this time in "Memorias" stresses Lira Pérez's precarious political position. Though the local sociopolitical circumstances of the forced flight are not intimated, my grandfather indicates that as an associate of the hacienda elite his father was viewed as an enemy of the insurgents, and that he left his ancestral home because soldiers were planning to execute him. (As I will explain in the next section, Lira Pérez paid protection money to the insurrectionists for a time; but in early 1914, perhaps a few months before the April 2 Battle of Torreón, his agreement with the rebels fell apart.)

The legend of his 1914 flight, which had fascinated and disturbed me as a college student, as well as the less than heroic reasons for the exodus, I can now see are plainly inscribed in the margins of my grandfather's memoirs. My earlier desire to reconstruct an ideologically acceptable version of my past had led me to dismiss these passages as youthful "adventures," largely extraneous to my grandfather's romantic narrative of origins. In his account of events in early 1914, my grandfather describes how his father hid in a well for three days without food while the soldiers searching for him sacked and burned his property at San Juan de las Calabasas. Several of Lira Pérez's employers had been executed by the insurrectionists. The haciendas where his father had been employed for more than three decades were raided and burned. Stories by members of my grandmother's family, the Herreras—who lived on the nearby Tesorero and Víboras haciendas—recount pitched battles between troops and rebel soldiers on the hacienda grounds. Salvador Herrera—Concepción Pérez's eldest brother and a man who lived to be ninety-seven—described these engagements in a tape-recorded interview with Esther. He recalled soldiers from opposing sides screaming epithets at each other in the midst of a battle at Tesorero. His wife, Jesusita, remembered the battle as having occurred in and around the hacienda chapel. (Salvador and Concepción's sister, María, became Lira Pérez's fourth wife and bore a child by him in 1912. Though Concepción was ten years older than her husband and therefore likely to be more familiar with Lira Pérez's life and reputation in Jerez, my grandmother never mentioned his name to anyone. When I asked her for information about him during an interview, she said she knew nothing.)

Before escaping from the town, my great-grandfather, according to the myth written by his son, only narrowly evaded his pursuers. When the fallen patriarch emerged from his last hiding place, he escaped with his six-year-old son under the cover of night. What now strikes me in this section of my grandfather's otherwise nostalgic reconstruction of his childhood is his lasting resentment that "when the revolutionaries, those blood brothers of ours, arrived in Jerez, they executed people and they forced many others to flee. . . . They wanted to kill my father, too. Many times he escaped by the skin of his teeth . . . a week later we all escaped through the mountains by burro, one for each of us" (4).[30]

The image of his father escaping in the dark is my grandfather's sharpest memory of this journey through the mountains, and although Lira Pérez lived for another five years, and my grandfather remained in Mexico for two more after his death, this childhood trauma—the originary moment of separation from his ancestral Mexican community—serves in "Memorias" as what Padilla names the point of sociocultural rupture in the Mexican American autobiographical and historical consciousness. By fixating on the image of his father on that night, my grandfather cannot but nostalgically push aside the humiliating details of the previous days. Eighty years after his father's inglorious retreat, my grandfather remembers the tall figure in front of him on that night, restored imaginatively to an honored position within the idealized cultural geography of his settler ancestors. "There, fleeing from his ancestral home," my grandfather writes, "went an honorable and productive citizen . . . who at one time was a descendant of the most prosperous and propertied hacendados in the entire valley of Jerez" (4). Neither his father's exile, nor his own permanent displacement, can be viewed by my grandfather except in the light of the mythic hacienda past. His is the elite class perspective of a child whose secure and comfortable world was overturned by a ragtag group of peons. The peasant soldiers who sought his father, he suggests, were actually using their newfound power for short-term gain. As my grandfather ironically explains, "we left at night so that our loyal Mexican 'brethren,' people who one day were our employees and we the employers, couldn't detect us" (4).

We have come a long way from the family narratives of some Chicanos whose *antepasados* were said to have ridden a "raid or two" with Pancho Villa—but we must go further. As I would later learn from my Aunt Esther, who met and spoke with Berta, the Róbles family believes that when Juliana, my grandfather's mother, was pregnant in 1912–1913 with her third child, she was cared for in her home by her older sister Dominga. The Róbles family charges that Lira Pérez raped his sister-in-law, and then renounced his illegitimate son Paulo, primarily for legal and business reasons. Esther believed that the relationship was consensual, one that Lira Pérez broke off. According to the Róbles narrative, astute accountant that he was, Lira Pérez may have realized that legally recognizing the male child would create a web of financial difficulties for his other sons and family in Jerez. Yet, this suggests that if Lira Pérez had only supported and acknowledged the boy, the accusations of rape would perhaps have been forgotten. Obviously, he did not foresee his forced departure from the town a year or so later. He may even have been forced to leave before the child was born.

But this was not the end of the tale that Lira Pérez, while in Jerez, had written for himself. The fierce nostalgia that imbues my grandfather's account of the escape from town also obscures and suppresses yet another side of his father's life during the 1912–1914 period: a secret relationship with a woman named María Herrera (my grandmother's elder sister) who would later become his fourth wife, but who at this time lived with her family twenty miles from Jerez at the hacienda known as Víboras. (After Francisco's father's death in 1919, María and her siblings were extremely important to Francisco; her family took care of him, and, as mentioned earlier, he eventually married María's youngest sister, Concepción.) As my grandfather perhaps unintentionally acknowledged in a tape-recorded interview in 1987, when his father left Jerez in early 1914 on short notice, he took Francisco, his mistress/wife María, and their two children— a boy named Lucas, born in 1912, and a baby girl named Diega, born a few months before the family's flight. Although "Memorias" does not mention María as part of Lira Pérez's life in Jerez, in this interview María appears in my grandfather's description of their 1914 journey. After they left the mountains, they boarded a train, but were forced to ride on its roof because it was filled with soldiers on their way north to do battle with Villista and Maderista rebels. The episode recalls the train rides described in Galarza's *Barrio Boy*, whose early chapters are also set at the height of the revolution. My grandfather remembered María sitting on the curved roof at night, holding on to Diega, struggling to keep herself and the baby from falling off the shaking train. Clearly contradicting this taped recollection, "Memorias" instead states vaguely that it was "during his father's stay" in Torreón, where he lived on and off between early 1914 and his death, that both Lucas and Diega were born. By suggesting that Lira Pérez met María after leaving Jerez, the text erases the secret affair with María. Since this third relationship means that between 1912 and 1914 Lira Pérez had four children by three women—Paulo by Dominga Róbles; Lucas and Diega by María Herrera; and Marcos II, who died in infancy in 1913, by his wife Juliana (see family tree)—Berta's impassioned complaint at the funeral becomes all the more credible and compelling. And yet, although María could presumably have been blamed for Dominga's abandonment by Lira Pérez, the Róbles family narrative doesn't mention her at all, suggesting that the Róbles accusation centers upon Lira Pérez's abuse of Dominga, rather than his decision, if this is in fact what occurred, to take María, rather than Dominga, with him.

The Róbles narrative instead draws other conclusions from the events of this time. Both Dominga and Juliana died at a young age, Juliana in 1913 and Dominga, who was at least fifteen years older than her sister, in 1922. Esther, who for a time mistakenly believed that Dominga had died in 1916, once joked that the aging patriarch may have poisoned these sisters to extricate himself from the legal and personal morass he had created; and while this theory is chronologically impossible in the case of Dominga, I obviously have no way of determining the complete truth of Lira Pérez's complex relationship with the Róbleses. As Galarza, quoting Henry Adams, cites in the epigraph of *Barrio Boy*, "the memory was all that mattered" for the Róbleses. Yet my aunt's passing remarks do perhaps throw added light on the origins of the Róbles narrative, for as Berta's and Nico's comments insinuate, the Róbles family may have excoriated Lira Pérez not only for his rape of Dominga and repudiation of Paulo, but also for the deaths of both sisters at an early age. Juliana apparently died of natural causes while recovering from childbirth. After losing their second daughter Dominga nine years later in 1922, however, the Róbles family may have concluded that any of their daughters who came in contact with Lira Pérez would meet a tragic end—or perhaps that the Pérezes simply brought tragedy to the family. I have not yet determined with any certainty the class status or political sympathies of the Róbleses when they lived near Jerez. Though certainly not associated with the hacendado elite, it is not clear they were impoverished campesinos. Many did not leave Mexico until the 1950s.

By preventing further contact between the Pérez and Róbles families, the revolution settled the issue of the illegitimate child—or so it seemed. For my purposes, the appearance of insurrectionists in Jerez in 1913 serves two important functions. First, by destroying Lira Pérez's career, dispossessing him of his property, and forcing him into permanent exile, it gave

him the comeuppance the Róbles family believes he deserved for his treatment of their daughters and perhaps for his decades-long role in the hacienda caste system. This financial ruin explains my grandfather's
socioeconomic and cultural "orphanhood." Had his father not left Jerez
nor lost his property, my grandfather probably would not have needed to
emigrate to the United States. Second, the civil war ensured that the mystery of Lira Pérez's relationship to the Róbles family would not be fully
revealed for many decades. The Róbleses never had the opportunity to
confront the despised founding father of one line of their family, nor—
because many of them remained in Mexico until after World War II—his
immediate heirs. Though eighty years had passed, Chavela's funeral offered the Róbleses an occasion to meet the descendants of Don Lira Pérez,
who, owing to their own unique construction of the past, knew almost
nothing of the other side of their patriarch's life and reputation.

I have only recently learned from Esther what is perhaps the most
tragic irony in my family narrative. My grandfather always blamed his
mother's death in 1913 on her sister Dominga! Refusing to imagine his
father as anything but heroic, he came to view this older sister as a wily
temptress and seducer of a distinguished and reluctant patriarch. According to this improbable twist, my grandfather's bedridden mother died
of a "broken heart" brought on by the shock of her own sister's betrayal.
Not only does this turn of plot make for a dramatic denouement to the
family narrative; in this way my grandfather transferred the blame for
Lira Pérez's apparent crimes onto the Róbles family, thus allowing him to
embrace a long-dead father and mother by salvaging untarnished memories of them from the chaos of family history—his most ambitious narrative sleight of hand.

The Maderista Rebellions

In the dining hall of the workers' camp at Rancho Sespe, I heard a [Mexi-
can] "bracero," a plebeian, make the following comment while he ate:
"One must eat the gringo's food, but one should throw the plate in his
face." I leave this statement to your critical judgment. In difficult times,
all things are acceptable. . . .

All of this is a part of a past that is filled with memories and not a
few sufferings, but today I am proud for having surmounted them. . . . I
was a child in Mexico, then a youth in the United States, a man, a
mature man, and now I am an old man. . . . I am so old I already have

one foot in the "other world." And what more than this is the inheritance of mankind? Today I am content that the maker of the infinite universe has granted me and my family the divine grace of living for so many years.

—Francisco R. Pérez, "Memorias"

Memory—how we remember and what we choose to remember, since we cannot remember everything—is intimately tied to a culturally organized discursive habitat.

—Genaro M. Padilla, *My History, Not Yours*

After Chavela's funeral, what struck me about my grandfather's text was not just its evasion of the Róbles complaint and nostalgic aggrandizement of Lira Pérez, but the multitude of absences, silences, gaps, and suppressions that now seemed to determine the narrative's representation of family history. The series of tales through which my family came to imagine its historical origins and cultural identity had been constructed on the buried ruins of the anti-nostalgic Róbles counterhistory and this "other" history might be said to signify more than the forgotten grievance of a single family. It represented as well the displaced histories of groups marginalized within Mexican society itself—such as women, Indians, and campesinos—who were systematically victimized by the feudalistic hacienda system and institutionally erased from the historical record. By focusing narrowly on the modern period without acknowledging the "trailing" historical qualifiers that Mexican Americans carry with us, some Chicano literary and historical studies unintentionally construct nineteenth-century (hacienda) history like my own family genealogy. In the interest of recovering our buried Mexican (American) past, they overlook the complexity, contradiction, and discontinuity inherent in this nineteenth-century social experience, thereby erasing our historical links to the hacienda as a social and cultural institution. Berta's complaint, which transgressed the traditional Mexican codes of respect and honor paid to elders and ancestors, provoked key questions about Chicano origins and history that my earlier readings of historical narratives had raised but not yet fully distilled.

The Róbles family narrative illuminates, from the perspective of the invisible victims of the Porfirian hacienda system, the class-based social contradictions as well as the gender-defined conflicts in hacienda society that formed the roots of the civil war and revolution, but that my grandfather's nostalgic idealization of his father's life effectively suppressed.

My grandfather alludes to his father's local political predicament and forced exile, but his single reference to the events leading up to the 1913 "well" episode is tellingly brief—a brevity that elides the painfully sublimated reality of the family's exodus: the Constitutionalist forces who gained ascendancy in rural Zacatecas in 1913 wished to put Lira Pérez to death because of his association with the *patrónes* (bosses) in the region.

The rebellions recounted in "Memorias" occurred in the summer of 1913. Since my grandfather was only five years old at the time, his interpretation of the political landscape within which these violent clashes took place must have come from stories told by his father until his death in 1919. Over the years since then, these stories, like all of the others in "Memorias," were subject to the vagaries of memory. Gore Vidal (1995) characterizes memory as a palimpsest: one never remembers an actual event, but rather one's earlier remembrance of the event, until late in life one has only memories of earlier remembrances of earlier recollections, and so forth. Like other contemporary writers of historical fiction both in the United States and Latin America, E. L. Doctorow (1993) too rejects the notion that imagination and memory are ever independent of each other.

By drawing from the historical scholarship on the period, however, one may sketch a picture of the turbulent political events that shaped the lives of Francisco and his father. The violence in Jerez was one of a multitude of lesser uprisings throughout the rural region around the capital occurring during mid-1913, skirmishes that preceded by a year the major battles between Federal troops and northern (Villista) and local revolutionary forces in the cities of Torreón and Zacatecas. The actions were carried out by groups that were a part of the early Madero movement—the first phase of the Madero Revolution in Zacatecas—a movement that came to prominence in the state two years earlier. The Maderistas opposed the Díaz dictatorship, and began armed activities to end the regime in the border region of Zacatecas and Durango in February 1911. Led by José Luis Moya, Pánfilo Natera, Martín Triana, and Trinidad Cervantes, the Maderistas sought a transformation of the political system and a role in the governmental decision-making process (Flores 1996, 157). "The immediate effects of the Madero Revolution in the [region] were limited: the removal from office of the governor and his replacement by one who fully represented the cause of Maderismo . . . and the replacement of various functionaries in the occupied regions by revolutionary officers" (157). Although Zacatecan Maderistas claimed that the 1911 Ciudad Juárez agreement, which ended the Díaz regime, did not change the political structure of the Mexican government, up to the summer of 1911 none of the Maderista groups in Zacatecas espoused any ideas other than those set forth by Maderismo (157).

Even before the February 1913 coup that ended the Madero presidency, the Zacatecan Maderistas were disappointed with the Madero presidency. By the time the president was assassinated, opposition to the government was widespread throughout the region and expressed in the form of rebellions and banditry (158). And while the official state political apparatus recognized the new administration of Victoriano Huerta, local functionaries with Maderista ties, who held either civil posts or positions in the rural forces, immediately rebelled (158). Led by Natera—the greatest Zacatecan hero of the revolution whose his giant bronze statue today stands atop the Bufa alongside that of Villa—the Maderista militants began armed actions to carry out the Constitutionalist revolution. Their forces quickly took control of most of the state. At this point, Lira Pérez's status as an associate of the hacendados marked him as an opponent of local, perhaps newly recruited rebels in Jerez. Some of the insurrectionists he faced could well have been former peons recruited from the very haciendas where he had worked for more than three decades.

The objective of the "second phase of the Madero revolution" in Zacatecas was the end of *cacicazgo*. Hacienda society, whose contradictions Porfirian modernization and industrialization amplified, was controlled for generations by *caciques* (local landowners or bosses), who wielded absolute power over peons, servants, and tenants. Even before the well-known depredations of the hacienda system under the Díaz dictatorship, in its mid-nineteenth-century manifestation, cacicazgo meant serfdom for the great majority of Mexican citizens. Speaking at the Mexican constitutional convention of 1856, the same year that Lira Pérez was born, reformer Ponciano Arriaga denounced the injustices of the landowning and peonage structure:

> the rich Mexican landowner . . . or the majordomo who represents him, may be compared to a feudal lord of the Middle Ages. On his domain, with more or less formality, he makes laws and executes them; administers justice and exercises civil powers; imposes taxes and fines; has jails, chains, and jailers; inflicts punishments and tortures, monopolizes trade and forbids any other business than that of his estate to be carried on without his consent. As a rule the judges and other public officials on these estates are the landowner's servants or tenants; they are henchmen incapable of acting freely, impartially, or justly, or of enforcing any law other than the absolute will of the master. (1993, 97)

As mentioned earlier, the economic policies enacted under Díaz aggra-vated these contradictions. The second phase of the Madero movement thus constituted a social revolution with more radical goals than those of the first phase. Not only did diverse sectors of the Zacatecan population participate in the movement, but, in seeking an end to *cacicazgo*, they "radicalized the substance of [earlier] demands, which now included sub-stantial changes in rural and mining work conditions, higher living stan-dards, a redefinition of the structure of private property . . . and a desire for more effective, honest, and respectful government administrations" (Flores 1996, 156).

In the summer of 1913, Zacatecan Constitutionalist forces responded to Huerta's coup by carrying out reprisals and other military actions against groups identified with the hacienda system—"landlords, *caciques*, Federals, sometimes clerics, and Spaniards (though rarely Americans)" (Knight 1986, 42). Accounts of these revolts in northern Zacatecas capture what prob-ably happened in nearby Jerez, where Lira Pérez was employed:

> [Justo] Avila, a small rancher at odds with the Lobatos hacienda, raised the latter's peons in revolt, recruiting 500 men. . . . Lobatos was a haci-enda with an absentee owner and, more important, a notoriously harsh *administrador*. Other properties suffered: the huge, Spanish-owned El Saucillo, near Rincón de Ramos, was sacked; peons were reported to have taken over estates at Pinos, to the east, where the *rurales* had mutinied. Soon, towns became targets. At the mines of Los Tocayos the entreaties of the miners' wives prevented the triumphant rebels from dynamiting the company building; at Sombrerete, the *jefe* and his men held off the rebels for a while, but finally the town was taken and sacked. (43)

Rural grievances and recruitment were all-important in these uprisings (43). Since landowners and caciques had exploited their peons, servants, and tenants, Constitutionalist recruitment among the ranks of hacienda laborers in Zacatecas continued apace throughout early 1913. By the sum-mer of 1913, the Constitutionalist army had grown to a point where "the governors and military commanders of Zacatecas, San Luis and Coahuila admitted that they could not police beyond the major cities, and they urged landowners to undertake their own defense" (45). Executions and other reprisals against officials, landowners, and merchants were com-mon. Yet some smaller towns and villages, choosing to acknowledge the defeat of the Federals, "gave up appealing for troops and made terms with the rebels instead" (45). Lira Pérez attempted this strategy. His brother-in-law Salvador Herrera told Esther that Francisco's father made an agreement with the rebels in Jerez, paying money to them in return for a guarantee of his safety.

The Federal withdrawal from the countryside during the summer of 1913 was paralleled by a general exodus of middle and upper class groups (45). His agreement broken in the fall of 1913, Lira Perez's life was in peril. Pursued by Maderista soldiers, he next found himself among the thousands of "well-to-do" refugees fleeing to the major cities of the northeast (45). He made his way to Torreón, where he hoped his anonymity, as well as the city's geographic distance from Jerez, would provide a measure of protection. (Instead, with the arrival of Pancho Villa's Division of the North only a few months later in March 1914, Torreón would be the site of one of the bloodiest battles of the revolution, witnessed by Lira Pérez and his family. Later, in August, Natera's Zacatecan forces joined up with Villa's army to lay siege to the city of Zacatecas, killing 6,000 Federal troops in three days.)

By the end of 1913, the Zacatecan Constitutionalists controlled most of the state, with the exception of the capital, where the Huertistas remained in power (Flores 1996, 158). The haciendas surrounding Jerez were "left in the hands of overseers or of peons, sharecroppers and villagers, and most of the smaller towns in the region were stripped of their *caciques*, officials and elite families" (Knight 1986, 46). Lira Pérez's exile thus represents the widespread and random nature of the process of military and political dissolution in Mexico during 1913–1914. As Knight explains:

> Historians of the Revolution are wont to trace its advance with an eye on the major cities. But their fall came at the end of a long sequence, beginning with the mountains and remote hamlets, then the villages and scattered mining camps, finally the provincial towns and state capitals. The major revolutionary armies of the north, it is true, advanced on Mexico City in 1914 in a roughly progressive, geographical fashion. But long before—and also while—this advance took place, there was a complementary revolutionary advance which cannot be mapped, save metaphorically. This took the form, not of a tide sweeping the country, but rather of an insidiously rising water level, which first inundated the rural areas . . . and finally swamped [the cities] to cover the face of the earth like Noah's flood. (46)

By the beginning of 1914, Lira Pérez's situation was desperate. Now in his late fifties, he had several young children to provide for as well as a son by a previous marriage fighting in the Federal army. Though freed from the

Maderista threat in Jerez, he was now a refugee bereft of property and a means of employment. When by chance he landed in Torreón in time to witness one of the great battles of the civil war, he too must have felt helpless before the flood.

Orphans of History

> I do not buy all the myths of the tribe into which I was born. . . . I will not glorify those aspects of my culture which have injured me and which have injured me in the name of protecting me.

> —Gloria Anzaldúa, *Borderlands/La Frontera*

The further information that Berta Róbles provided in her definitive deconstruction of the Pérez patriarchal legend—a dismantling completed by my family's knowledge of Lira Pérez's affair with María Herrera as well as the political context provided above—suggests that my grandfather's father abused his privileged status in Jerez not only to violate the young Róbles daughter sexually, but also to evade responsibility for his actions. In the male-dominated, economically polarized hacienda world, Lira Pérez's elite peers may well have viewed his actions as an "indiscretion." The marginalized status of women in nineteenth-century Mexico would certainly support this view. Describing the condition of women in Mexico City during this period, Sylvia Marina Arrom observes that:

> the pater familias exercised his authority without restraints, unencumbered by tradition or competing power; he completely controlled his wife's legal acts, property and person, being able to claim her domestic services, obedience and sexual fidelity (although the double standard granted him sexual freedom); he made all important decisions to enforce his will upon its members using whatever means he deemed necessary. (As quoted in Griswold del Castillo 1989, 86)

As Lira Pérez's story demonstrates, an important aspect of the ideal of patriarchal authority in Mexico involved the subordinate position of women, one defined by tradition. Richard Griswold del Castillo explains that:

> In the Iberian Catholic and the pre-Columbian traditions, women were supposed to accept absolute male authority in the household. Spanish laws, including the *Siete Partidas*, frequently described the relationship

between husband and wife in monarchical terms. . . . Men were the "rulers," women the "subjects"; husbands were the "absolute monarchs" of the "nation" of the family. (88)

The feudalistic social structure of the Porfirian hacienda system, controlled by patriarchs who passed their property and *patrón* status on to the eldest son, intensified the subordination and exploitation of female peons, servants, and tenants. By depicting the rapes committed by the cacique Páramo as well as by his teenage son, Miguel, Rulfo's *Pedro Páramo* foregrounds the crisis of abused campesino women under the hacienda system.

When local Maderistas rebelled in the summer of 1913, Lira Pérez's "indiscretion" was likely only one of the many moral transgressions held against the Jerez hacendados and their associates. I have learned from interviews with other family members that Dominga must have been at least twenty-five years younger than Lira Pérez, and while my relatives today refuse to discuss the topic, the evidence seems convincing that Lira Pérez raped Dominga. Only such an action would account fully for Berta's outburst and Nico's comment at the funeral, as well as the other corroborating stories that I have subsequently gathered.[31]

The silencing of Dominga's voice in my family history emblematizes that elaborate suppression of submerged power relations and social antagonisms found in many of the early Mexican American autobiographies. In such texts, nostalgia for an idealized past is often the narrator's dominant self-fashioning technique. Though a highly subjective narrative constructed by deeply interested individuals over three generations, Berta's anti-nostalgic denunciation of the Pérez patriarch lays bare fundamental class and gender conflicts buried deep within the imaginary pastoral sociocultural terrain of "Memorias." Lira Pérez's elite class status before the civil war, a position bolstered by the capitalist modernization of the Mexican hacienda economy under the Díaz regime, probably would have protected him from any accusation by the Róbles family, apparently people of a lower, though not necessarily peasant, class whose own economic situation worsened considerably during the war. Working for hacendados for more than thirty years would have ensured for my grandfather's father the protection of those men who for decades had wielded political and economic authority in the region. Even a university-educated crony of the hacendados, however, could not in 1912 have foreseen the uprisings in Jerez only a year later, let alone the coming social upheaval.

Padilla's study of early Mexican American autobiographies has informed my attempts to describe the range of contradictory socioideological and cultural meanings inscribed in my grandfather's autobiography. Padilla adroitly positions Mexican American autobiographies in relation to their authors' sociohistorical and cultural condition under Anglo American domination. He also demonstrates the complex strategies by which they forge an identity for themselves out of their marginalized lives. Valuable not only as foundational Mexican American literary texts, the heroic, self-told stories of formerly unknown Mexican American writers also disclose the monumental injustice Mexican American society has suffered through the exclusion of Chicano works from mainstream American literary and cultural discourse. Beginning as early as 1848, the sustained institutional suppression of such works within the context of U.S. sociocultural domination suggests how great a challenge critics and theorists of Mexican American literature face as they conduct their recuperative and interpretive projects. *My History, Not Yours* is the culmination of a substantial body of research and criticism on Mexican American autobiography. To those who would dismiss the writings of these early autobiographers for their presumed "hacienda syndrome," Padilla replies with a distinctly historicized sense of the complex imbrication of these autobiographers' private and public struggles as Mexican American "orphans" in a land that was once their cultural, spiritual, and geographic home. Rosaura Sánchez's recent scholarship on nineteenth-century Mexican American writing follows in the path created by Padilla's retrieval project and particularly the historicist impetus that informs it. Yet Sánchez's work expands on Padilla's theoretical paradigm as well as on his treatment of the socio-ideological and political context of the Californio narratives. As Sánchez puts it, her study is "rooted in cultural politics," and thus considers "cultural production as inseparable from structural and agential relations." For that reason, it "takes on and examines the issue of representation by a subaltern population within the context of relations of production, social restructuring, and collective agency" (1995, x). Because Sánchez offers a more comprehensive study of that body of testimonials by Californios collected by Bancroft in the 1870s, and takes Padilla's historicist premises an important step forward through its dialectical analysis grounded in feminist, postcolonial, and especially Marxist theory, her work will prove to be indispensable to the future study of nineteenth-century Mexican American literature.[32]

Sánchez's aim in *Telling Identities* may be said to parallel my own. As Berta Róbles's narrative powerfully suggests, such historicizing as Padilla's may still leave the voices of other victims and orphans of history suppressed. They must no longer be silenced. Although the story of Dominga Róbles has been elaborately sublimated within my own family consciousness for more than eighty years, her distant voice, if not yet fully retrieved, has finally been acknowledged. Berta's dramatic statement at the funeral, as well as the other family secrets presented in this essay, should thus remind scholars intent on recovering marginalized texts and establishing the discursive genealogy of suppressed (Chicano) literary traditions that the powerfully disruptive autobiographical impulse to self-invention is always at work. The same may be said of many historiographic texts. Her confrontation with my grandfather's narrative, and her implicit challenge to Padilla's autobiography model has a more fundamental purpose as well. Just as her story has profoundly influenced my own interpretation of my grandfather's text, as students of Mexican American autobiography, literature, and history we must recognize and identify the omissions, inaccuracies, misrepresentations, and lies—both conscious and unconscious—in other foundational Mexican American narratives, if we wish to move toward a version of history closer to the "truth" than we can ever approach through "close" readings of Mexican American autobiographies and other historical works. As I've suggested, Sánchez's research on the California testimonies has already begun to move Chicano autobiography and historical studies in this productive direction. Engaging the socio-ideological suppressions of nineteenth-century autobiographers, and particularly their pre-American nostalgic sublimations, will help scholars both recuperate and critique how their subjects represent the existential and cultural dilemmas of their fragmented existence. Though Berta's disclosure does not necessarily provide a more representative version of the Mexican American past, it certainly reveals the remarkable energy of my grandfather's retrospective desire, after a life in exile as a cultural "orphan" torn between Mexico and the United States, to resist his community's "present" sociocultural erasure and fragmentation by imaginatively restoring and tenaciously repressing the social reality of his Mexican ancestors.

Padilla notes that Mariano Guadalupe Vallejo's autobiography operates as a eulogy to a Mexican "social and cultural subjectivity stranded in the past over and against a colonized subjectivity accommodating and acquiescent toward an American social formation that had exploited and displaced [Mexicans]" (1993, 87). Like many modern Mexican immigrant narrators, Vallejo and other nineteenth-century Mexican American authors write from the cultural perspective of a marginalized community dislocated and excluded by colonizing American institutions. Just as my grandfather's orphanhood symbolizes his immigrant community's sociocultural break with the past *and* a continued alienation from both Mexico and the United States, Vallejo and early autobiographers write as culturally and economically deracinated *huérfanos* (orphans), compelled to reconstruct in narrative an earlier "heroic" world that American society has denigrated, destroyed, or simply forgotten. Undeniably, like Vallejo and other early autobiographers, my grandfather struggled in his writings to negotiate his "bicultural" status in the United States without rejecting Anglo American culture in toto. My grandfather honored this country; and he was in turn very proud of being an American citizen. As a Mexican exploited and dispossessed by United States social formations, however, he also resisted this political and sociocultural hegemony. Along with the family of Dominga Róbles, a true orphan of history, we can only wish that my grandfather had also been capable of speaking to similar repressions in the hacienda sociocultural economy of his Mexican forebears. His nostalgic recovery of his father's life story today instructs others who continue to pursue the recuperation of our Chicano origins.

Epilogue

> On the second day, a sail drew near, nearer, and picked me up at last. It was the devious-cruising Rachel, that in her retracing search after her missing children, only found another orphan.
>
> —Herman Melville, *Moby Dick*

Since October 17, 1994, when my grandfather left on a trip to Mexico, my family has received no word from him, nor any other information that would tell us what may have happened to him or whether he is still alive. A missing person's report was filed with the U.S. and Mexican police, and the disappearance was publicized in several newspapers in Los Angeles and along the United States-Mexican border. In late 1994, the Ventura County Police Department informed us that my grandfather did arrive on October 17 at the Los Angeles bus depot downtown, where he purchased a ticket to the Mexican border city of Tijuana. The police, however, could not determine whether he boarded the bus that would have taken him to Mexico. Just as the California and Mexican authorities have been confounded by this case, my family has been frustrated in its efforts to find out what may have become of my grandfather. Our relatives in central and northern Mexico have heard nothing from him; hospitals, funeral homes, and public institutions that we have contacted in Mexico and the United States have no record of his admittance; media announcements of his disappearance ultimately yielded no rewarding clues. After almost five years of exasperation and grief, we have grown resigned to the likelihood that the circumstances of his death will remain a mystery. On the anniversary of his departure later this year, we will hold a memorial service to honor my grandfather.

When he boarded a bus in Fillmore, California, at a location just down the road from where, as a young farmworker seeking employment at the Sespe Ranch, he had arrived sixty years earlier, my grandfather was not carrying any luggage and, as he was wont to do in his old age, probably had no identification. He was eighty-six years old, underweight, and in poor health. His adopted community of more than half a century must have seemed strangely different from the town that he had first seen in his youth. After his wife died, he lived alone in a tract house that he never considered his true home because it was "far away" (five miles) from the Mexican community at Sespe Village where he had reared his children and where, against their wishes, he continued to live until 1970. Beginning in the late 1940s, the children had all left the village for Los Angeles; his grandchildren and great-grandchildren, all of them assimilated and urban, were now further removed from their patriarch's Mexican rural community and culture.

Some would probably never know what the workers' camp at Sespe meant to my grandfather. The Mexican village, built above the banks of a river and set amid citrus and avocado orchards as well as eucalyptus and oak trees, had once been a thriving and self-sustaining community filled with well-tended homes and productive gardens—a place where for decades the language, customs, and culture of Mexico were practiced and maintained in the midst of an Anglo-dominated environment that was hostile toward and exploitative of Mexicans. My grandfather was proud of the town and of the people who had been a part of it. When he first arrived there, he knew that the village, from its houses to its trees and flowers, was owned by the Spalding family, and that Mexican workers and their families could be evicted on short notice at the whim of its owners.[33] Yet its rural and pastoral qualities must have attracted my grandfather from the outset, perhaps reminding him of his secure and idyllic hacienda childhood alongside his father and grandmother Hipólita at San Juan de las Calabasas near Jerez. My Aunt Esther's version of her childhood at Sespe supports this very characterization of the physical setting of the rancho. Though Esther is elsewhere highly critical of the feudal nature of ranch society, she describes its physical setting nostalgically in her essay as a "little paradise that was surrounded on three sides by lemon and orange orchards and completely isolated from the American community five miles away . . . a place where the skies were clear, the air fresh, the nearby mountains high and majestic, and the river that bordered the village a haven for a man and his three growing sons."

Until it was demolished five years ago, Sespe Village remained a functioning workers' camp for Mexican agricultural laborers and their families. One year before the camp was razed, my parents, grandparents, and I visited the town for the last time. Access to the village was the same as it had been fifty years earlier, a bumpy dirt road whose entrance was barely visible from the highway and which wound for a half mile through a thick grove of orange and avocado trees and then along the Sespe River to the dusty outskirts of the town. Amid the 150 shotgun houses in disrepair and decay, we found the house where my father and his brothers and sisters spent their childhoods. My grandparents and my father were upset and disappointed at the condition of the dilapidated house, and especially the growth of weeds and vegetation engulfing it and the other homes. My father recalled this home, and the Mexican village of his youth, in a manner reminiscent of his father's own nostalgic recollection of the bountiful hacienda landscape where Juan Lira Pérez had lived.

Though most of its full-time residents had already deserted Sespe Village, as we drove through the town, we met an old man, Pancho Casas, Nico's brother-in-law and a close friend of my grandfather, whose family had lived in the camp since the time of my grandfather's arrival in 1936. Pancho had been evicted from Sespe for participating in the 1941 strike; he returned to the village several years later. Knowing that the last inhabitants of the workers' camp were young immigrants from Mexico, I was astonished at meeting, at that late date, a distant relative and an original resident from my grandfather's generation. I half-expected other ghosts from my grandfather's past to appear—perhaps, as I now reflect on that visit, his lost half-brother Paulo, whose distant cousins (Nico and his siblings) had lived in Sespe Village from the 1920s through the 1960s. But, as it turned out, Mr. Casas was at that moment preparing to move. His departure marked the end of my family's decades-long residence in Sespe Village. Although the history of the community was erased from the official record, it lives in the collective memory of Sespe's Chicano descendants.

Chronology: The Life of Francisco Róbles Pérez

1908   Born in Jerez, Zacatecas, Mexico, to Juan Lira Pérez and Juliana Róbles Pérez.

1911   Thirty-five year reign of Porfirio Díaz ends.

1912   Half-brother/cousin Paulo Róbles Pérez and half-brother Lucas Herrera Pérez born in Jerez.

1908–13 Childhood in Jerez and San Juan de las Calabasas.

1913   Mother dies. Maderista rebels take Jerez.

1914   Half-sister Diega Herrera Pérez born. Civil War breaks out throughout rural Zacatecas. Flees with father and step-mother María Herrera. In Coahuila, father and son witness the Battle of Torreón.

1914–17 Moves with father throughout north-central Mexico. Francisco attends school to the third grade.

1917   Half-sister Paula Herrera Pérez born in Torreón.

1919   Father dies in Gómez Palacios, Durango. Francisco works as a servant for a wealthy family.

1920   Works as a servant for a North American dentist in Gómez Palacios.

1921   Emigrates to the United States with the Herrera family, in-laws to his father.

1922   Dominga Róbles dies in Jerez.

1923   Works as a farm laborer in Orange County, California. Lives with the Herrera family.

1924   Marries Concepción Herrera in Whittier, California.

1925   Daughter Esther Brígida Herrera Pérez born in Placentia.

1927   Son Juan Francisco Herrera Pérez born in Placentia.

1930   Son Antonio Cirildo Herrera Pérez born in Placentia.

1933   Son David Herrera Pérez born in Placentia.

1936   Citrus workers strike in Orange County.

1935   Blacklisted by ranchers for organizing Mexican agricultural workers, Francisco is forced to leave Orange County. Moves family to Ventura County. Takes a job as a farm laborer at Rancho Sespe, owned by the Spalding sports equipment manufacturing family.

1937   Daughter María Celia Herrera Pérez born in Sespe Village.

1935–77   Works for the Spalding family at Rancho Sespe.

1957   Grandson Vincent Anthony Pérez born.

1977   Retires from job at Rancho Sespe.

1985   Begins taped narration of his autobiography to grandson Vincent. Paulo Róbles Pérez dies in Jerez, Mexico.

1990   Begins work on a written autobiography.

1992   Funeral of Isabel "Chavela" Róbles.

1994   Leaves on trip to Mexico. Reported missing and believed dead by family.

Notes

This essay is excerpted from "Heroes and Orphans: Testimonial Memory as Resistance and Repression in Francisco Róbles Pérez's 'Memories';" which appeared in *Biography* 20, no 1 (Winter 1997). An earlier version of this article was presented in December 1994 at the Recovery Project Conference.

I would like to acknowledge the help and support of my aunt, Esther Pérez Doran in the writing of this essay. The daughter and eldest child of Francisco Róbles Pérez, and the first Pérez of her generation to attend college, Esther is today a marriage, family, and child counselor and a clinical specialist in psychiatric nursing. She is employed at the Los Angeles Veterans Administration Medical Center's Post-Traumatic Stress Disorder Unit. Without her love, inspiration, knowledge, and guidance, the truths that I have tried to bring to light in this article could not have been recovered.

1. Two studies of Mexican American autobiography, both of which draw upon previous research on the nineteenth-century origins of Chicano literature, are Genaro M. Padilla's *My History, Not Yours,* and Rosaura Sánchez's *Telling Identities: The Californio Testimonies.* Padilla's model provides the discursive framework for my analysis of modern Mexican American immigrant autobiography. For two recent articles that engage issues linked to Padilla's discussion, see Rebolledo (1990) and Goldman (1992). The first studies to deal specifically with Chicano autobiography as a genre are Márquez 1984, Padilla 1984, and Saldívar 1985.

2. See Saldívar 1990 and 1985, particularly chapter seven. Following Bruce-Novoa's (1990) assessment of recent developments in Chicano literary theory and particularly works by Ramón Saldívar and José David Saldívar, my examination of Mexican American autobiography takes as its underlying critical assumptions the need for "dialectical analysis that takes history into consideration as another text," and the idea "that true dialectical thought is always self-critical" (Bruce-Novoa 1990, 171).

3. The "Recovering the United States Hispanic Literary Heritage" project, under the direction of Nicolás Kanellos at the University of Houston, has been at the forefront of this recuperative endeavor. See Gutiérrez (1993) and Gonzáles-Berry (1996) for anthologies of critical essays collected and published through this project.

4. Francisco Róbles Pérez's "Memorias" is an unpublished manuscript. All subsequent paginations refer to the seventy-page text that I have compiled from my transcription of two notebooks from the original handwritten manuscript. All translations of this text are mine.

5. Though called "aunt" by my father, Isabel "Chavela" Róbles was actually my grandfather's first cousin, the niece of Juliana Róbles and first cousin of Berta Róbles (see fig. 4).

6. Raymund A. Paredes uses this term to highlight sociocultural and ideological contradictions in writings by early New Mexican "Hispano" writers, and to call attention to what he views as the works' "contrived and derivative romanticism" (1982, 52–53).

7. For Chicana feminist approaches to Chicano/Mexicano culture and history that intersect my analysis of the Róbles critique of Mexicano patriarchy, see the distinguished body of writings produced over the past ten years by Rosaura Sánchez (1995), Norma Alarcón (1993), Gloria Anzaldúa (1987), Ana Castillo (1994), Cherríe Moraga (1983), María Herrera-Sobek (1990), Tey Diana Rebolledo (1993), and Adelaida R. del Castillo (1990). Because of the Chicana's position within a patriarchal society, many Chicana writers are keenly attuned to the historical and ideological issues that I raise throughout this article. Their writings have in turn helped me to interpret and historicize my grandfather's narrative. Yet, at the same time, several Chicana cultural critics have posited a unitary Mexican homeland and therefore apparently created ideologically self-contradictory texts. As Padilla has explained, "Anzaldúa and other recent Chicano/a autobiographers, although recognizing themselves as occupying a social space of multiple identities, speak another (contradictory?) desire for a unitary and collective cultural economy imagined in the past, or on the other side of the border" (1993, 238).

8. For an analysis of this question as it has arisen in Chicano poetry, see Pérez-Torres 1995, chapters two and three.

9. Sociologist Mario Barrera notes the diverse socioeconomic origins of early twentieth-century Mexican emigrants to the United States: "the background of the immigrants prior to migrating is a little explored topic. The impression most writers have is that the immigrants during this period were largely agricultural workers in Mexico, notwithstanding the fact that the Mexican

Revolution of 1910–1920 also caused people of higher occupational categories to migrate. Still, there are indications that the immigrants were not necessarily representative of the largely rural, agricultural population in Mexico at that time" (1979, 67). Barrera cites a 1944 survey in San Bernardino, California, of men who had come to the United States from Mexico in the early part of the century, which indicated that only about a third of them had been engaged in hacienda work in Mexico.

10. Doroteo Arango (Francisco "Pancho" Villa) (1877–1922) was the legendary general of the famous Division of the North, which sought to overthrow the Mexican government beginning in 1913. In March to April of 1914, in the town of Torreón, Coahuila, my grandfather and his father crossed paths with Villa's army, as they were caught in "the most grueling and bloody contest in the long annals of the Mexican Revolution" (Knight 1986, 143) "Memorias" describes the artillery and infantry siege by Villa's Constitutionalist army from the perspective of a child barricaded in a house with his family. After days of explosions that included, according to my grandfather, the destruction of a nearby train filled with ammunition, and several days more of street fighting, the battle ended with the Villistas victorious. My grandfather and his family emerged from their house to search for food and water. "In the street there were mountains of dead bodies," my grandfather writes, "both soldiers and their horses, thousands of dead piled on each other in the streets, all shot and covered with blood . . . the plumes of smoke and soot made the sky look yellow, because all of the *fincas* (ranches) near the town had been burned and all of the businesses and stores in town had been sacked and burned in just a few days" (17). As John Reed observes in his firsthand account of the battle, after the fighting ended there were "vultures gorging themselves on dead horses; the prolific executions of prisoners, the faint smell of corpses and the rising smoke of dozens of funeral pyres" (Reed as quoted in Knight 1986, 143). While my grandfather walked through a street near his house, he discovered a revolver. He recalled dragging the gun home to give to his father. Grandfather's most vivid memory of this event is of his father, after seeing the gift, angrily throwing it outside. He admonished his son harshly for drawing attention to their family during a dangerous time.

11. See, for example, Ramón Saldívar (1990) and José David Saldívar (1991). For historical studies that examine Mexican American history but do not foreground links to the Mexican period in the Southwest, see Acuña (1988) and De Leon (1982). Though delving critically into Mexican hacienda society in Texas, Montejano (1987) focuses on Mexican American dispossession after the United States takeover. Of the book-length histories written by Mexican American scholars, only Ramón A. Gutiérrez (1991) and Armando C. Alonzo (1998) delve at length into the history of the Mexican period.

12. Ramón Gutiérrez examined how Chicano historiography has traditionally structured the past in a recent lecture at the University of Texas at Austin. He identified five "typologies" based on the ideological perspective of the historian and the period chosen as the "inception" of Chicano history. According to Gutiérrez, the "bourgeois" version selects 30,000 B.C. as the point of origin; the "proletarian," 1910; the "internal colonial," 1848; the "Feminist," 1519; and the

"conjunctural or postmodernist," 1836. The "proletarian" model, according to Gutiérrez, dominates the written record, demonstrating that Chicano historical scholarship has been governed and defined by studies of the modern period. See his "Time, Space, and Becoming: Narratives of Chicano History," a lecture presented at the University of Texas at Austin, March 11, 1999.

13. Quoted in Martin (1989, 260–61).

14. I will refer to "Memorias" throughout as an autobiography rather than as a *testimonio* (testimonial). The collaborative nature of my genealogical project implies, however, that my grandfather's account may also be classified as a testimonial. Rosaura Sánchez has distinguished testimonials from autobiographies by identifying their collaborative and mediated qualities. According to Sánchez, while autobiography "offers a self-generated/agential discursive construction of 'self' within particular social spaces," the testimonial is the product of a collaboration involving an interviewer/editor. The production of the testimonial is "mediated and filtered through a second, more powerful agency" so that its narrating voice "is othered in terms of production as well as at the discursive level." In works of this type, "narrating agency . . . is thus not simply that of the speaking subject but also that of the editing and writing subject" (1995, 8). Both the "production" and recuperation of "Memorias" are obviously mediated by my own involvement as an interviewer, editor, critic—as well as a relative of the interviewee. The final manuscript will, for instance, include transcribed oral responses to questions posed to my grandfather during tape-recorded interviews.

15. The scale of this social upheaval and its impact on the Southwest United States are suggested by Meier and Ribera (1993) in their history of Mexican Americans:

> The 1910 revolution, a period of incredible violence and confusion, directly affected the Southwest. Out of fifteen million Mexicans, an estimated one million lost their lives in the decade of revolution, and there was a large-scale displacement of people. Thousands fled from the countryside into the larger towns and cities of Mexico; at the same time other thousands fled northward to the United States. No one knows precisely how many Mexicans were involved in this great exodus; one estimate holds that more than one million Mexicans crossed over into the Southwest between 1910 and 1920. (108–09).

As for my grandfather, "Memorias" suggests that he was abandoned. Any blood relatives of his father had apparently remained in Jerez during the revolution, and the war prevented communication with them. My grandfather mentions a sister (mother of the three Ramirez daughters), but she is spoken of only in passing. Except for several half-siblings, no other living Pérez blood relatives are identified in the text. As I mentioned earlier, another family, the Herreras, in-laws to my grandfather's father and also from Jerez, were extremely important to my grandfather after Lira Pérez died in 1919—in fact, Francisco came to the United States with the Herreras. However, he did not consider them "family"; he always felt like an outsider and "orphan" among them. Lira Pérez apparently married the last of his four wives, María Herrera, by whom he had three children, after he settled in Torreón in 1914, but he had his first child by her, named Lucas, in 1912, while he was married to Juliana Róbles. (It is also possible that both my family and the Róbleses are a year off on the date of Juliana's death; if she died in 1912 rather than 1913, Lira Pérez could perhaps have married María just after his wife died and then had Lucas later that year.) The reason my grandfather felt "abandoned" by his Herrera in-laws was because, two years after his father's death, his step-mother María, rather than embracing her husband's son as a family member (he had been supporting himself as a servant for two years), instead handed him a train ticket to the United States and "gave" him to her brothers who were then preparing to emigrate. She and her own children never emigrated. (My Aunt Esther believes that María sent Francisco to the United States so that only she and her children would be able to claim Lira Pérez's property in Jerez.) So, although my grandfather was by definition an orphan when he journeyed to the United States, he came here with members of the Herrera family and therefore was not alone and abandoned. Though not mentioned by name in "Memorias," one of the Herreras must have been the person who bought him a pair of shoes at the border (in Mexico he wore only *huaraches*, or sandals). Francisco eventually lived with the Herreras in California for several years, and in 1924 married María's youngest sister, Concepción. "Memorias" states that when my grandfather arrived in 1921 at the Herrera home in Yorba Linda, he had to explain to them who he was. In the middle of a celebration, someone asked for quiet, and, pointing at Francisco, asked, "And who is he?"

16. For a description of Sespe Village, see the epilogue of this article.

17. I use "colonial" in quotes because colonialism actually ended in 1821 with Mexican independence from Spain; Lira Pérez was born in 1856.

18. Jerez de la Frontera, the Andalusian town famous for its sherry wine, was the birthplace of Álvar Nuñez Cabeza de Vaca (1490–1560), the first Spaniard to explore a large region of North America. Fernández and Favata explain that Cabeza de Vaca's account of his journey, *La Relación* (1542), is one of the first Spanish descriptions of the New World that "calls for a compassionate and tolerant policy toward the natives of the Western Hemisphere" (1993, 11).

19. The subjugation of the indigenous peoples of Mexico during the colonial period took on a distinctly modern (i.e., positivist) cast during the era in which Lira Pérez prospered as a business associate of the Zacatecan hacendados. As Meier and Ribera (1993) observe, between 1880 and 1910:

> The economic policies of the government were promoted by a group of positivists, who planned and worked for a modern, scientifically run Mexico which [they believed] would take its rightful place in the world. They accepted that certain races were less advanced because of heredity and environment; they believed that Indians and their culture were inferior and therefore not a sound base on which to build a modern Mexico. In the name of progress they set out to Europeanize Mexico's Indians, partly as a result of positivist ideas. . . . Indians were brutally hounded, and many were sold into virtual slavery to large landowners. (104)

20. My grandfather foregrounded his alienation from Anglo American as well as Mexican society, and therefore contradicts recent theoretical projections

of a transcultural subject who easily traverses cultural borders. Several passages in "Memorias," however, suggest that my grandfather recognized in Mexican American cultural formations a new bicultural subject who occupied a borderlands space. In what may well be one of the earliest written references to a distinctive "Chicano" language and culture, my grandfather recalled one of his first encounters, as a Mexican immigrant, with "pochis" (acculturated, or "faded," Mexicans). On Sundays in 1922, the Mexican American community in Whittier, California, would gather for social events. As my grandfather explained,

> It was there that I made a few friends, two of whom were young *pochas* born in the United States, Rosa and Luisa. One day while we were talking, one of them asked me, "Oye, por qué no nos tritéas?" (Hey, why don't ya treat us?) To which I answered, "Y eso, qué es?" (What do you mean?) The other said, "Pues, que nos des una raspada o una goma." (Well, buy us a snow cone or some gum.) What they meant to say, of course, was "una copa de hielo raspado" (a cup of shaved ice) and "un paquete de chicle" (a pack of gum). The two spoke very poor Spanish. The pochos also called automobiles *carruchas*. The following week, I went out on my first date with Rosa. We went to a *borlote*, which is the word the pochos used for "dance." (22)

Although one might expect my grandfather to have labeled the culture of the "pochos" inferior to his "aristocratic" Mexican hacienda culture, he didn't judge the Americanized "pochos" for their cultural hybridity, and even befriended them and their families.

21. In a passage that links my grandfather's sense of cultural superiority over Anglo Americans—because of his "aristocratic" Mexican childhood—to the racism faced by Mexican Americans of that period, "Memorias" depicts the efforts of Mexican immigrants in the late 1930s to attend a movie at a local segregated theater in Fillmore, California:

> In the movie theater in town, which is still in business today, the racists segregated us from the whites. This, after we had worked perhaps sixty hours during the week—and six days a week. They did the same to the Mexican children; there was a separate school for them. We, of course, protested both of these actions. As we told the whites, we paid money for these services like anyone else in town. . . . In any case, the "theater" was a cheap little shack filled with "white fleas" compared to the theaters in my own country. I came from a culture where even the burros sang opera! You see, almost every large town in Mexico has an opera house, quite unlike the United States. (36)

22. Keith Spalding, the multimillionaire co-owner of the Spalding Corporation and hacendado of Rancho Sespe, died in 1963. He left $3,000 in his will to my grandfather, who had been a loyal worker at the ranch for nearly thirty years.

23. According to Acuña:

> By 1910, foreign investors controlled 76 percent of all corporations [in Mexico], 95 percent of mining, 89 percent of industry, 100 percent of oil, and 96 percent of agriculture. The United States owned 38 percent

of this investment, Britain 29 percent, and France 27 percent . . . [and] in contrast, 97.1 percent of the families in [the state of] Guanajuato were without land, 96.2 percent in Jalisco, 99.5 percent in Mexico (state), and 99.3 percent in Puebla. (1988, 149–50)

24. Elsewhere in "Memorias," my grandfather used the same phrasing to describe the Pérez side of his family, and as my Aunt Esther told me in a telephone call in May 1995, he always signed his name Francisco Róbles Pérez. In the same conversation, Esther told me that, although my grandfather only briefly mentioned these Róbles forebears in "Memorias," she believes he was as "proud" of the Róbles ancestors as of the Pérez. Nonetheless, the emphasis throughout the early part of "Memorias," the only section in which my grandfather discussed his origins, is on the nobility of the Pérez line. Based on my conversations with him and Esther, I don't think this was entirely conscious, however. As I've pointed out, the only mother he ever knew was the Róbles "matriarch," Doña Hipólita, and "Memorias" clearly shows that he has fond memories of life with her. His remembrances of the Róbles grandparents—conveyed in "Memorias" as well as in conversations with me and with Esther—were completely removed from the Róbles-Pérez clash later initiated by Lira Pérez, and rekindled in 1992 by Berta Róbles. Esther's recollection of her father's castigation of Dominga, when considered alongside Francisco's refusal to acknowledge Paulo at a funeral in 1984, as well as the subsequent revelations brought to light by the Róbles narrative, have led me to conclude that my grandfather must have viewed Paulo as a bastard and interloper—and a legitimate member of *neither* side of his family. Though Paulo was in fact a closer "blood" relative than half-brother, since their mothers, Juliana and Dominga, were sisters, from my grandfather's perspective, as he expressed it once to Esther, Dominga was to blame for a great many of his father's troubles, and most significantly the death of Juliana; this would explain why she is set apart in "Memorias," and in his conversations with family members, from his cherished memories of the Róbles "matriarch."

25. Following his father's example, my grandfather portrays Díaz in a flattering light. He is described in several passages as a benevolent dictator and national hero. The revolutionaries who rose up against Díaz and this dictator's legacy, says grandfather, thus "fought against a government that was unique in the history of Mexico . . . one which had maintained the country at the high social and economic level of the other great nations in the western world at that time" (4). Not surprisingly, Casimiro—Lira Pérez's first son, the product of his second marriage, to Matilde—joined the federal army to fight against the Maderista and Villista insurrections.

26. See Adams (1990), Eakin (1985), and Couser (1989). Couser has summarized the development in recent autobiography studies in the wake of the structuralist and poststructuralist critiques of the subject:

The trend in autobiography studies has been to erode the distinction between fiction and nonfiction and to deconstruct the apparent relation between the self and its textual embodiment. . . . Autobiography, then, is seen not as produced by a preexistent self but as producing a provisional and contingent one. Indeed, that self is seen as bound and (pre)determined by the constraints of the linguistic resources and narrative tropes available to the "author." (19)

27. Though Paulo later adopted Pérez as his legal name, he was reared by the Róbleses and never had contact with members of the Pérez family. So, while Berta Róbles married a "Pérez," she wed into a family known by her own as Róbleses.

28. In his Last Will and Testament, Lira Pérez names as his "only heirs" four sons (including Francisco), two daughters, and his fourth wife, María Herrera, who was also his executor. My translation of part of the will reads as follows:

> In the city of Gómez Palacios, in the house on North Morelos Street, on the thirteenth day of May 1919, in the presence of the witnesses Mr. Don Filemón Turado and Mr. Don Antonio Correa, I state that, being gravely ill, and feeling that I am on the brink of death, it is necessary to set forth the following terms [of my will] . . .
>
> I am the owner of a house in Jerez, Zacatecas. The house is comprised of a corner room, bedroom, kitchen, hall, living room, corral, and waterwheel/well. [I own] two tracts of land in San Juan de las Calabasas and a granary in the same location. The granary [is situated] on a smaller piece of land toward the south, but since I do not have the [proper] papers before me, I cannot specify the measurements [of any of these properties].
>
> It is my wish to leave as my only heirs my wife María Herrera and my children, named Casimiro Pérez, Marcos Pérez, Francisco Pérez, Lucas Pérez, [and] Diega and Paula Pérez. I assign to my wife the role of guardian and administrator [of my estate], whose function will be to divide the shares [of my property] in equal parts, in a manner that she is best able to carry out.
>
> With nothing more to express, I conclude the present private disposition [of my will]. Since I have no other recourse and am in a foreign region, I have not written this document in the proper legal manner before a Notary Public.

29. Although he had two elder half-brothers, the oldest, Casimiro, disappeared in 1914 while serving in the Federal Army, and may have died in one of the battles of that year, while the second, Marcos, the one in the photo, was incapacitated by mental illness and drug addiction during adolescence. My grandfather told me that in 1913, while on leave, Casimiro returned to ask his father for his portion of his inheritance. Lira Pérez sold a tract of land and gave Casimiro the money from the sale. The story from my grandfather is that Casimiro believed he would be killed in the civil war and wanted to spend his inheritance. It seems very likely that he *was* killed in one of the battles of 1914—possibly in Torreón, where his father was living. If Casimiro had ever returned to Jerez after 1921, my grandfather would have learned of it through his younger half-siblings or perhaps through María Herrera's family. As for Marcos, if he had gone with Lira Pérez when he was forced to leave Jerez, my grandfather probably would have mentioned it. Apparently, Marcos was later brought to his father in Torreón. Marcos is mentioned in "Memorias" for his

odd behavior as a teenager in Torreón—namely, public nudity and petty crime. The last we hear of this half-brother is when my grandfather, leaving in 1921 to go to the United States, says goodbye to him at the train station. My grandfather says the Herrera family never knew what became of Marcos; the story I have heard is that he left town when still a teenager and wasn't heard from again.

30. A number of parallels between my grandfather's childhood and the life of the Mexican novelist Juan Rulfo stand out. Though born ten years after my grandfather in 1918, Rulfo was from the state of Jalisco, which borders Zacatecas. (The name "La Bufa," the mountain landmark near the city of Zacatecas described in my grandfather's account, comes from the hill's resemblance to an animal's bladder—an allusion used in the Rulfo quote [see page 27]). Both writers were born into the upper class, and both were orphaned as young children during the civil war. Rulfo's hometown, Apulco, was sacked and burned by armed insurgents, and his father was murdered in 1923 while fleeing. According to some scholars, Rulfo's father was killed by peasant insurrectionists, though in an interview the author denied knowing who was responsible. *Pedro Páramo*, Rulfo's nostalgic recreation of the hacienda community of his childhood, addresses orphanhood and "origins" as central themes. A more remarkable coincidence is Rulfo's family name. After his mother died in 1927, Rulfo was taken in by her relatives in Mexico City, who required that he use their name—Pérez (the author's full name was Juan Pérez Rulfo).

31. Two stories that provide circumstantial evidence are my grandfather's narrative of Lira Pérez's forced flight due to his expected execution by local insurrectionists, some of whom could have been Róbleses, and his suggestion that Dominga Róbles was responsible not only for her relationship with his father, but also for his mother's death. The latter narrative tells us that my grandfather may well have always known about the Róbles complaint, and perhaps of the rape accusation. His claim that Dominga caused Juliana's death may have been a response to the rape accusation. This also makes it easier to see why he could never acknowledge Paulo as his half-brother.

32. Sánchez discusses but does not foreground the suppressions and exclusions in the Californio testimonios. Her study argues that the nineteenth-century world of Alta California "was not an idyllic 'pastoral' society," but rather a "labor-intensive . . . economy with a largely 'unfree' labor force made up of Indian men and women whose ancestors had lived on those lands for generations." (1995, 168) Thus, all Californios, according to Sánchez, do not get equal time in the testimonials. "The nonpropertied classes and what [Hubert] Bancroft calls the plebeian 'humble *ranchero*' are largely absent or mentioned only in passing. Significantly, the Indians are very visible as the Other of the Californios. . . . In every case, representation [in the testimonials] follows the ideological perspectives of dominant segments of the Californio population, perspectives often at odds with those of other factions, given regional and social divisions of Californio society. (10)

33. According to my father, Anthony Pérez, during one week in 1941, 80 percent of the families in Sespe were evicted because of their involvement with a labor strike against the Spalding-owned ranch. See Menchaca (1995, 83–89).

Works Cited

Acuña, Rodolfo. 1988. *Occupied America: A History of Chicanos.* New York: HarperCollins.

Adams, Timothy Dow. 1990. *Telling Lies in Modern American Autobiography.* Chapel Hill: University of North Carolina Press.

Alarcón, Norma. 1989. *The Sexuality of Latinas.* Berkeley: Third Woman Press.

———. 1991. "The Theoretical Subject(s) of This Bridge Called My Back." In *Criticism in the Borderlands: Studies in Chicano Literature, Culture, and Ideology,* ed. Héctor Calderón and José David Saldívar, 28–39. Durham, NC: Duke University Press.

———, ed. 1993. *Chicana Critical Issues.* Berkeley: Third Woman Press.

Alonzo, Armando C. 1998. *Tejano Legacy: Rancheros and Settlers in South Texas, 1734–1900.* Albuquerque: University of New Mexico Press.

The Americas Review: A Review of Hispanic Literature and Art of the USA 16, no. 3–4 (Fall–Winter 1988). Special issue on "United States Hispanic Autobiography."

Anzaldúa, Gloria. 1987. *Borderlands/La Frontera: The New Mestiza.* San Francisco: Spinsters/Aunt Lute.

Arriaga, Ponciano. 1993. "The Dispossessed of Rural Mexico." In *Latin America, Conflict and Creation: A Historical Reader,* ed. E. Bradford Burns. Englewood Cliffs, NJ: Prentice Hall.

Barrera, Mario. 1979. *Race and Class in the Southwest: A Theory of Racial Inequality.* South Bend, IN: University of Notre Dame Press.

———. 1990. *Retrospace: Collected Essays on Chicano Literature.* Houston: Arte Público.

Bruce-Novoa, Juan, ed. 1980. *Chicano Authors: Inquiry by Interview.* Austin: University of Texas Press.

Cardoso, Fernando Henrique, and Enzo Faletto. 1979. *Dependency and Development in Latin America,* trans. Marjory Muttingly Urquidi. Berkeley: University of California Press.

Castillo, Ana. 1994. *Massacre of the Dreamers: Essays on Xicanisma.* Albuquerque: University of New Mexico Press.

Couser, G. Thomas. 1989. *Altered Egos: Authority in American Autobiography.* New York: Oxford University Press.

del Castillo, Adelaida R., ed. 1990. *Between Borders: Essays on Mexicana/Chicana History.* Encino, CA: Floricanto Press.

De León, Arnoldo. 1982. *The Tejano Community, 1836–1900.* Dallas, Texas: Southern Methodist University Press.

Doctorow, E. L. 1993. *Jack London, Hemingway, and the Constitution: Selected Essays, 1977–1992.* New York: Random House.

Doran, Esther Pérez. 1965. "Death in the Mexican American Community." Unpublished essay.

Eakin, Paul John. 1985. *Fictions in Autobiography: Studies in the Art of Self-Invention.* Princeton, NJ: Princeton University Press.

Faulkner, William. [1932] 1959. *Light in August*. New York: Random House.

———. [1936] 1972. *Absalom, Absalom!* New York: Vintage.

Fernández, José B., and Martin A. Favata. [1542] 1993. Introduction to *The Account: Álvar Núñez Cabeza de Vaca's Relación*. Houston, Texas: Arte Público.

Flores Olague, Jesús, Mercedes de Vega, Sandra Kuntz Ficker, and Laura del Alizal. 1996. *Breve Historia de Zacatecas*. Mexico D. F.: El Colegio de México.

Foucault, Michel. 1977. *Language, Counter-Memory, Practice: Selected Essays and Interviews*, ed. Donald F. Bouchard. Ithaca, NY: Cornell University Press.

Galarza, Ernesto. [1971] 1986. *Barrio Boy*. Notre Dame, IN: University of Notre Dame Press.

García Márquez, Gabriel. [1970] 1991. *One Hundred Years of Solitude*. New York: HarperCollins.

Goldman, Anne. 1992. "'I Yam What I Yam': Cooking, Culture, and Colonialism." In *De/Colonizing the Subject: Politics and Gender in Women's Autobiographical Practice*, ed. Sidonie Smith and Julia Watson, 170–82. Minneapolis: University of Minnesota Press.

Gonzáles-Berry, Erlinda, and Chuck Tatum, ed. 1996. *Recovering the United States Hispanic Literary Heritage*. Houston, Texas: Arte Público.

González, Jovita, and Eve Raleigh. 1996. *Caballero: A Historical Novel*. College Station: Texas A&M University Press.

Griswold del Castillo, Richard. 1989. "Patriarchy and the Status of Women in the Late Nineteenth-Century Southwest." In *The Mexican and Mexican American Experience in the 19th Century*, ed. Jamie E. Rodriguez O. Tempe, AZ: Bilingual Press.

Gutiérrez, David G. 1995. *Walls and Mirrors: Mexican Americans, Mexican Immigrants, and the Politics of Ethnicity*. Berkeley: University of California Press.

Gutiérrez, Ramón A. 1991. *When Jesus Came, the Corn Mothers Went Away: Marriage, Sexuality, and Power in New Mexico, 1500–1846*. Stanford: Stanford University Press.

Gutiérrez, Ramón A., and Genaro Padilla, ed. 1993. *Recovering the United States Hispanic Literary Heritage*. Houston, Texas: Arte Público.

Haas, Lisabeth. 1995. *Conquests and Historical Identities in California, 1769–1936*. Berkeley: University of California Press.

Herrera-Sobek, Maria, and Helena Viramontes, eds. 1996. *Chicana Creativity and Criticism: New Frontiers in American Literature*. Albuquerque: University of New Mexico Press.

Karl, Frederick. 1988. *William Faulkner: A Biography*. New York: Knopf.

Knight, Alan. 1986. *The Mexican Revolution, Volume 2: Counter-revolution and Reconstruction*. Lincoln: University of Nebraska Press.

Leal, Luis. 1973. "Mexican American Literature: A Historical Perspective." *Revista Chicano-Riqueña* I, 1: 32–44. Reprinted in *Modern Chicano Writers: A Collection of Critical Essays*, ed. Joseph Sommers and Tomás Ybarra-Frausto, 18–30. New York: Prentice-Hall, 1979.

Márquez, Antonio C. 1984. "Richard Rodriguez' *Hunger of Memory* and the Poetics of Experience." *Arizona Quarterly* 39, no. 4 (Winter): 130–41.

Martí, José. 1975. *Inside the Monster: Writings on the United States and American Imperialism*, ed. Phillip S. Foner, trans. Elinor Randall. New York: Monthly Review Press.

Martin, Gerald. 1989. *Journeys through the Labryinth: Latin American Fiction in the Twentieth Century*. New York: Verso.

Meier, Matt S., and Feliciano Ribera. 1993. *Mexican Americans/American Mexicans: From Conquistadors to Chicanos*. New York: Farrar, Straus & Giroux.

Menchaca, Martha. 1995. *The Mexican Outsiders: A Community History of Marginalization and Discrimination in California*. Austin: University of Texas Press.

Montejano, David. 1987. *Anglos and Mexicans in the Making of Texas, 1836–1986*. Austin: University of Texas Press.

Moraga, Cherrie. 1983. *Loving in the War Years: Lo Que Nunca Pasó Por Sus Labios*. Boston: South End Press.

Moraga, Cherrie, and Gloria Anzaldua, eds. 1981. *This Bridge Called My Back: Writings by Radical Women of Color*. Watertown, Pennsylvania: Persephone Press.

Padilla, Genaro M. 1993. *My History, Not Yours: The Formation of Mexican American Autobiography*. Madison: University of Wisconsin Press.

———. 1984. "Self as Cultural Metaphor in Acosta's *The Autobiography of a Brown Buffalo*." *Journal of General Education* 35: 242–58.

Paredes, Raymund A. 1982. "The Evolution of Chicano Literature." In *Three American Literatures*, ed. Houston A. Baker Jr., 33–79. New York: Modern Language Association.

Pérez-Torres, Rafael. 1995. *Movements in Chicano Poetry: Against Myths, Against Margins*. New York: Cambridge University Press.

Rebolledo, Tey Diana. 1990. "Narrative Strategies of Resistance in Hispana Writing." *Journal of Narrative Technique* 20, no. 2 (Spring): 134–46.

———. 1995. *Women Singing in the Snow: A Cultural Analysis of Chicana Literature*. Tucson: University of Arizona Press.

Rebolledo, Tey Diana, and Eliana S. Rivero. 1993. Introduction to *Infinite Divisions: An Anthology of Chicana Literature*, ed. Rebolledo and Rivero. Tucson: University of Arizona Press.

Revueltas, José. [1943] 1990. *Human Mourning* [E luto humano], trans. Roberto Crespi. Minneapolis: University of Minneapolis Press.

Rulfo, Juan. [1955] 1987. *Pedro Páramo*. New York: Grove.

Saldivar, Jose David. 1991. *The Dialectics of Our America: Genealogy, Cultural Critique, and Literary History*. Durham, NC: Duke University Press.

Saldívar, Ramón. 1990. *Chicano Narrative: The Dialectics of Difference*. Madison: University of Wisconsin Press.

———. 1985. "Ideologies of the Self: Chicano Autobiography." *Diacritics* (Fall): 25–34.

Sánchez, Rosaura. 1995. *Telling Identities: The Californio Testimonios*. Minneapolis: University of Minnesota Press.

Semo, Enrique. 1993. *The History of Capitalism in Mexico: Its Origins, 1521–1763*. Austin: University of Texas Press.

Vallejo, Mariano Guadalupe. 1994. "Recuerdos históricos y personales tocante a la Alta California de Mariano Guadalupe Vallejo." In *Nineteenth Century Californio Testimonials*, eds. Rosaura Sánchez, Beatrice Pita, and Bárbara Reyes, 138–43. San Diego: Crítica Monograph.

Vidal, Gore. 1995. *Palimpsest: A Memoir.* New York: Random House.

The Measure of a Cock:
Mexican Cockfighting, Culture, and Masculinity

Jerry Garcia

> I don't want to play a macho! What does that word mean? See, a macho
> has no questions. A macho is self-assured. He has no doubts . . . When
> I say macho, I see my grandfather, a man: good, kind, gentle, and strong.
> He was a macho. He raised fighting cocks.
>
> —Rick Najera, *The Pain of the Macho*

I have no memory of the first time I saw my father measuring his cock. I
remain, however, keenly aware that at a young age I was initiated into a
world of manliness unlike any other. Often, I would watch in amazement
as my father held and caressed the red bobbing head in his hands. As I
recall those adolescent years I remain curious about the fixation my father
had as he deliberately, tenderly, and with subtle care stroked and admired
his cock. There were times when I saw him place his salivating mouth
over the head and run his lips back and forth along the shaft as if trying to
will it to new life. This ritual, almost religious in nature, of checking for
hardness, softness, strength, and weakness, became a familiar practice. I
found it strange, even as an adolescent, that someone would pay such attention to this symbol of masculinity. As I came of age, I soon realized that
Mexican culture valued strong, courageous, aggressive, and virile men and
that the cock represented these traits. Thus, in my childhood, the cock
became a master symbol of manliness and of characteristics valued by
Mexican culture. It became clear that my father had a deep psychological
identification with his cock, a bond that appeared obsessive. My intent is
not to make ethical arguments for or against my father's behavior, but to

focus on this experience and to question why some men, Mexican men in particular, are overly devoted to their cocks. I hope it is evident that I am speaking of the cocks used in cockfights, or *peleas de gallos*, as my father calls them. The double entendre is difficult to avoid, as it is relevant and important in discussing Mexican men and cockfights.[1]

Historians, anthropologists, sociologists, and scholars from other fields have, intentionally or unintentionally, largely ignored Mexican culture and cockfighting. This study is an attempt to fill this void, and is based on my personal experiences growing up in a cockfighting family in the Pacific Northwest, on interviews with other sources from a similar background, and on the relevant existing scholarship on cockfighting.

First introduced into North America in the early colonial era, cockfighting continues to serve an important but controversial role in Mexican culture within the United States. Spain introduced the sport to regions of Latin America and to what is now known as the American Southwest, where it has continued to flourish as a culturally important tradition in Mexican American communities. The British meanwhile introduced cockfighting along the Eastern Seaboard, from where it spread to the American South. Cockfights persist in the United States even though most states impose severe penalties on individuals arrested in conjunction with cockfighting, amid a well-vocalized public contempt for the sport.

People of Mexican origin, a historically marginalized ethnic group in the country, have tried to maintain a strong sense of their culture despite extensive efforts by U.S. society at deculturalization. The willingness of ethnic Mexicans to engage in illegal activity through active participation in, and support of, cockfighting can be seen as an attempt to minimize and resist this deculturalization and marginalization. This resistance may manifest itself in a distinctive form of masculinity outwardly expressed through cockfighting. Mexican cockfighting may also be encouraging transnationalism as Mexicans negotiate their marginalization on both sides of the border. For all these reasons, cockfighting plays a unique and significant role within the Mexican community in the United States. At the same time, it stands as one of the cultural barriers between people of Mexican origin and mainstream U.S. society. If this conflict is to be resolved, there is a need to better understand the underlying reasons for the persistence in selected communities of this usually illegal and always ethically controversial sport.

Of Gallos and Galleros

Cockfighting is considered one of the oldest organized forms of recreation. Its origins can be traced to Southeast Asia, to around 3000 BC with the domestication of the chicken (McCaghy and Neal 1973, 15).[2] Admiration for and even adoration of the *Gallus sonneratii* unquestionably reaches far into antiquity. The gamecock was an object of worship among the Babylonians, ancient Syrians, and Greeks. In Rome it was idealized as a symbol of courage in battle, and Roman authorities in Gaul minted coins bearing a representation of a Gaulish helmet with a cock on its crest (Ingersoll 1923, 45). In fact, it is with the Romans that the notion of "blood sport" emerges (Plass 1995).

In the Christian era, some scholars attribute the first comments on the deeper meaning of the cockfight to St. Augustine (AD 354–430), who asked, "Why do cocks fight and why are men so fascinated by cockfights?" (1942, 49). Although St. Augustine was writing on a larger theme, in *De Ordine* (About Order) he nonetheless touched upon some fundamental elements of cockfighting that have perplexed scholars to the present. St. Augustine describes witnessing a cockfight in a barnyard, and says that he and his companions were drawn to the spectacle. In the end he asks:

> Why do all cocks behave this way? Why do they fight for the sake of supremacy of the hens subject to them? Why did the very beauty of the fight draw us aside from this higher study for a while, and onto the pleasure of the spectacle? What is there in us that searches out many things beyond the reach of the senses? And on the other hand, what is it that is grasped by the beckoning of the senses themselves? (51)

Although not universal, cockfighting flourished in many parts of the world. There appears to be no record, however, of game fowl (chicken) in the Americas before the arrival of Europeans. Nevertheless, Alfred Crosby, in *The Columbian Exchange*, does refer to a "type" of chicken in existence before colonization:

> The acceptance of a pre-Columbian American chicken probably also means acceptance of pre-Columbian trans-Pacific contacts with areas where the chicken was first domesticated. Whatever the truth may be, there is no doubt that most of the chickens in America by 1600 were of European descent. (1972, 95–96)

Whether or not the indigenous people had chickens, there is no doubt that they were familiar with blood sports. Scholars have studied sport, competition, and violence among indigenous tribes of pre-Columbian America, most notably the Aztecs, and have compared them to the sports of other ancient cultures, such as the Roman. For example, Inga Clendinnen in *Aztecs* relates that "the Mexica male self was constructed in competition," and that most men lived in a precarious position, especially those from the warrior class who were constantly challenged (1991, 142). Although not a sport in the traditional sense, gladiatorial sacrifices were conducted throughout the Aztec empire and provided spectacles for entire cities. In most cases those being sacrificed were captured warriors or nobles:

> The captive was taken to the round sacrificial stone, where he was painted with stripes. He was given four cudgels to throw, a shield, and a sword with its obsidian blades replaced by feathers. After drinking octli, he fought warriors—several, if he was a great warrior. First he fought four warriors of the military orders in a row—two jaguars and two eagles—and if he triumphed, then he fought a left-handed warrior. He fought until he was felled, whereupon he was stretched on his back, his chest was cut open, and his heart was torn out and dedicated to the sun. Then the body was flayed, and the priests wore the skin. (Hassig 1988, 200–02)

Another competitive sport in Mesoamerica that has gained some attention is the "ballgame." It is believed to have been first played in the Olmec civilization around 1500 BC. The game was usually played for ceremonial purposes, to resolve conflicts, or for gambling, and at times became a game of death. Several detailed paintings and stone carvings from Mesoamerica depict entire teams being decapitated after losing to an opponent (Carrasco 1998, 179–80).

The people of Mesoamerica were thus well accustomed to violent competitions and sports, and the participation of the public in such events. This tradition found new expression in the sport of cockfighting, introduced into the Americas after the European conquest and colonization. Like the Balinese cockfighting examined by anthropologist Clifford Geertz (1972, 101), Mexican cockfighting can be seen as a continuation of a cultural past in which sport often involved a blood offering or even human sacrifice.

Cockfighting came to the Western Hemisphere and eventually to what is now the American Southwest via conquest and colonization by Spain and England in the fifteenth and sixteenth centuries. The European conquest of the Americas brought not only violence and destruction, but also a resettling of the region. This resettling was coupled with a restructuring of society, a process of cultural modification that varied depending on the intent of the colonizer. By the late colonial period in the Americas, various forms of European culture and entertainment had found their way into the daily lives of those living in the conquered territories. The sport of cockfighting was one aspect of this societal transformation.

Space constraints prevent a detailed comparison of the different forms of cockfighting introduced by the English and Spanish. However, it is interesting to note that the English introduced gaff fighting, using an instrument that resembles a rapier with a sharpened point and a round body. The American gaff fight requires that one gaff be tied to each leg of the cock. The Spanish and Mexicans brought in a tradition of "slasher" or knife fights, with a blade resembling a curved single-edged razor blade tied to the cock's leg. Both forms are popular in the United States, but Mexican cockfighters have traditionally favored the knife, quite possibly because it increases the risk and somewhat neutralizes the level of skill, creating the possibility of an upset by a less-skilled cock.

Cockfighting flourished throughout Latin America and the Caribbean in such places as Mexico, Venezuela, Cuba, the Dominican Republic, and Haiti. By the early nineteenth century gambling associated with cockfighting was well entrenched in Mexico. In fact some sources claim that the infamous General Antonio López de Santa Anna was addicted to cockfighting and opium (Wasserman 2000, 17).

In *Cocks and Bulls in Caracas*, Olga Briceño provides a colorful description of a cockfight in Venezuela during the early twentieth century:

> The audience consisted of country people in their Sunday best, muleteers, vagabonds, and sprinkle of respectable men in hunting clothes ... There were not more than ten country women, for women do not enjoy that kind of occasion ... The rival cocks faced each other, their combs erect. As their owners had done, they eyed each other for a moment before attacking in a savage moment ... The old man soothed his cock with a mother's tenderness, whispering in its ear between the rounds as he wiped blood from its head ... The old man took a mouthful of vinegar and standing near the bird spurted it over the injury, in an attempt to bring it to. (1945, 138–40)

Cuba has also sustained a vibrant cockfighting culture. In fact, some of the earliest documented cockfights in the Americas took place on the island. Cockfighting in prerevolutionary Cuba was not only a form of popular culture in which all social groups participated, but was also a source of income for the government:

> Cockfighting, also supervised as a government monopoly, was next to the lottery in general gambling favor. All degrees of people, including the poorest farmers, not a few priests, and royal officials as high as an occasional captain general, had been raising, training, and fighting cocks ever since early in the sixteenth century. During some prosperous and feverish years mains [cockfights] were held at several public and official pits almost daily. High and low, black and white crowded into the enclosure, elbowing, sweating, shouting, and betting. Thousands of dollars were bet upon each occasion while the government, which placed a small tax upon each pair of birds set in the ring, thus obtained about fifteen thousand dollars annually. (Bradley 1941, 266)

Cockfighting became so popular in Cuba that when it was banned for ten years in the late nineteenth century, José Míguel Gómez ran for president on a platform that included lifting the ban. He kept his promise when he became president in the early twentieth century (397–98).

As cockfighting increased in popularity throughout the Americas it created a sense of identity for individuals and countries. After Haiti gained independence in 1804 it embraced the cock as a symbol, thus following the lead of France, which had adopted the rooster as a symbol of its revolution in the late eighteenth century (Wucker 1999, 13). In Haiti and the Dominican Republic, which share the island of Hispaniola, cockfighting not only remains a passion but has come to symbolize each country's nationalistic fervor and their historic rivalry. The cockfight has been used metaphorically to describe politicians and their sometimes adversarial relationships, as Michele Wucker writes in *Why the Cocks Fight*:

> On one level, the scraggly fighting rooster makes sense as a politician's symbol: politics, after all, is a battle of strategy, endurance, and aggression played out on a national stage. It inspires the same emotion and scheming that the cockfight does in spectators and gamblers. Look closer, however, and the political rooster dissolves into other images with entirely different meanings in religion and daily life. In other contexts, the rooster of aggression becomes a bird of sustenance, a symbol of the dawn and new beginning, and, most important, a guardian of territory. (10–11)

Thus, the cock in Haitian and Dominican cultures not only represents independence, but also remains a potent political symbol that resonates in both countries.

The United States inherited the practice of cockfighting from Mexico—after its conquest of Mexico's northern territories—as well as directly from Europe. American cockfighting was most widespread in the colonial and early modern era, when it was not yet considered deviant or illegal (Scott 1983).

> By the nineteenth century the first formal complaints against cockfighting in the United States emerged. In the 1820s and 1830s various states were considering anti-cockfighting bills. Registered complaints were most pronounced in the North. Letters to the editor proclaimed that "cockfighting was unfriendly to morals, occasioned idleness, fraud, gambling, profane swearing, and hardened the heart against the feelings of humanity." (123)

The first state to outlaw cockfighting was Pennsylvania, in 1830 (McCaghy and Neal 1973, 559). Today all but two states prohibit cockfighting, on the principle that the fights are inhumane and cruel to animals. The sport remains legal only in Louisiana and New Mexico, home to many established back-road pits (Kilborn 2000). Oklahoma banned cockfighting in 2002, but legal challenges have been filed and the fights continue. All states allow the breeding of gamecocks, which are often exported to states where fighting is legal despite federal law prohibiting interstate transport of fighting birds. Despite the laws passed against it, the sport continues underground and remains a popular form of culture or subculture in various parts of the country. It is particularly entrenched in rural America, but it is not unheard of in urban areas, as recent cockfighting raids in New York City attest (Chivers 2000; Kilborn 2000; Ross 2003).

To my knowledge there is no published literature on cockfighting in the Pacific Northwest, where my case study is set. However, we can assume that cockfighting emerged in the region, mostly likely around the turn of the nineteenth century, as a result of European and American settlement. European colonization of the Pacific Northwest was mainly by non-Spaniards, and with some exceptions that have been noted by scholars, Spanish culture did not consolidate itself in this region. Cockfighting therefore was principally with the gaff, traditionally preferred by European Americans, rather than with the knife, which was chiefly used by Spaniards and eventually Mexicans in what is today the American Southwest. However, exceptions can be found, and my father and uncle began their cockfighting careers using the gaff.

Mexican Masculinity and Cockfighting

Of cocks and men . . . this phrase from Geertz's seminal essay "Deep Play: Notes on the Balinese Cockfight" (1972) comes to mind as I reconstruct

visions of the cockfights I attended as a child, as well as those I still occasionally see. Attendance at a cockfight leaves little doubt that this sport is
a space created, regulated, and dominated by men. Indeed, the picture is
one of unabashed masculine sexuality: the sensuous dance of the two cocks,
mirrored by the similar movements of their human handlers, and the frenzy
of the spectators, all within the confines of a pit fifteen feet in diameter.
Men gather in a corner drinking and talking of an upcoming fight, while
others huddle around a cock, admiring it, in awe of its power. Mexicans
often refer to the gamecock as a *gallo*, and this term is also used metaphorically to describe someone who exemplifies Mexican manhood. Although
no sexual act is performed, there is no mistaking the aura of masculinity,
sex, and sexuality that hangs over the cockfighting pit.

At the same time, within this exclusively male-to-male preserve, an
element of homoeroticism can be seen at play. To begin with, the cockfight
arena is, as Varda Burstyn argues in *The Rites of Men*, an example of
homosociality, or the desire and custom of men to be in male company
exclusively (1999, 294n41). It goes beyond that, though, to encompass an
experience and spectacle of intense physical interaction between males of
two species that can indeed be described as homoerotic. This interaction
begins with an intense male-to-male "gaze" that has also been noted in other
sporting arenas. For example, it has been chronicled that in the late nineteenth century homoeroticism may have inspired the sporting male-to-male
gaze, providing a nonverbal language of desire. This gaze is evident at the
beginning of any boxing match, as the two boxers stand face-to-face within
inches of each other. In the cockfight, the human handlers use this male-to-
male gaze in an attempt to intimidate before the fight begins.

In some ways the cockfight can be interpreted as a homoerotic dance
between the cocks themselves, between the two human handlers, and between cock and man. The highly charged atmosphere and the symbolism
involved in sustaining the cock's life by sucking, blowing, caressing, and
stroking create a great web of homoeroticism. I described this intimacy
between my father and his cock at the beginning of this paper. These techniques are almost universal, and though only meant to resuscitate a gamecock, they partially explain why cockfighting has often been associated
with sexuality. Another example of this interplay is described in *The Day
of the Locust*:

> When the dwarf [Abe] gathered the red up, its neck had begun to droop
> and it was a mass of blood and matted feathers . . . He spit into its gaping

beak and took the comb between his lips and sucked the blood back
into it. The red began to regain its fury . . . Abe, moaning softly, smoothed
its feathers and licked its eyes clean, then took its whole head in his
mouth. The red was finished, however. It couldn't even hold its neck
straight. (West 1969, 154)

What makes all this unusual is that it takes place within a Mexican working-class environment that is usually linked with homophobic men. Is it
possible, as Dundes suggests, that in cockfighting one proves his maleness
by feminizing the opponent (1994, 250–51)?

The sport of cockfighting is not exclusively male. But women are
underrepresented and are usually relegated to spectator status, and are not
intimately involved in handling the cock. The gamecock "handler" and
the "cockpit" are roles and spaces generally reserved for males.[3] This is
largely true across cockfighting cultures. Geertz, in his study of Balinese
cockfighting, observed that women were discouraged from attending cockfights. Wucker, writing of cockfighting on Hispaniola, reports that cockfighting is a male ritual in the region but, ironically, "the most enduring
Dominican legends of strength and redemption are female" (1999, 7).
According to my uncle, in his more than fifty years of cockfighting he has
never seen a Mexican female "handler." Although he has witnessed Anglo
women performing this task, he says it is a rare occurrence.[4]

This domain is for the interaction of man and man, cock and man,
cock and cock. Both the gamecock and the cockfighting man have been
described as the embodiment of courage, commitment, dominance, and
aggressiveness. In Bali, Geertz notes, "*Sabung*, the word for cock, is used
metaphorically to mean 'hero,' 'warrior,' champion,' 'man of parts,' 'lady
killer,' or 'tough guy'" (1972, 99). A cock without these virtues is considered impotent. According to some social scientists, Mexicans' manliness is
often compared to that of roosters: "the better man is the one who can
drink more, defend himself best, have more sex relations, and have more
sons born by his wife" (Madsen 1973, 22). If the cock and the cockfight
can be considered an extension of Mexican masculinity, the reverse is also
true. For the cock to be considered aggressive and domineering, it has to
be "handled" by a man who possesses the same qualities. Thus masculinity
becomes an important element of the cockfight, whether actually displayed
by the man or imagined for the rooster.

Scholarship examining Mexican masculinity is in short supply and
some of what has been done is deeply flawed. Critics have examined both
old and recent scholarship on masculinity and its expression among ethnic

Mexicans residing in the United States. For example, the concept of machismo, which is actually inherent in most cultures, is strongly associated with Mexican and other Latino men. Américo Paredes writes that the characteristics of machismo are "the outrageous boast, a distinct phallic symbolism, the identification of a man with the male animal, and the ambivalence toward women—varying from an abject and tearful posture to brutal disdain" (1993, 215). Another scholar observes:

> *Machismo* has been used by scholars and authors to describe male assertiveness and control over everything from nature to society. In its most succinct form, machismo is defined as a template for male behavior that reifies aggression and domination as uniquely male attributes and reprojects them to every area of culture. The behavioral traits most commonly associated with machismo include hypermasculine bravado and posturing, willingness to confront physically any perceived slight, domination of women and other men through act and language, drinking to excess, sexual conquest, and siring children. (Klein 2000)

Alfredo Mirandé, in *Hombres y Machos* (1997), and Alan Klein, in his insightful article "Dueling Machos: Masculinity and Sport in Mexican Baseball" (2000), shed some light on the origins of the equation of machismo with Mexican masculinity. According to their studies, the person most responsible for the fusion is essayist and poet Octavio Paz in *The Labyrinth of Solitude* (1950). Klein observes that *Labyrinth* contained "a definition of masculinity that wed psychoanalytic elements with history":

> The original conquest of Aztec forebears by conquistadors was seen, by Paz, as so traumatic as to imprint itself on all subsequent generations. Overall Spanish brutality toward Aztecs was converted into the sexual act of raping Aztec women, and with it came the implication that Aztec men were unable to prevent it." (Klein 2000, 68–69)

Mirandé argues in similar fashion:

> Native men developed an overly masculine and aggressive response in order to compensate for deeply felt feelings of powerlessness and weakness. Machismo, then, is nothing more than a futile attempt to mask a profound sense of impotence, powerlessness, and ineptitude, an expression of weakness and a sense of inferiority. (1997, 36)

Some scholars have described Mexican working-class masculinity as a "protest masculinity" that responds to economic disadvantage. According to this theory, Mexican males who feel inferior because they lack economic mobility or political clout conceal those feelings behind a substantial display of power and virility (36). Baca Zinn considers this point in her article "Chicano Men and Masculinity." While acknowledging that male dominance does exist among Chicanos, she contends that the culture argument is oversimplified: "research suggests that in the realm of marital decision making, egalitarianism is far more prevalent than macho dominance" (1982, 29–43).

Other scholars, such as Lionel Cantú, have argued that examining Chicano masculinity through the lens of studies conducted on males in Latin American distorts the reality of Chicanos and, more importantly, represents Chicano culture "as if it were fixed or static" (2000, 227). Along these same lines, he maintains, studying Chicano sex roles from the perspective of the machismo/*marianismo* model found in traditional or mainstream analysis perpetuates stereotypes of Latino culture (228). Finally, Cantú asserts that "the static and monolithic definition of the Mexican 'macho' is problematic both in its failure to capture the diverse social locations of Mexican men and in its assumption that Mexican gender identities transcend time" (228).

As can be seen, the conceptualization of masculinity for ethnic Mexicans, as for other men of color, has been problematic. What does appear true is that Mexican men do not fit into a traditional or stereotypical form of masculinity, but exhibit multiple forms, as R. W. Connell has observed:

> It follows that in multicultural societies such as the contemporary United States there are likely to be multiple definitions of masculinity . . . There are for instance differences in the expression of masculinity between Latino and Anglo men in the United States . . . The meaning of masculinity in working-class life is different from the meaning in middle-class life, not to mention among the very rich and the very poor. (1996, 208)

I agree with Connell's assessment that ethnic Mexicans in the United States exhibit various forms of masculinity. I would argue that those who participate in the underground and illegal sport of cockfighting are challenging hegemonic masculinity, which Connell defines as "the configuration of gender practice which embodies the currently accepted answer to the problem of legitimacy or patriarchy, which guarantees the dominant position of men and the subordination of women" (1995, 77). Or, put another way, nonhegemonic masculinities are "subordinated by the ruling, or 'hegemonic,' masculinity of Western white, heterosexual, middle-class men" (Cantú 2000, 226).

One can see a parallel in the behavior of some black males in American society who adopt the "cool pose," defined by Majors and Billson as "a ritualized form of masculinity that entails behaviors, scripts, physical posturing" (1992, 2–3). This is also thought to be a coping mechanism that provides "a means to show the dominant culture that the black male is strong, proud, and can survive, regardless of what may have been done to harm or limit him" (Majors 1990, 111). Like African Americans, ethnic Mexicans living in the United States occupy a marginalized status, one shaped by political and cultural exclusion and economic discrimination as well as by the concept of "otherness" based on race and ethnicity (Connell 1995, 79–80). By challenging hegemonic masculinity, cockfighting, I argue, is a form of "resistance masculinity" by which Mexican men assert their own masculine values based on a traditional sport. Like the "cool pose," it is a survival mechanism that empowers the Mexican male; "it eases the worry and pain of blocked opportunities" (Majors 1992, 5). And through the cockfight, Mexican males construct a masculine identity that garners respect within the Mexican family and local Mexican community, even though it does not live up to the ideal form of masculinity established in the dominant culture.

"Resistance masculinity" does have some limitations, however. For example, scholars argue that public displays of masculinity or machismo are not only a form of resistance against class and race oppression, but also a means of oppressing women. Hondagneu-Sotelo and Messner state that "gender is commonly viewed as … an effect of the dominant class and/or race relations [and] what is obscured, or even drops out of sight, is the feminist observation that masculinity itself is a form of domination over women" (2000, 68). Some of these limitations emerged when I interviewed various individuals for this project and they will be illustrated in the following case study. Nevertheless, the sport of Mexican cockfighting provides an opportunity to examine ethnic Mexicans within a sphere rarely seen by the majority of the public and it offers investigators an unusual opportunity to observe displays of masculinity within this realm.

Cockfighting in the Pacific Northwest: A Case Study

Investigating Mexican cockfighting in the United States requires one to navigate the blurred boundaries of Mexican and Mexican American ethnicity and culture. Most of my life experiences have taken place in the Pacific Northwest, almost two thousand miles from the U.S.-Mexican border. The Pacific Northwest has a long history of Spanish, Mexican, and Chicano influences, yet it remains detached from what many Chicana/o studies scholars consider the cultural center of Mexicanness, namely the U.S.-Mexico border region.[5] As a result, Mexicans and Mexican Americans who live in the Pacific Northwest and other regions outside the Southwest have had to cope with distance and the lack of a "critical mass" of Mexicans locally, making their experiences diverse. Nonetheless, I agree with Adelaida del Castillo when she writes, "The affinity between things Mexican and Mexican American/Chicano has a basis in common history, border space, culture, and language long renewed by migration and immigration, which more recently has come to signify the mexicanization of the United States" (1996, 207). In addition, the concept of borders has changed in the last twenty years and no longer refers simply to the political boundaries between countries. The new conceptualization of borders encompasses illusory and metaphoric constructions of demarcations, borderlands, and "borderlessness." I submit that Mexicans living in the Pacific Northwest exist in a similar multidimensional space. Even here, Mexican culture thrives with the continued renewal of traditional values and customs through immigration/migration and through the activities of those Mexican Americans who cling to their Mexican heritage.

The co-existence of the Mexican and Mexican American communities within these various border constructs has obscured many of their cultural differences. Offsetting this are the counter-pressures for Mexican acculturation and assimilation to the dominant society. For example, in order to survive in the United States, my father has had to acculturate economically as a laborer. Despite this workplace assimilation, however, and the fact that he is a naturalized U.S. citizen, my father maintains primary relations with his own ethnic group and has only secondary interaction with individuals and institutions of the dominant culture (see fig. 1). Some sociologists have called this process "selective acculturation" (Portes and Rumbaut 1996, 250–51).

This selective acculturation partially explains why Mexican culture remains intact among those who engage in cockfighting at the level of my elders. First-generation immigrants such as my father and uncle find in the cockfight a cultural cocoon to protect them from alienation, domination, and isolation within American society and culture. It is thus the equivalent of the "cool pose" discussed earlier. My father and uncle take part in this tradition as a means of maintaining their cultural identity as Mexicans, part of which includes the notion of machismo and masculinity, an important aspect of Mexican cockfighting.

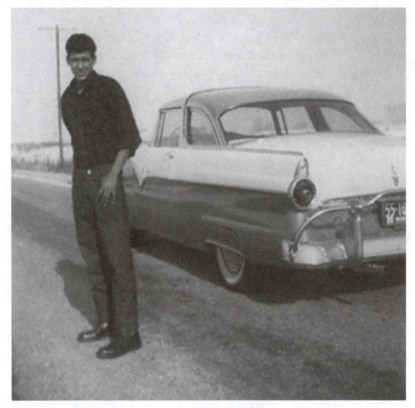

Fig. 1. The author's father, R. Garcia, with his first car, a Ford Crown Victoria, in Granger, Washington, 1956. Photo taken by his brother R. Garcia. Garcia family photo collection.

My father and his brother are cockfighters, or *galleros*, par excellence. They display the near-obsessive behavior toward their cocks that Geertz described among Balinese cockfighters:

> Balinese men, or any large majority of Balinese men, spend an enormous amount of time with their favorites, grooming them, feeding them, discussing them, trying them out against one another, or just gazing at them with a mixture of rapt admiration and dreamy self-absorption. (1972, 99–100)

As a child and as an adult I witnessed similar behavior. At family functions my father and uncle would discuss their favorite cocks, training and care of the birds, game strategy, and upcoming matches. These gatherings often featured impromptu friendly matches in the front yard or a challenge from a rival appearing unannounced, as happened on a number of occasions. My father's and uncle's time away from home increasingly included tending to their gamecocks for an upcoming season of cockfights. It is important to note that within my working-class Mexican family, cock-fighting was never seen as deviant or barbaric. My mother never complained about its cruelty, only that my father spent too much time and money on it. On numerous occasions my mother complained of the depletion of family income and to a certain degree, of neglect by my father. When I interviewed my aunt she expressed no alarm about the treatment of gamecocks or her husband's participation in a sport deemed inhumane, low-life, and criminal. Like many Mexicans, she had a relative who was involved with cockfighting long before she met my uncle and so she was familiar with the sport.[6]

Very early I came to the realization that my father and uncle were not simply spectators. Instead, they were actually men of prominence and importance in the cockfighting world. By the time I had reached the age of twelve my father and uncle had garnered the respect and admiration of fellow *galleros* and aficionados of the sport. Although it is now illegal in all but two states, cockfighting has its own promotional magazines with thousands of subscribers. The most prominent of these are *Gamecock* and *Grit and Steel*, with one lesser-known publication called *The Feathered Warrior*. In fact, my father and uncle were once featured in an issue of *Gamecock* for having won a significant number of their cockfights.[7] In the cockfighting world this is the equivalent of being featured in *Sports Illustrated*, and is considered quite an honor.

When the daily lives of my father and uncle are juxtaposed with their status as respected cockfighters, a stark contrast emerges. They were born three years apart in a place called El Rancho de Agua Fresca, on the outskirts of Monterrey, Mexico. You will not find this community on any map; in fact, when I interviewed my uncle he was uncertain whether it still existed. Growing up, I always enjoyed hearing this name and knowing that it was also my place of origin. There is a certain mystical and divine quality to the sound of the name, and I want to believe that it is an actual place. More likely, however, El Rancho de Agua Fresca was simply a few houses located in a rural site with a fresh-water well, as my uncle put it, and has long since disappeared or turned into a ghost town. Nonetheless, that was the place my father and uncle left when they emigrated from Mexico to Texas in the late 1940s. As Mexican immigrants, they survived by moving frequently within Texas in search of farm work. At the age of about twelve, my uncle was paid $2.50 per day, he recalls. By the early

1950s my father and uncle and their families began another long migration, this time to the Northwest. They followed long-established migration routes that took them through Montana, where they worked sugar beets, then to Idaho to pick potatoes, and finally to the Yakima Valley in Washington, where they worked sugar beets, hops, and potato crops.

Their motivation for this arduous journey was economic. Texas growers tended to pay wages by the day; in the Northwest, however, growers paid laborers by the hour. In the early 1950s, when my father and uncle arrived in the Northwest, the prevailing wage for a farm laborer was $1.00 per hour, a significant income for a family of migrant workers. Because they were both immigrants and undereducated, the two brothers worked as farm laborers for most of their lives, along with their families. Although my father and uncle eventually went from unskilled to semi-skilled work and finally to skilled blue-collar positions, and were generally well respected in the community, they never received the admiration or respect on the job that they achieved as cockfighters and breeders. Thus, the cockfight became a world of acceptance and success for my uncle and father, a place where each became a clear winner, and where they could display their self-worth, have a sense of accomplishment, and practice a nontraditional form of masculinity.

Racial discrimination was another aspect of the exclusion experienced by my father and uncle in their relations with the dominant culture. For example, my uncle elaborates on how they were regarded as they migrated to various communities in west Texas to pick cotton:

> There were many Mexicans, but it was mostly Anglo people living in this region. I will never forget that we once went to the movies and after getting my popcorn and soda I went to sit in the center of the theater. Shortly after, a young white girl poked me on the shoulder and said, "You are not supposed to sit here. You are supposed to sit up there in the balcony." In those days we did not know our rights and we did as we were told.

Both my father and uncle recall a significant change in treatment after leaving for the Northwest, where they did not experience the overt forms of racism and discrimination they were subjected to in Texas. Other Mexican American migrants who came to the Northwest during the same period have made similar statements. The only explanation I have to offer for this variation in treatment between regions is the small number of Mexicans in the Northwest at the time. Without a critical mass of Mexicans,

Mexican culture posed no threat to the dominant culture. It might also be argued that still fresh in the minds of many Anglo families and growers were the Mexican braceros who came to the Northwest during World War II to harvest their crops.

My uncle became interested in cockfighting at a very early age, having attended his first cockfight at the age of about four or five in Mexico during a fiesta (see fig. 2):

> I don't know who in the hell took me, but they used to make a few fights during fiestas near Monterrey in Nuevo Leon. I remember, like in a dream, when they used to fight those chickens. I think that is why I have this in my blood. I was about fourteen when I fought my first rooster. It was a gaff fight. I actually won my first fight against an old timer. I guess this is why I got hooked. However, I don't think I got real serious

Fig. 2. *The author's uncle, R. Garcia, with one of his first roost-ers, in the Crewport Labor Camp in Granger, Washington, circa 1953. He is holding a young Mcallahan rooster. Garcia family photo collection.*

about cockfighting until after I got married at age twenty and was making enough money. At this time I had maybe four roosters. Right now I have over two hundred that I breed and fight.

My uncle introduced my father to cockfighting. By the time my father entered the sport my uncle already had a decade of experience as a breeder and handler. According to my uncle, when he and my father arrived in the Pacific Northwest, Anglos were the dominant cockfighters in the region, though that changed as more Mexicans arrived. My uncle mentioned that within the region an economic cross-section of society participated in cockfighting, but I sense that he may have derived this impression from observing the sport as practiced by Anglos in other areas of the country. Among Anglos, it is clear that cockfighting does appeal to a wide socioeconomic circle. The sport's various trade magazines as well as the (limited) scholarship on the topic and statistical data gleaned from surveys provide evidence that a cross-section of U.S. society participates in cockfighting. However, among Mexicans, working-class males dominate cockfighting in the Pacific Northwest, with very little representation from other socioeconomic groups. While very few surveys on cockfighters have been done, either in the United States or in Mexico, a 1991 survey of cockfighting in the United States found most cockfighters to be

> white male Protestants from small communities or rural areas in the general southern region of the United States, who were likely to have grown up in similar localities. They were usually married, had slightly more children than the national average, with a median age of 42, and an average educational attainment of high school graduation or 1 to 2 years of college. For the most part, they were skilled craftsmen, managers, or owners of small businesses. (Bryant and Li 1991, 199–202)

In contrast to this socioeconomic diversity, my observations at Mexican cockfights and discussions with Mexican cockfighters suggest they have similar rural backgrounds and occupational levels, although because of regional differences Mexicans residing in eastern Washington tend to be in agricultural occupations. Furthermore, at the two dozen fights I have attended, Chicano (as opposed to Mexican) males were noticeably absent, and the few who attended were there as spectators.

My uncle further observed that Mexican immigration to the Pacific Northwest changed not only the ethnic makeup of cockfighting there but also the very nature of the fight. When my family arrived in the region in the 1950s cockfighting was primarily done with the American gaff. However, as Mexicans began arriving and supplanting Anglo cockfighters, they introduced the Mexican knife described earlier. This surprised me, since I was under the impression that my father and uncle had always fought with the knife. However, my uncle remembers that it was a difficult transition— switching instruments of death—and at first he could not accept the change. In fact, my uncle and father had no experience using the Mexican knife and had to have others show them how to tie it on a rooster's spur. Using a Mexican knife demands a tremendous amount of care and skill from both trainer and handler. Because the knife is razor-sharp, one wrong move can slice off a human finger or slash a wrist. In comparison to the American gaff, the Mexican knife also changes the dynamics of the fight. With the gaff, a well-bred and conditioned gamecock has a clear advantage. The Mexican knife diminishes this advantage due to its "slashing" capacity and the amount of damage it can inflict in a short time. If they wished to continue fighting cocks, my uncle recalls, he and my father had to modify their approach and adapt to the Mexican knife, since it was the preferred style of the Mexican cockfighters coming into the region. Ultimately he and my father did adapt, and by the late 1980s and early 1990s they were still considered the most successful cockfighters in the region.[8]

In my discussions with my father and particularly with my uncle, neither displays much modesty about his cockfighting abilities. My uncle, when discussing his skills as a master breeder, demonstrates the confidence one would expect from a successful cockfighter with fifty years of experience. He is self-assured and states without hesitation that he and his brother raise and fight the best cocks in the Northwest. He also states that he continues to prefer the American gaff fight and compares a gamecock fighting with a gaff to a boxer. "We breed our cocks to have some stamina and power and remain kicking like a boxer, but with the knife it's just one or two 'flys' and one is a winner and the other a loser." I have witnessed numerous cockfights that use the Mexican knife: most end rather quickly, with one cock mortally wounded or killed. With the gaff, by contrast, fights can last for thirty minutes or longer and oftentimes a handler will pull a cock before it is killed.

My father and uncle were both concerned with the public image of the Mexican cockfighter. However, they tended to disagree with that image somewhat. In fact, my uncle became defensive when I posed a question regarding cockfighting and machismo:

A Mexicano who fights roosters is any goddamn Mexicano. He doesn't have to be no macho. The cockfighter wishes for his roosters to be macho, but he doesn't have to be. The songs about cockfighters I think are just pretend, that is not the reality. A man can never be as brave as rooster.

Later, after I explained to my uncle that I have seen him and my father display forms of machismo, he told me that cockfighters must maintain a certain mystique about themselves. In his estimation, a gamecock is only as good as its breeder and handler, and both bird and human must have an air of confidence and toughness. These contradictory statements are not difficult to understand, given the unsavory image of cockfighting in the media. Furthermore, it also reinforces my argument that the arena of cock-fighting provides ethnic Mexicans a sense of control over their lives.

To further explore the interplay between cockfighting and Mexican culture, I have examined my family's rural background in Mexico, and interviewed other *galleros* of similar origins to gauge similarities or differences in culture continuity. Juan Gómez-Quiñones explored the meaning of culture, stating, "Culture is a central concept in all societies and one that encompasses the customs, values, attitudes, ideas, patterns of social behavior and arts common to members of a group. Culture, ethnicity, identity, language, history, nationhood, and nationality are all related" (1979, 55). Almost all of the *galleros*, including my father and uncle, practiced a traditional form of Mexican culture, with its most prominent element being a hierarchal structure. Men are the heads of the households, the main breadwinners and powerbrokers, while women have the roles of mother, homemaker, nurturer, and child bearer.

I was raised in this traditional family structure. My father, although dominant, was not domineering; nonetheless, the notion of machismo remained strong in my family, and it shaped my own masculinity during my adolescent years. My father played a major role until my fourteenth year, when my parents divorced. Thereafter, my mother became the primary role model and I gained much of my identity from her. Cockfighting reinforced a patriarchal notion of masculinity in my family, suggesting another limitation to the concept of "resistance masculinity." For example, although this study argues that some ethnic Mexicans use cockfighting as a form of liberation, other scholars have argued against such a view, stating, "in foregrounding the oppression of men by men, [some] studies risk portraying aggressive, even misogynist, gender displays primarily as liberatory forms of resistance against class and racial oppression" while ignoring that masculinity itself is domination over women (Hondagneu-Sotelo and Messner 2000, 69–70). Furthermore, although my relationship with my father was not antagonistic, I had decided that I would seek respectability outside of the cockfighting world.

I had sensed early on that my father might be grooming me to follow in his footsteps and carry on the cockfighting tradition in our family. At a very early age he allowed me to attend cockfights, witness the training sessions, and sit in on discussions with my uncle—in other words, to be present in a very adult-oriented sport. I recall one incident that speaks to this point. As a young teenager I had accompanied my father and uncle to a large cock-fighting derby. In an attempt to give me a sense of belonging and acquaint me with some of the intricacies of cockfighting, my father put me in charge of handling the gaff/knife case. I took this responsibility very seriously, for the case carried all the necessary instruments of destruction needed to win the derby. I proudly followed my father, carrying the case, and at the right moments I opened it so my father could retrieve a gaff or knife. Sometime during the match someone yelled either *policía!* or *la migra!*, signaling a raid by the police or the immigration service or both. It really didn't matter which, since either word brought pandemonium to this illegal sport, where police raids were a constant threat. In most cases these fights took place in remote secret locations known only to the participants within the "circle of trust." In this instance men and gamecocks scattered, but I remained to protect the sacred gaff/knife case and a deputy sheriff apprehended me. My father, see-ing his son in police custody, came forward and took full responsibility. In the end my father was fined and had to hire an attorney to retrieve the weapons case, which had been confiscated. I, in turn, had to testify in court about why I was carrying a case full of gaffs and knives. This turned out to be my rite of passage in which I indirectly earned membership in the under-ground world of cockfighting.

A Mexican cockfight can take place anywhere that men gather (see fig. 3). They can be spontaneous events. For example, because my father and uncle are well-known cockfighters, they are constantly being chal-lenged by new arrivals, possibly up-and-coming *galleros* or others who hold a grudge from a fight lost long ago. In one particular "grudge match," sev-eral Mexicanos arrived at my father's home while we were enjoying a bar-becue, and the usual challenge ensued. These matches are somewhat unusual because they involve only one fight with, in most instances, a sizeable wager. Mexican cockfighting is conducted for two purposes: first, to determine who has the finest cocks, and second, for financial gain. I

Fig. 3. A typical cockfight in the Pacific Northwest, 2001. The two roosters are Bonanza Black breeds out of Okalahoma, also known as the gallo negro. The spectators are predominantly male. Photo taken by R. Garcia. Garcia family photo collection.

have attended cockfights in which the wager amounted to thousands of dollars. Typically two types of betting take place: one in the center between the owners of the cocks, and others on the side among the spectators. Although betting can be more complicated in other cultures, such as in Bali, at Mexican cockfights the system is relatively simple. Rarely are odds given: both the center and outside bets are straight up. However, the center bet tends to be the larger and normally involves a number of supporters pooling their resources. The outside bets, made on a one-to-one basis among the spectators, are usually smaller.

The grudge match I witnessed involved a center bet determined by the principals without side bets being conducted. To an outsider it may appear that the cockfight, because of its illegal status, has no rules or etiquette. However, it is self-regulated and structured by the participants, and rules of engagement and etiquette are strict. Betting makes it more complicated. For brevity, let me just say that on this day a dispute over the rules turned into a shouting match between a dozen or so cockfighters that almost led to violence—always a danger in a grudge match because of the inflated egos at stake. The bravado of the cockfight, and of the *galleros* themselves, can at times reach the absurd rhetorical level of an argument about who possesses the largest *cojones* (balls). The danger, of course, is that masculinity will be expressed through behavior in which men inflict violence upon themselves and others. Emulating their cocks, they do their utmost to avoid showing tameness, meekness, or a lack of balls. I watched my father in the midst of this dispute, wondering whether I myself would be pulled into this surreal event. As my father and the other cockfighter came closer to each other, it seemed as if they had become the cocks. Their words were reminiscent of the sounds cocks make as they battle and their body language resembled that of cocks ready to plunge in for the kill. In this case, however, cooler heads prevailed, a draw was declared, and the challengers left without serious incident.

At another cockfight in which my father's cock was pitted against another Mexican cock, the fight began, as they all do, with the two male handlers in the middle of the pit, slowly dancing with their cocks in their hands, inciting the birds by allowing them to "bill" at each other. This makes the cocks aggressive and signals that the action is about to begin. However, as I watched my father's opponent handling his cock, I noticed a pistol tucked under his belt. After the match I asked my father about this, and his explanation, although simplistic, speaks to the essential symbolism of cockfighting. The pistol, according to him, was simply an element of bravado. Mexican cockfighters carry weapons to intimidate their opponents and to display bravery, and a few fights later, I saw a pistol tucked under my father's belt.

In retrospect, these incidents seem typical of cockfights. Cockfighting, like any other sport, can have its unsavory elements and moments, but most individuals involved are there to simply enjoy the sport. I have seen heated discussions and disagreements at cockfights, but never have they escalated into physical violence between people, an observation substantiated by my uncle. Moreover, my father and uncle have always been respected for their fairness and incorruptibility, so unpleasant incidents were rare.

Nevertheless, cases have been recorded where violence and shootings have occurred. For example, in Wapato, Washington several men were shot and one killed while attending a cockfight. From the newspaper account is difficult to determine whether this incident involved cockfighters or spectators, and whether the dispute was over cockfighting or something unrelated. According to the *Seattle Post-Intelligencer* (2001), "Detectives believe the shooting occurred as the result of 'some long-standing hostilities' between [Noe] Sanchez and others at the cockfight." Again, this example serves to illustrate the complexities of my argument regarding "resistance masculinity." It is apparent that in this case masculinity was expressed through violence. Furthermore, displays of masculinity at these matches can transcend the boundaries of cockfighting and spill over into private space, intersecting not only with race and class differences but also with gender. In other words, ethnic Mexicans display multiple forms of masculinity: on the one hand, these can help them resist their marginalization in U.S. society, but on the other, these create a paradox in which Mexicans become the oppressors within their communities.

Yet bravado is an inherent element of the cockfight, particularly at the more formal events in which a *gallero* may be fighting six or eight cocks in one day. My father was a master of bravado and intimidation in the fighting pit, channeling this through the cock itself. He was the handler, while my uncle was the master breeder of the cocks. Each role is significant in its own right, but the handler metaphorically embodies the manliness that needs to be transferred to the cock in order to maintain the cock's fierceness. At the beginning of the paper I described a scene in which my father appeared to be performing a sexual act, but in fact was only tending one of his cocks during a lull in a fight. During such lulls, handlers inspect their cocks for any injuries and use a number of techniques to motivate the bird to fight on with increasing aggressiveness—attention and intimacy that creates an unusual bond between man and cock. Examples of such techniques can be seen in observations of an East Timorese cockfight:

> As the handler inspects his charge for wounds, any sign of glumness provokes gleeful howls from the rival's supporters. The others hold their peace. To revive an injured champion, a handler spruces up the comb, jowls, and fleshy flaps surrounding the ears and may even blow water into the bird's mouth. Each handler has his own favorite methods for effecting recovery. One man I noticed plucked out a tail feather and

stuck it down the bird's throat. Another rubbed his charge's back and thighs, stretched its legs, and blew into its open beak. A third, suspecting perhaps a ruptured lung, sucked blood from the stricken creature's mouth. Blowing on the head is also held by some handlers to be efficacious. (Hicks 2002)

The relationship is similar to the one between a boxer and his trainer, although that bond lacks the intimacy a handler shows a cock. My father and uncle each spoke of the need to display a strong sense of confidence while in the pit. My father believes that the gamecock can sense this confidence and will in turn display similar qualities:

> The handler must enter the pit not showing any fear. The rooster does not know fear so the handler cannot fear the other handler. If the handler is not confident this will help the rooster lose.

Elements of masculinity as defined by Mexican culture are kept alive within the arena of the cockfight. They then manifest themselves throughout the community in both negative and positive forms; for example, the aggressiveness and bravado of a cockfight can carry over into general public space, where negative forms of machismo, such as fistfights, are displayed. On the other hand, Mexican males who see masculinity as a positive mechanism for overcoming discriminatory structural forces in the United States display forms of assertiveness, responsibility, and selflessness. As a result, the cockfight becomes the means by which Mexican males are able to create a space of their own in a world far from their origins, and, in some way, slow down the process of assimilation. This "resistance masculinity" thus becomes a defensive mechanism against the devaluation of Mexican culture.

This dynamic was very evident within my own family. My father, having lived in the United States for over fifty years, could easily slip back into Mexico without missing a cultural beat. After five decades in the United States he has remained culturally Mexican, and the same can be said of my uncle. Their commonalities consist of an intense interest in cockfighting and continued association with like-minded Mexican men. Although by strict definition my father is a U.S. citizen of Mexican ancestry, because of his naturalization some fifty years ago, he nonetheless remains culturally a Mexicano. By this I mean that he practices a culture that is imbued with his Mexican heritage. He has continued speaking Spanish, socializes frequently with other Mexicans, and maintains ethnic awareness and loyalty—key criteria of Mexican cultural identification, according to Moore and Pachon. (1985, 130–31). This is not to say, however, that assimilation forces have not affected my family's first generation. For example, my father and uncle speak both Spanish and English, but read and write only English. This is explained by the limited formal education they received while in Mexico and the United States; for all practical purposes, my elders were *forced* to learn how to read and write only in English. My uncle even admits that his literacy skills in English and Spanish are limited, which is common among first-generation immigrants.

As successful cockfighters, my father and uncle enjoy a sense of accomplishment and respect they could not easily obtain otherwise, given the realities of their position in U.S. society. Cockfighting publications have featured them, individuals seek their advice on all facets of the sport, and within the Mexican community they are honored with the title of "Don," a term that recognizes them as important elders. Thus, for my elders and others, the sport of cockfighting transcends the arena itself and creates a parallel world for its participants. Like *fútbol*, baseball, bullfighting, and the *charreada* (rodeo/variety show), cockfighting is as much about culture and identity as it is about the sport itself. These national pastimes provide participants and spectators a space to practice their culture of origin without ridicule or shame. For Mexican cockfighters, the beloved sport is a connection to their Mexicanness and to a land left behind.

Conclusion

As my uncle stated, "We will keep fighting roosters until the very end. It's in our blood." Historians, sociologists, and anthropologists who have studied cockfighting throughout the world would recognize these words. This devotion to cockfighting is what makes the sport appealing and intriguing as a subject of study. For the Mexican men who breed, train, and fight cocks, the sport appears to have a meaning that reaches beyond watching two roosters battle to the death. Although money and betting are crucial elements, they do not fully explain the devotion displayed by my father and uncle.

Cockfighting in the Mexican community in the United States has a long history. For rural Mexican males in this country, maintenance of the cockfighting tradition has created a buffer against assimilation by providing a gendered space for displays of masculinity. The masculinity on display couples elements of traditional Mexican masculinity with a form of resistance masculinity, and carries over from the sport into the larger Mexican community. Cockfighting, at least for those men I have described in this article, has provided a sense of community and cultural continuity in a place far distant from their place of origin. Considering the limited opportunities and structural barriers that my father and uncle encountered, cockfighting has allowed them to experience a kind of economic and social upward mobility that their working class status in mainstream society did not provide or allow. Lastly, when I see my father's cock matched up against an opponent's cock, I can see that it has an equalizing effect. In the cockfighting pit, it is all about skill and aggressiveness; place of origin, socioeconomic background, race, and ethnicity are effectively neutralized.

In the end, my father was not adamant, forceful, or even concerned when my interest waned and I decided to be a spectator and not a cockfighter. As a second-generation Chicano, I have had opportunities not afforded to my father or uncle, and thus have been able to challenge oppression and discrimination in other ways. In hindsight, my father may have seen cockfighting as an old tradition that he did not want his children to follow, just as he insisted that his children break the cycle of poverty. Still, there are days I realize that when my father and uncle finally stop fighting gamecocks a family tradition will end.

Notes

I began this essay in the fall of 2001 and subsequently presented a portion of it at the III Congreso Internacional de Literatura de Chicana in Malaga, Spain, in May 2002. I want to thank Sharon Bird, Iowa State University Department of Sociology, for the many discussions we had on masculinity and for her insightful suggestions on fine-tuning this essay. Also, I thank Sidner Larson, director of the American Indian Studies Program at Iowa State University, and Andrejs Plakans, chair of the History Department at Iowa State University, for their support and editorial suggestions. A word of thanks to the anonymous peer reviewers at *Aztlán* for their helpful suggestions and comments. Cathy Sunshine, the copyeditor at the UCLA Chicano Studies Research Center Press, worked her magic throughout this paper. Finally, to my father and uncle—thanks for the unique childhood experiences that continue to resonate with me and for keeping many aspects of our culture alive.

1. In choosing among the various terms describing Mexicans in the United States, I make use of David G. Gutierrez's definitions (1993, 520n1). In this essay, when I speak of *Mexican Americans* I am referring to American citizens of Mexican descent, regardless of their length of residence in the United States. The term

Chicano refers to persons of Mexican descent who used that term as a self-referent during the 1960s and 1970s. I use the term *Mexican immigrants* when referring to citizens of Mexico residing in the United States. Although all of these groups historically have recognized important distinctions among themselves, all have been subject to varying degrees of prejudice and discrimination in the United States, regardless of their formal citizenship status. Thus, when referring to the combined population of all persons of Mexican ancestry or descent living in the United States, I employ the term *ethnic Mexicans*.

2. See also Dundes 1994 and Scott 1983.

3. The handler, formerly called a *setter* or *setter-to*, is supposed have expert knowledge of preparing cocks for battle and handling them during the actual fights. For terms associated with cockfighting see Scott 1983, 188–93.

4. Statements in this essay attributed to my uncle were obtained in an interview I did with him on January 3, 2003. My father and uncle are still active cockfighters and to protect their identities I cannot use their names or disclose their whereabouts. After all, this is an illegal sport.

5. There remains a paucity of literature on the Mexican diaspora in the Pacific Northwest. Further discussion on ethnic Mexicans in this region can be found in Maldonado and Garcia 2001, 1–7. For insight into the Spanish exploration of the Pacific Northwest see Weber 1992, and for additional readings on the origins of Mexicans in the Pacific Northwest see Gamboa and Baun 1995.

6. I interviewed my aunt and uncle on January 9, 2003.

7. Under normal circumstances I would provide a citation to the issue of *Gamecock* in which my elders appeared. However, for security purposes I am unable to provide any information that could reveal the identities of my father and uncle.

8. For an excellent description of a cockfight see Clifford Geertz's article (1972) on Balinese cockfighting. The Mexican cockfight and rules of engagement are similar to the Balinese.

Works Cited

Baca Zinn, Maxine. 1982. "Chicano Men and Masculinity." *Journal of Ethnic Studies* 10, no. 2: 29–43.

Bradley, Hugh. 1941. *Havana: Cinderella's City*. New York: Doubleday, Doran.

Bryant, Clifton D., and Li Li. 1991. "A Statistical Value Profile of Cockfighters." *Sociology and Social Research* 75, no. 4 (July): 199–209.

Briceño, Olga. 1945. *Cocks and Bulls in Caracas: How We Live in Venezuela*. Boston: Houghton Mifflin.

Burstyn, Varda. 1999. *The Rites of Men: Manhood, Politics, and the Culture of Sport*. Toronto: University of Toronto Press.

Cantú, Lionel. 2000. "*Entre Hombres*/Between Men: Latino Masculinities and Homosexualities." In *Gay Masculinities*, ed. Peter Nardi. Thousand Oaks, CA: Sage Publications.

Carrasco, David, with Scott Sessions. 1998. *Daily Life of the Aztec: People of the Sun and Earth*. Westport, CT: Greenwood Press.

Chivers, C. J. 2000. "Police Storm Cockfighting Tournament in a Derelict Bronx Theatre." *New York Times*, June 5.

Clendinnen, Inga. 1991. *Aztecs: An Interpretation*. Cambridge: Cambridge University Press.

Connell, R. W. 1996. "Teaching the Boys: New Research on Masculinity, and Gender Strategies for Schools." *Teachers College Record* 98, no. 2 (Winter): 208.

————. 1995. *Masculinities*. Berkeley and Los Angeles: University of California Press.

Crosby, Alfred W. Jr. 1972. *The Columbian Exchange: Biological and Cultural Consequences of 1492*. Westport, CT: Greenwood Press.

del Castillo, Adelaida R. 1996. "Gender and Its Discontinuities in Male/Female Domestic Relations: Mexicans in Cross-Cultural Context." In *Chicanas/Chicanos at the Crossroads: Social, Economic, and Political Change*, ed. David R. Maciel and Isidro D. Ortiz. Tucson: University of Arizona Press.

Dundes, Alan. 1994. *The Cockfight: A Casebook*. Madison: University of Wisconsin Press.

Gamboa, Erasmo, and Carolyn M. Baun. 1995. *Nosotros: The Hispanic People of Oregon, Essays and Collections*. Portland: Oregon Council for the Humanities.

Geertz, Clifford. 1972. "Deep Play: Notes on the Balinese Cockfight." *Daedalus: Journal of the American Academy of Arts and Sciences* 101, no. 1 (Winter): 1–37. Reprinted in *The Cockfight: A Casebook*, ed. Alan Dundes. Madison: University of Wisconsin Press, 1994.

Gómez-Quiñones, Juan. 1979. "Toward a Concept of Culture." In *Modern Chicano Writers: A Collection of Critical Essays*, ed. Joseph Sommers and Tomás Ybarra-Frausto. Upper Saddle River, NJ: Prentice Hall.

Gutiérrez, David G. 1993. "Significant to Whom?: Mexican Americans and the History of the American West." *Western Historical Quarterly* 24, no. 4 (November): 519–39.

Hassig, Ross. 1988. *Aztec Warfare: Imperial Expansion and Political Control*. Norman: University of Oklahoma Press.

Hicks, David. 2002. "Blood and Feathers: Masculine Identity in East Timorese Cockfighting." Retrieved February 12, 2004 from the World Wide Web: http://www.etan.org. First published in *The World and I Magazine*, January 2001.

Hondagneu-Sotelo, Pierrette, and Michael A. Messner. 2000. "Gender Displays and Men's Power: The 'New Man' and the Mexican Immigrant Man." In *Gender Through the Prism of Difference*, 2d ed., ed. Maxine Baca Zinn, Pierrette Hondagneu-Sotelo, and Michael A. Messner. Boston: Allyn and Bacon.

Ingersoll, Ernest. 1923. *Birds in Legend, Fable, and Folklore*. New York: Longman's, Green.

Kilborn, T. 2000. "In Enclaves of Rural America, a Cockfighting Industry Thrives." *New York Times*. June 6.

Klein, Alan M. 2000. "Dueling Machos: Masculinity and Sport in Mexican Baseball." In *Masculinities, Gender Relations, and Sport*, ed. Jim McKay, Michael A. Messner, and Donald F. Sabo. London: Sage Publications.

Madsen, William. 1973. *Mexican Americans of South Texas*. New York: Holt, Rinehart, and Winston.

Majors, Richard. 1990. "Cool Pose: Black Masculinity and Sports." In *Sport, Men, and Gender Order: Critical Feminist Perspectives*, ed. Michael A. Messner and Donald F. Sabo. Champaign, IL: Human Kinetics Books.

Majors, Richard, and Janet Mancini Billson. 1992. *Cool Pose: The Dilemmas of Black Manhood in America*. New York: Lexington Books.

Maldonado, Carlos S., and Gilberto Garcia. 2001. *The Chicano Experience in the Northwest*, 2d ed.. Dubuque, IA: Kendall/Hunt.

McCaghy, H., and Arthur G. Neal. 1973. "The Fraternity of Cockfighters: Ethical Embellishments of an Illegal Sport." *Journal of Popular Culture* 8, no. 3 (Winter): 557–69.

Mirandé, Alfredo. 1997. *Hombres y Machos: Masculinity and Latino Culture*. Boulder, CO: Westview.

Moore, Joan, and Harry Pachon. 1985. *Hispanics in the United States*. Upper Saddle River, NJ: Prentice Hall.

Najera, Rick. 1997. *The Pain of the Macho and Other Plays*. Houston: Arte Público.

Paredes, Américo. 1993. *Folklore and Culture on the Texas-Mexican Border*. Austin, Texas: University of Texas, Center for Mexican American Studies.

Paz, Octavio. 1950. *El laberinto de la soledad*. México: Cuadernos Americanos.

Plass, Paul. 1995. *The Game of Death in Ancient Rome: Arena Sport and Political Suicide*. Madison: University of Wisconsin Press.

Portes, Alejandro, and Rubén G. Rumbaut. 1996. *Immigrant America: A Portrait*. Berkeley and Los Angeles: University of California Press.

Ross, Brian. 2001. "Roosters with Razors: Cockfighting Still Legal in Three States, Gambling Persists." March 30. Retrieved February 17, 2004 from the World Wide Web: http://www.abcnews.com

Scott, George Ryley. 1983. *The History of Cockfighting*. Hindhead, Surrey, U.K.: Saiga.

Seattle Post–Intelligencer. 2001. "Victim Likely Had Been Bystander at Shooting." December 5.

St. Augustine, Bishop of Hippo. 1942. *Divine Providence and the Problem of Evil: A Translation of St. Augustine's De Ordine*, trans. Robert P. Russell. New York: Cosmopolitan Science and Art Service.

Wasserman, Mark. 2000. *Everyday Life and Politics in Nineteenth Century Mexico: Men, Women, and War*. Albuquerque: University of New Mexico Press.

Weber, David J. 1992. *The Spanish Frontier in North America*. New Haven, CT: Yale University Press.

West, Nathaniel. 1969. "California Cockfight." In *The Day of the Locust*. New York: New Direction Books.

Wucker, Michele. 1999. *Why the Cocks Fight: Dominicans, Haitians, and the Struggle for Hispaniola*. New York: Hill and Wang.

Testifying

Activist Latina Lesbian Publishing:

esto no tiene nombre and *conmoción*

tatiana de la tierra

esto no tiene nombre: *this has no name: the way a look says desire, the way love spirals into DNA, the way dancing happens with one finger, the way that sisterhood travels, the way in which we walk with certainty even when there's not a word to stake a claim. ¿Qué quieres? What is your desire? esto.*

—de la tierra, "Las Sinvergüenzas"

From 1991 until 1996, two Latina lesbian magazines, *esto no tiene nombre* (this has no name) and *conmoción* (commotion + in motion) were published. I was one of the founders and editors of both of these periodicals. For the sake of herstory and with the intent of exposing and analyzing the reality and implications of publishing these magazines, I unearthed three boxes that contain the archives of *esto* and *conmoción*.

The files are messy and incomplete. The story that unfolds will be detailed with the raw materials that created it, including documents from the archives and the magazines themselves, as well as interviews with key people and my own perception and memory of the events, geography, politics, and "characters" involved. This is not an impartial narrative, though I do intend to be as factually accurate as possible and it will be easy for the reader to distinguish between fact and interpretation. I don't expect that everyone who was engaged with *esto* and *conmoción* will agree with or even appreciate my point of view. Still, I was at the center of these publications from the beginning until the end, and I am the holder of the archives.

I think this is a story that needs to be told—we really did create history with the act of publishing. We left documents behind, we added to the

Latina lesbian body of work, and we did so, in my opinion, with a rawness and vibrancy that had not existed to date and has not been repeated since within the world of Latina lesbian literary expression.

This story begins in Miami, Florida, circa 1991.

I remember reading a classified ad in *New Times*, a weekly entertainment paper. It went something like this: "Latina lesbians, let's get together." Close to twenty of us congregated one Saturday afternoon in someone's hot and crowded living room. We voiced our need to be together as Latinas and as lesbians, to have barbecues, to have positive reinforcement for our existence. We wanted to be able to talk in Spanish among our own. Many of us did not connect with the white lesbian organizations and were deemed invisible and/or undesirable by our own families. Some were in the closet. We passed around a piece of paper and put our names and telephone numbers on it. It seemed like the Beginning of Something Good.

We never met again.

Las Salamandras de Ambiente

Months later, I heard about a new Latina lesbian group that was started by Angie and Ena. The word spread and soon Everyone made the scene, including many of the same ones who attended the other meeting. It was obvious to all of us that there was a great need for a Latina lesbian organization. As far as we knew, such a group had never existed in Miami. While there had always been a teeming Latina lesbian presence in the gay and lesbian bars and probably on every street in Miami, there had not been an official, public declaration that united sexual and ethnic identity. The weekly meetings were being held in a room in a warehouse district that had been converted into "women's space." By the time I got there, the group had been meeting for several months and was due for a party. I phoned every lesbian on the list from the original classified ad meeting to tell them about the party. One of them, Margarita, offered to pick me up and I agreed, not realizing that it was a Date.

The party was a smash. It took place at Ena and Isabel's large, fancy house in Hialeah. Salsa music blasted, ham croquetas and pasteles de guayaba were eaten up, Spanish was spoken, and everyone was decked out to the hilt, Latin style. I think all of us knew that the group was really happening, that it would be long-lasting and fruitful. I got a ride back home from someone else, as Margarita terrified me. She was a loud, obnoxious, Cuban old-time butch who was so forthright in her sexual energy that I didn't know how to respond to her.

Soon after, the group had a name—Las Salamandras de Ambiente. "De ambiente" is Latin queer code for "in the life." And salamanders were, according to research conducted by Vanessa and Patricia, amphibians whose reproduction was female-centered. Female salamanders hatched eggs without any male intervention and, thus, were "lesbians." In addition, they were blessed with the mythical ability to live in fire. Therefore, salamanders were not only lesbians—they were hardy survivors. The name was happily adopted. Later, Vanessa and Patricia discovered that their initial research was flawed and that the "lesbian" reptile was a close cousin to the salamander. But it was too late—Las Salamandras de Ambiente had already been baptized by all of its members. Angie designed the group's logo, two lusty salamanders encircling a palm tree within a triangle.

Las Salamandras reflected the diversity of Miami's Latin community. Members were from all over—Cuba, the Dominican Republic, Puerto Rico, Colombia, Mexico, Venezuela, Costa Rica, and Ecuador. We were all immigrants and fluent in Spanish and English. We were of working and middle-class extraction, mostly mulatas and light-skinned, from twenty to forty-something years old. We were students, teachers, accountants, counselors, saleswomen, massage therapists, bank tellers, federal employees, musicians, writers, and housewives. Typical of Latinas, we were family-oriented. The Cuban Salamandras were fierce anti-comunistas. Overall, I would classify the group as "conservative." This was not a flag-waving rabble-rousing ensemble at all, and was not ever linked with any social movement or "activism" beyond existing as a publicly recognized Latina lesbian organization.

In practical terms, Las Salamandras was a support group that met every Thursday evening at 8:00. We rapped about coming out, about family and lovers, about who we were. We met in each other's apartments at times, though once the group got settled, the meetings were held at the Metropolitan Community Church and, once it opened, at the Lesbian and Gay Community Center in Miami Beach. The true "support" that Las Salamandras offered anyone was questionable, but if you could measure a group's success by the parties, Las Salamandras was over the top. We had parties in each other's homes, at rented halls, at the Unitarian church, at clubs, in celebration of New Year's, Halloween, Valentine's, or whatever—and not one of them was a dud.

Most of us in Las Salamandras were true Miamians: we were born in another country but, in the United States, Miami was our only home. I had lived in Miami most of my life and had completed my undergraduate degree in Gainesville, north Florida. Before moving back to Miami, I had traveled throughout the United States. Several other Salamandras had relocated from Boston and a few other cities in the northeast. I mention these distinctions because there were noticeable differences between the Miami natives and those who had also resided in other metropolitan areas. Miami Salamandras, it seemed, viewed lesbianism in practical and narrow terms. To be able to live in a fashion that allowed lesbianism to coexist with being a functioning member of family, society, and the workforce was the ultimate goal. Parties on weekends were a plus. But being a lesbian did not include challenging the social construction that kept lesbianism a private matter or exploring beyond the Miami shores. And Miami Latinas, due to culture and geography, were alienated from the Anglo gay and lesbian "community" and its corresponding national concerns and internal politics. I saw Miami, in a sense, as an island unto itself.

Those of us who had lived elsewhere, though, had participated in or at least been exposed to a wider gamut of lesbian culture, including women's bookstores, music festivals, feminist politics, and lesbian herstory and literature. By 1991, I had been "out" for eight years and had gone through my own worldwide lesbian awakening. I was a barefoot traveling lesbian in search of an exotic secret society. I had participated in several Latin American lesbian feminist gatherings, beginning with the first one that was held in Mexico in 1987 (see de la tierra 1988). And I had attended women's gatherings in the United States, including numerous women's music festivals. For years, I had been negotiating my identity within all of these spaces. The lesbians I encountered at home in Colombia and in Latin America were often educated and wealthy daddy's girls whom I could not easily identify with. Besides, I was a Latina from the United States, which put me in a different class altogether. I had been influenced by angry white separatist feminist vegetarian dykes who danced to the goddess's tune, which didn't help me blend in with South American sisters.

In the United States, on the other hand, I was eventually alienated from the whiteness of mainstream culture and allied myself with women of color. I had read and connected with some of the defining literature of the 1980s—*This Bridge Called My Back* (Moraga and Anzaldúa 1981), *Loving in the War Years* (Moraga 1983), *Chicana Lesbians* (Trujillo 1991), and *Compañeras* (Ramos 1994), where I had my first poem, "De ambiente," published. I had also written articles about Latin American lesbians and had begun to compile lists of international Latin lesbian organizations. I was a natural networker and collector of Latina lesbian culture—flyers, books, music, photographs, posters, anything.

I had been Desperately In Search of Latinas for many years, no doubt a search for my own self. After having internalized the ethnic and linguistic self-hatred produced by this country's racism and hatred of Others, I was ready to embrace my own. I don't think this was mutual, though. As I have felt my entire life anywhere that I have ever lived, I also felt alienated from Las Salamandras. I was more Americanized than most, and less fluid in social customs and graces. I could not even speak in public at the time without turning red. And worst of all, I could not dance. I did have nerve, though, and I was creative and persistent, as well as a budding writer, all qualities that led me to join the group's newsletter committee. It was the only place where I could possibly find a niche.

esto no tiene nombre

The first issue, dated 23 September 1991, was a basic black-and-white eighteen-page homegrown publication that was photocopied at Kinko's and sold for $2. We printed fifty copies, and then reprinted another batch. It debuted the evening of yet another sensational Salamandra party. We called it *esto no tiene nombre, revista de lesbianas latinas en Miami* (this has no name, Latina lesbian magazine in Miami) (see fig. 1).[1] We literally could not come up with a name, and on the editorial page we wrote, in bold letters, "Necesitamos un nombre" (we need a name). Of course, we liked the double entendre of not having a name, of not being able to name lesbian desire. It insinuated love in the closet. "*Esto no tiene nombre*" is also an expression of something being beyond words. It was the title of a Puerto Rican comedy TV show that aired in the 1970s. And it was charming, in a way. We could rationalize many things about being poetically nameless, and actually, we did just that. The name grew on us and it was there to stay.

But *esto no tiene nombre* was a source of conflict from the first. The headline on the cover asks, "Debut y ¿Despedida?" (debut and farewell?) This was also a play on words: it was the title of a song by Puerto Rican singer Lissette, yet it posed a pertinent question. A few Salamandras were concerned, even before we published anything at all, about the content, the editorial control, and the role that the publication would play in the community. They wanted a simple newsletter, one that would inform about the group's activities, and they wanted the final copy to be approved by the group as a whole before anything was published. But those of us on the

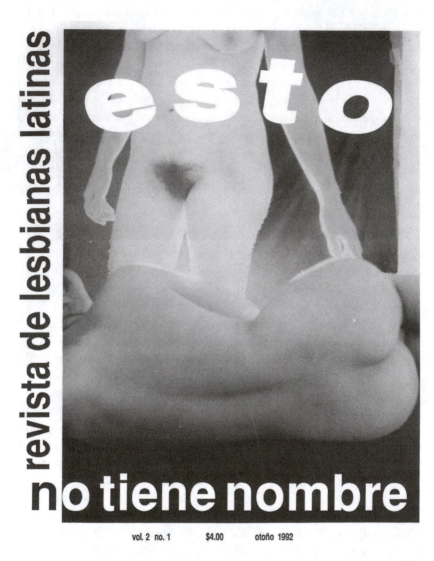

Fig. 1. *Cover of* esto no tiene nombre *(volume 2, number 1, 1992)*.

editorial committee wanted a magazine, one that would include as many voices as possible. We wanted to publish anything any of us had to say. We solicited writings, graphics, and ideas from the group, and these, compiled with our own writings and vision, were the raw materials for the first issue.

On the cover, in Spanish, we published the first editorial, one that acknowledged the conflict that preempted *esto*. "We understand that this is an internal struggle and part of the process of growth in our community. The editorial committee has decided to publish this first volume so that each woman can formulate her own responses." We defended freedom of creativity and expression and asked, "Is our community ready for our magazine? . . . Who has not enjoyed a clitoris, a nipple, a woman's kiss? It would be hypocritical and a form of internalized lesbophobia to exclude these images when they are the basis of our expression." The rest of the newsletter included brief pieces, written by nine Salamandra contributors. It included lots of (bad) poetry, a few very short stories and chronicles, a cartoon, a recipe (for onion rice), advice on natural pesticides, video and book reviews, news and announcements, and "Cuéntame," an anonymous interview that I conducted and edited. The majority of the content was in Spanish and most of the contributors were identified only by first names by their request.

The first issue of *esto* caused a commotion. There was immediate dissent about what we had published. At question was how Las Salamandras was being represented (one had written a first-person narrative about her experience with the group); the graphic use of language (we decided to publish an orgasm in every issue—poetry or prose that celebrated our sexuality); and the Cuéntame interview, where a black Latina talked about her preference for black women and boasted in crude detail about bringing her lovers to orgasm. Her language was strong. It was real. It was us. And by publishing her words, we were being true to our editorial policy, which read in part: "*esto no tiene nombre* publishes materials by Latina lesbians that reflect our diversity and rupture the stereotypes that have been nailed upon us. Our objective is to create a forum for words and images that contribute to the fortitude and pride of our community."

But Las Salamandras did not appreciate our inclusive philosophy. Heated discussions ensued. We met in Caridad's apartment, where Salamandras fumed about the trash we were publishing. Our response was: if it bothers you, write a letter to the editor; let it be a debate among us. We saw *esto* as a forum for discussion within our community. We worked earnestly to produce the second issue of *esto*, despite the controversy. This time, though, we expanded beyond the local network and invited lesbians from Latin America, whom we met when they came into town for an international environmental conference, to contribute writings and to help us spread the word.

The second edition of *esto* was twenty pages, dated 31 January 1992, volume 1, number 2. It was printed on lavender paper, also at Kinko's. The cover had an image of Argentinian rockers Sandra Mihanovich and Celeste Carballo dreamily gazing into each other's eyes, as well as the cute Salamandra logo. The graphics, created by Patricia, were light-years ahead of the first edition. *Esto* had a clean-cut and orderly look now, with a table of contents, an editorial and contributor's page, letters to the editor, news and announcements, two ads, seven poems, and wide-ranging content. Among the highlights were Amy's essay on death, an interview with a Costa Rican lesbian activist, Vanessa's take on the Latino "disease model" of lesbianism, Patricia's witty crossword puzzle (that required knowledge of Latina and lesbian history and culture), my review of two lesbian sex videos, and the Cuéntame. There were eleven contributors this time, including a poet from Costa Rica and one from Puerto Rico.

Again, *esto* caused an uproar. And, again, it was the sexually explicit material that generated controversy: Margarita's "orgasm," my reviews of the videos *Bathroom Sluts* (1991)and *Dress Up for Daddy* (1991), and the anonymous Cuéntame interview, which denounced feminists and praised tribadism. While these pieces did not even take up two full pages in the publication, they were the focus of a debate that quickly escalated in intensity. Some of the Salamandras felt we had betrayed the group's morality, and they screamed for censorship. We were staunchly opposed to censorship and supported the free expression of ideas and experience by Latina lesbians on any topic. And we were not just free thinkers; we were true lovers of literature and were writers ourselves. We regarded our roles as editors with utmost seriousness—we believed that publishing had the power to transgress invisibility, that we were creating and representing our community along the way, that expressing lesbian sexuality was good and fun and healthy, and that what we were doing was meaningful. We saw internalized homophobia as the real crux of the matter. Several of Las Salamandras were offended by the word "lesbian" on the cover. Many were not "out" publicly and did not intend to be.

But those of us at the core of *esto* were of a different breed. Margarita, who had come to Miami during the Mariel exodus in 1980, had walked the streets of La Habana arm-in-arm with her female lovers in a country where being homosexual was a crime. She lived by laws of her own making. She was, according to the biographical note that we published in every issue of *esto*, "an anti-communist, a Christian, and a lover of women, sexuality, and communication." She was also Eurocentric and thought President Bush and Pinochet were the greatest, and she was one of the strongest characters anyone could ever imagine knowing.

The rest of us were bleeding-heart liberals. Patricia was a Cuban–Puerto Rican with leftist tendencies who had a bachelor's degree in political science. Vanessa, her partner, from Puerto Rico, had studied economics at MIT in Cambridge, where the two had met. Vane and Patri were well read in lesbian literature and well versed in lesbian and liberal discourse, including identity politics, class issues, and environmentalism. They had been involved with the politically active lesbian community in Boston, including the Women's Community Center and lesbian organizations on MIT's campus. They had attended conferences on pornography and on race and ethnicity among lesbians. When we first met, Vane and Patri lived in a house in South Dade, set smack in the middle of a field of tomatoes. They had back-to-the-earth values and envisioned living off the land. I shared many of Vane and Patri's worldviews. And like Margarita, I lived by my own rules. We were, each of us, strong-willed, outspoken, and independent. The four of us were the creators of *esto no tiene nombre*, and even though we were not in complete agreement about the world, we were able to accept that there would be disagreements.

"There's an agreement to our morality in the group."

Las Salamandras was not willing to accept the disagreements, though, and more screaming matches took place. On Sunday afternoon, 8 March 1992, a special meeting was held at the Alice Wainwright Park, practically across the street from Madonna's lavish Miami home. We tape-recorded the meeting and I later transcribed it. Among the verbatim excerpts from this meeting: "There is no need to use derogatory language." "I don't want these words in a magazine I share with my friends." "You think I can show this to my mother? Where do we draw the line?" "If the idea of this group is to give lesbians a positive image, how are we doing that here?" "I don't have a penis. I don't fuck." "What happens in the bedroom shouldn't be published." "You can open up much more with tenderness and sweetness, not by trying to scandalize people." "With all the empowering things to write about, I don't see a place for pornographic reviews." "A pornography book, is that what you want?" "Is this going to be *Playgirl? On Our Backs?*" "There's an agreement to our morality in the group." "Would you like your family to look at those words? Is that how you want to be represented?"

During the meeting at the park that Sunday, it was decided that a greater number of Salamandras should become involved in *esto's* editorial process. But by now, outsiders were getting in on the debate, including a Cuban lesbian minister from the Metropolitan Community Church, Mari Castellanos. Many members of Las Salamandras also attended Mari's sermons; some were her "groupies." The Latina lesbian moral majority now had their own Oral Roberts. The official editorial committee consisted of Vanessa Cruz, Patricia Pereira-Pujol, and myself. Margarita Castilla took charge of the accounting from the beginning and was part of the core group. Her name appears in the editorial box as of the second issue, along with Sylvia's name, who never did anything that I can recall. In fact, suddenly people who never had any interest in publishing joined the editorial committee. The "real" editorial committee was joined by six others, including two *esto* contributors and four moral police agents. By 9 March, the new, expanded committee had approved sixteen official editorial policies. The Newsletter Committee Document has the word "woman" and "women" scratched out and replaced with "lesbian" and "lesbians." The policies, written originally in English, are presented here just as they appear in the document, misspellings and all:

> Majority rule; No quorum required; The committee is open to any latin lesbian that is in agreement with the editorial policy; The editorial policy is open to discussion and change; All writers must be lesbian; All writers must be latin with the following exceptions—letters to the editor, collaboration with other latin women; The writings may not be oppressive; The writings do not contradict the purpose of the group as stated in the articles of incorporation; The writings do not include profanity or vulgarity for it's own sake or for the purpose to shock or when it is demeaning and oppressive; The writings may be in spanish or in english with the exception that the Editorial Notes presented on the inside cover of the News Letter be written in spanish; There will be no translations of the writings; Preference will be given to issues related to latin lesbian; No editorial changes without the agreement of the author, except for changes related to grammar or syntax; The editorial committee will aspire to present a balance view as to form and content; Authors will have copyright privileges; and Pseudonyms are allowed, however, the Editorial Committee must know who the person submitting the writing is. The right of the person to be anonymous will be respected in all cases.

Two policies were rejected by the majority: "There will be a qualitative standard of good taste and form in presenting the writers views"; and "Writings giving exposure to pornography be not allowed."

A final note appears at the bottom:

> A test of how the approved editorial policies would work was performed by having committee members vote on whether or not the article "Video-View: Las Putas y Los Papis" would be included in a News Letter issue if each of the committee members would apply the approved editorial policies. The article was accepted by a vote of 6 members voting yes to include the article and 4 members voting no.

I remember Vanessa saying that she trusted the process; the members of the editorial committee would come to understand what it meant to publish and they would either naturally eliminate themselves or grow. But of the ten people on this committee, only four were there as "moral police," and they were outnumbered. They cried foul.

Several days later, Las Salamandras held a meeting behind our backs. I was tipped off by a friend. Before the next Thursday night group meeting, and in anticipation of what was to evolve, Vanessa, Patricia, Margarita, and I decided to withdraw from the group. That night, 12 March 1992, we were presented with the following petition written in English, signed by almost every Salamandra, including new "outsiders" and many of the original Salamandras, who were our friends, or so we thought:

To: Editorial Committee *"ESTO NO TIENE NOMBRE"*

We, the undersigned, individually and collectively agree to the following:

1. The content of the newsletter *ESTO NO TIENE NOMBRE* continues to be a source of conflict which greatly distresses all of us. Therefore, we hereby, demand that this newsletter be discontinued, and/or the presumed sponsorship of SALAMANDRAS DE AMBIENTE be withdrawn from any such publication until such a date when the proper mechanisms are set into place to insure that said newsletter is representative and respectful of the consensus, philosophy and standards of this group.

2. We consider that the problems that have ensued from the newsletter are symptomatic of a lack of clarity regarding the position and purpose of SALAMANDRAS DE AMBIENTE and the lack of any structure designed to implement such position and purpose. Therefore, we call for the creation of a task force to study this issue, to design a model and to present and propose their conclusions to the membership at large by a specific date. Said task force will be constituted by volunteer mem-

bers who are endorsed by a 2/3 majority of the membership to be selected at our next business meeting.

off our backs or *On Our Backs?*

> **Salamandras:** Lizard-like lesbianas who can't take the heat. They stay
> low to the ground and hump hidden in the shadows of shame.
> Salamandras are the riff-raff of the race, Christian comemierda pets of
> the right-wing machine, pious pendejas who become skittish in the pres-
> ence of potent sinvergüenzas.
> —de la tierra, "Las Sinvergüenzas"

We didn't take what happened lightly—it was an ugly scenario, to be
stabbed in the back by our own familia, and it was deeply painful, never to
be forgotten. Vanessa and Patricia completely shut Las Salamandras out,
while Margarita and I occasionally went to meetings and parties. Despite
what had happened, Las Salamandras was our main connection to the
local Latina lesbian community, and we still had friends among the group.
But it was the end of an era.

Getting kicked out of Las Salamandras expanded *esto's* horizon. The
way they did what they did—behind closed doors—and that they penned a
petition intended to silence us fueled our conviction in publishing. It served
as inspiration to continue with *esto*, and it strengthened our bond. By then,
Margarita and I were locked in a steamy and passionate relationship, and
Vane and Patri were as solid as partners can be. The four of us were in love
with each other, and we had a mission: this, which has no name.

We continued with the immediate task at hand: to publish the next
issue of *esto*. The spring 1992 edition, volume 1, number 3, came out about
six weeks after our rupture with Las Salamandras, and it was markedly
different. We ditched Kinko's for a real printer and had a print run of 200,
which cost us $150. The final product was a twenty-page glossy magazine
with a full-sized black-and-white photograph of an alluring woman in the
woods who looked you right in the eye. (Years later, I was to discover that
she wasn't even a lesbian.) The contributors were all local, and the contents were similar to the previous issue. The layout, though, was much
more sophisticated, with labryses, lesbian symbols, and kissing women
scanned into the background of selected pieces, as well as a variety of fonts,
gray and black boxes, and just the right amount of white space. But the
real difference was our focus. "Miami" was dropped from the official name,
which was now, simply, *esto no tiene nombre, revista de lesbianas latinas*.

There were still remnants from Las Salamandras, though, in the letters to the editor section which was entitled "en nuestras mentes" (on our minds). Mari Castellanos, the moral-majority-Cuban-lesbian minister, wrote (in Spanish), a letter that begins by congratulating us for our wonderful, professional-looking magazine and then continues to praise and attack every single one of our contributions. About the controversy, she wrote:

> What confuses me about the magazine is that at times I don't know if I am reading *off our backs* (a national feminist magazine) or *On Our Backs* (a pornographic lesbian magazine). Tatiana's fascination with pornography intrigues me.[2] It is not my place to determine if it is appropriate or not. This should be determined by the group as a whole, by consensus. This magazine belongs to all of us, right? . . . I don't think this is representative of the values of the group. Oh, the tyranny of minorities! For some people, vulgar language represents a progressive wave against the established order. For others, the use of obscenities only indicates a lack of vocabulary. This definitely does not respect the sensibilities of many and imposes criteria that cause unnecessary friction. To impact society, one needs cutting-edge ideas and valiant positions, not vulgarity.

I responded (in Spanish) by deconstructing several of the offending "vulgar" words, all of which were used within the context of the lesbian sex video reviews that I had written: "singar" (to fuck); "puta" (slut); and "dyke." I defended sexual vocabulary, sexual education, and sexual liberation. They were futile words, though. We would never agree.

The back cover of the magazine announced *esto's* new venture—"la estupenda *esto*-peña" (the stupendous *esto*-club). This was to be a cultural event, to be held the third Sunday of every month, that would feature poetry readings, art exhibits, and the like. It would be a fundraiser for *esto*, as well as a literary/artistic link to the local Latina lesbian community. In the end, though, the *esto*-peña flopped, as would all our local efforts. While we did have supporters in the community, most of the "out" Latina lesbians were somehow associated with Las Salamandras, and a significant number of these women were faithful churchgoers who abided by the moral mood of the time. So while we did have an audience for our events, it was a small one in comparison to the multitudes that turned out for parties. "Literature" did not draw crowds. And there was an undeclared yet palpable boycott of *esto* by Las Salamandras, symptomatic of a mutual bitterness that would endure.

Technically, Las Salamandras had never truly sponsored *esto*. Margarita had fronted the money for the first issue, and since we had no publishing funds to begin with, we had started selling subscriptions, $10 a year for four issues, since the first edition. By the time *esto* had been kicked out of the group, around twenty members of Las Salamandras had subscribed. (Margarita, Vane, Patri, and I had also paid for our own subscriptions.) Margarita had already started the subscription list on a spiral shorthand pad, and she had been keeping a ledger for incoming funds and expenses as of 6 February 1992.

Esto No Tiene Nombre, Inc.

It was clear to us that in order to pursue our vision our efforts would have to have a national focus, not a local one. I had always envisioned a national magazine to begin with, and this turn of events paved our path. We didn't know much about distribution, publicity, or publishing, but we did know that we needed money to do anything at all. Our plan for *esto* involved establishing an existence as a legal entity and associating with an organization that had tax-exempt status so that we could apply for grants. We wanted to be independent, though, with the ability to manage our funds and activities. I consulted with Brenda Stout, an accountant who knew the gay community well, and she put us in contact with Brian Geenty, the director of Lambda Community Center of Greater Miami, Inc. Soon after, Brenda helped us fill out the Articles of Incorporation and Brian, via Lambda, became our fiscal sponsor. Lambda had tax-exempt status but was not active at the time, so it was a perfect match. We hoped eventually to establish tax-exempt status for *esto*, but since this would take a long time, we began by forming this alliance. The terms were simple. We would write grants and if we were awarded funds, Brian would receive them for us and hand them over. Subscriptions and any other funds would be directed to Lambda Community Center and the funds would go directly to *esto*.

We mailed the Articles of Incorporation for Esto No Tiene Nombre, Inc. to the Florida Department of State on 12 May 1992. On 20 May we received a letter requesting that we "provide an English translation for the corporate name." We complied and on 9 June 1992, ESTO NO TIENE NOMBRE, INC., "the English translation of which is 'This Has No Name, Inc.'," became "a corporation organized under the Laws of the State of Florida." The four of us were directors, and Vanessa was the registered agent. Soon, Esto No Tiene Nombre, Inc. had an independent bank account.

Becoming a legal entity was frightening. It was a defining moment for us. We didn't know a thing about corporations. But then, we didn't know a thing about publishing, either. We just did it by examining the ways that other publications seemed to do things and considered that our starting point. Then, we talked about it and came up with our own version. Thus, we created the editorial policy, call for submissions, table of contents, contributor notes, photo releases, and everything else. We made decisions by consensus, which was not always pretty, as we differed in ideology and in our approach to the actual work involved. Still, we worked with great mutual respect.

I remember one dispute about selection of material. Our policy was to publish anything by any Latina lesbian, regardless of point of view, unless we considered the writings "oppressive." In the beginning, we were desperate for enough material to fill the pages, so getting published in *esto* was practically a done deal for anyone who contributed. We did not have much quality control at first, though we did edit and doctor up shoddy writing when possible. Then came the poem in Spanish called "Como una mujer . . . como una rosa" (like a woman, like a rose):

A woman is like a rose: With her soft and delicate lips . . . there is nothing like a woman, only a rose.

The rose is like a woman: With its satin petals so delicious to touch.

The woman is like a rose: With so many mysteries of nature. . . .

There it was, the Latina lesbian cliché from hell. We hated it. I didn't want to publish it. But Margarita was adamant about being true to our all-inclusive policy. After much yelling, policy prevailed over quality and we put it in volume 1, number 3. It was not the first "bad" piece of writing that we published and it wouldn't be the last, but it put our values to test.

We collectively called ourselves "las publicadoras que hacemos todo en esto" (the publishers who do everything in *esto*), yet our fields of responsibility and interest were well defined. I was the networker, the one who maintained the mailing list, whose job it was to Find Stuff to Publish from any Latina lesbian, anywhere in the world. I was also one of the writers in the background; I grew up as a writer with *esto no tiene nombre*. Vanessa was the other writer in the group, a great writer, actually, sharp and creative with wonderful style. She typeset the materials that we all selected as a group, and edited most of the pieces. I don't know where she learned to edit, but she was an excellent editor, with a Zen sensibility in knowing where, exactly, to cut. Patricia was the graphic artist; she taught herself PageMaker and grew more skilled with each edition. It was impressive to witness her skill as a graphic artist evolve, issue by issue. Also worthy of note is that Vane and Patri didn't own a computer at first; they used the Macintosh computers at Miami-Dade Community College for the first four issues. And Margarita kept the books, collected the mail in her private mailbox, sold subscriptions, and proofread the writings in Spanish.

Grants and Golden Opportunitie$

After incorporating, we directed our attention to the next task at hand— grant writing. None of us had ever written or seen a grant proposal before. While we were serious about publishing, writing grant proposals added a new dimension to our commitment. The process forced us to reconsider our vision, to search within for the words that fully portrayed our intent. The proposals would also put us in the view of a different audience—people who would consider our vision and the products that resulted from it, and who would decide if our project was worthy of their funds. We were not aware of local funding sources and so we prepared ourselves to be assessed on a national level, most likely by individuals far removed from our island in mayami (Miami). We wondered if foundations would understand the unique situation of lesbian immigrants who existed without the support of national organizations, publications, centers, editorial houses, or gatherings, of if they even cared. We knew that we were outside the mainstream of everything white and gay and everything heterosexual and Latino, and that venturing into these territories was inherently risky. But we also thought that it was our best alternative for taking *esto* on the high road. And we knew we were ahead of our time and hoped that astute people would see this and would want to support us. We had heard that Astraea, the National Lesbian Action Foundation in New York City, funded lesbian organizations. We wrote our first proposal for Astraea, which included the following declaration:

> The goal of Esto No Tiene Nombre, Inc. is to foster cultural exchange and all forms of expressions by Latina lesbians. We intend to serve as a vehicle for the dissemination of ideas and information about and from Latina lesbians. We feel it is important to have a space to explore who we are, what we do, what we want, what we think and where we are going. We want to establish a dialogue among ourselves without fear, censure, or having to justify ourselves in order to talk about what is important to us. With *esto no tiene nombre* we want to open minds, provoke discussion, create controversy,

break isolation, celebrate the diversity of our communities, provide space where there is none and nurture a passion for our roots.

Astraea believed in us—they awarded *esto* $1,000 in 1992, and $1,000 in 1993, and $2,500 in 1994. Through Astraea we found out about other foundations that supported gay and lesbian nonprofit organizations, and we applied to a few of them. Thus, we were awarded $700 by Open Meadows Foundation on 6 October 1992, and $800 by RESIST on 23 October 1993. These funds would turn out to be absolutely essential to *esto*'s evolution, a trajectory that would lead far away from Miami.

'Selling" *esto*

Expanding our network to the point of establishing a national and international presence within our community required lots of legwork and outreach. I was more than happy to take on this responsibility—making connections and converting them into tangible, useful parts of a whole is one of my innate abilities. Key to making *esto* an organic part of the national Latina lesbian community was to go where the Latina lesbians were—sprinkled throughout white lesbian enclaves in the United States and concentrated within Latina lesbian organizations.

In addition to covering routine publishing expenses such as postage, photocopies, office supplies and such, grant moneys permitted us to invest in other areas that we previously could not consider. The expenses were relatively small at first, but they were critical. We placed subscription ads in *Lesbian Connection*, for instance, and a call for submissions in *Poets and Writers*. We paid for an exhibit at the National Latina Lesbian and Gay Conference, held in Houston in 1992. I contacted Latina lesbian organizations such as Lesbianas Unidas in Los Angeles, Mujerio in San Francisco, Ellas in San Antonio, and Las Buenas Amigas in Manhattan. Where possible, *esto* subscription flyers were sent to everyone on each group's mailing list, either directly by us or by the organization itself. I sent flyers to lesbian and gay organizations, archives, and publications in the United States, Mexico, Latin America, and the Caribbean.

It wasn't all about money, though—it was about following any lead that could generate national visibility for *esto*. We needed material to publish, and we needed an audience for the final product. I had had an innate love and understanding of the media since I was young—I had been the features editor of my high school newspaper. I knew that editors appreciated the offbeat, that they had the means to make items of their interest visible, and that, through them, the word would eventually spread. I used the media in any way that I could conjure. I traded my writings, mostly columns, for advertising for *esto* in publications such as *Outlines* in Chicago and *The Fountain* in Miami. I established exchange subscriptions with many gay and lesbian periodicals, from *Sojourner* to *Calyx* to the *Washington Blade*. I contacted bookstores and asked them to place our flyers on their bulletin boards, or to sell *esto* on consignment. I sent sample copies of *esto* to women's presses, such as Kitchen Table Women of Color Press, Naiad, and Firebrand, and requested that they place us on their mailing lists.

I even went on national television myself, for The Cause. The first time was on Telemundo's magazine-format *Contacto* show for a segment called "Cuando su hijo es gay" (when your child is gay). I got my mom to go on the air with me. (There we were, the Radical Lesbian and her Accepting Christian Mother.) The stipulation was that the producers had to mention *esto no tiene nombre* and publicize our contact information, which they did.

And when I was arrested in front of the Colombian consulate in Coral Gables on 9 March 1994, an act that attracted media attention, my immediate concern was how to keep the reporters away from *me* and use them in favor of The Cause. I was the sole counter-demonstrator in a throng of Cubans who were threatening to boycott Colombian products because Colombia was negotiating the sale of petroleum to Cuba. Thousands of Cubans were protesting when I showed up with the Colombian flag, a "Free Cuba" T-shirt, and a "Down with the Cuban Embargo" sign. The crowd attacked me, I fought back, and the police whisked me to jail. It was a highly publicized rally and all the local news stations were there. The melee was filmed for the world to see. I experienced, unwittingly, my fifteen seconds of fame. The image of a dueling tatiana made it to Canada, Mexico, Colombia and back. And since my arrest was the only authentic event of the protest, reporters ambushed me for interviews. I declined— my views on Cuba would not get me anywhere—and offered to give them interviews about Latina lesbians instead.

A few Colombian reporters took me up on it. This is how I ended up on Colombia's national television show, *El Noticiero de las Siete,* and on other national Colombian media: *El Tiempo,* a newspaper (Shanahan 1994); *Revista Semana,* a weekly newsmagazine (1994, my interview appeared right after a piece on Princess Diana, to my aunt's shock); and Caracol, a national radio station (de la tierra 1994). The interviews didn't generate subscriptions, but they presumably had positive effects for queer visibility in Colombia. They also brought me out to all my Colombian relatives, an after-effect I had somehow overlooked. But my strategy was flawed; I was terrible on screen, very self-conscious and liable to spontaneously say the wrong thing. One day, I finally decided to Just Say No to television. (For an in-depth account of the arrest, see de la tierra 1999a.)

My biggest and most successful campaign in reaching Latina lesbians took place on the phone. I would somehow get the phone number of Some Latina Lesbian Somewhere in the United States, and I would call her. I wanted to know who the local Latina lesbian writers and artists were, where Latina lesbians congregated, what organizations they were involved in, who was good at what, where local information was published, who had the central mailing list—anything that could possibly lead to my being able to obtain either contributions of writings or graphics for the magazine, or new subscribers. I don't know if I was good on the phone or just persistent, but I know that I stayed on the phone for as long as my unknown Latina lesbian victim would permit. Maybe they complied just to get rid of me, but I was able to establish many connections this way, and to get my foot in the door of some of the Latina lesbian organizations (all but Las Salamandras, of course, who wouldn't agree to sending *esto* subscription flyers to its mailing list).[3] Eventually, since the world is indeed as small as they say, I would meet in person some of the women to whom I had previously spoken on the phone. Making the scene at conferences and gatherings here and there was another one of my methods of "selling" *esto*. (Unfortunately, though, *esto* was never able to fund any of us for travel.)

Personal contact is the most powerful way to engender trust and commitment to a cause from people. Others can always sense when you truly believe in what you do; the enthusiasm is contagious. I was very focused on soliciting materials for publishing and on selling subscriptions. I would do anything, even unwise things.

Once, I got a phone call from a Cuban lesbian who lived in Miami Beach. She had gotten my phone number from the Telemundo show and she wanted to know more about *esto*. Smelling a possible subscription sale, I volunteered that, next time I was on South Beach, I could stop by her place and show her the magazines. One day, that's exactly what I did. She cracked the door open a bit and checked me out before unhooking the security chain. I walked in and she locked the door, snapping each of the seven deadbolts into place. That's when I noticed that, even though it was the middle of the afternoon, there was no natural light in the house; incandescent bulbs lit the place. The windowpanes were covered with aluminum foil. Each piece of furniture was draped with a white cloth. The woman herself was wearing a housedress akin to a white sheet, and she said incom–prehensible things and shook. I pretended that everything was normal, showed her the magazines, and counted the minutes until I could find a way out. She never did subscribe.

"Ask me for your hunger, in Spanish"

We published nine issues of *esto no tiene nombre*, a total of 182 pages, a pile half an inch thick, with the collaboration of sixty-eight contributors. The volumes are slim; they average twenty 8 1/2" x 11" pages each. It doesn't seem like much; *esto* was small, by any standard. Yet it was significant—each issue carries its weight proudly, adds pages to the Latina lesbian archives of the future, to the herstorical records of the recent past.

As part of the "research" for this paper, I got in bed with all the issues of *esto no tiene nombre* and read them all over again, cover to cover. I'm not sure why I did this, but I read them in reverse order, beginning with volume 3, number 1, published in 1994, three years after the first edition. I am not an objective reader—each magazine reminded me of the writers and artists who contributed, of the particular circumstances behind the scenes of each edition, of the political topic of the moment, of my love life, my friendships, my health, my dreams. But if I can possibly extract the personal associations that I have with each issue, I can make some general observations about *esto*.

There are noticeable changes from issue to issue. The first major shift begins with the fourth edition (volume 1, number 4, summer 1992) which has an image of Coyolxauhqui, the Aztec moon goddess, on the cover. Miami is suddenly replaced with Aztlán—Chicanas make themselves at home in *esto*. I remember not knowing much about Chicanas until we started publishing their voices. I had read some of the literature, and had even traveled to Mexico, but Chicanos were still mythical beings who existed very far away from Miami, Latin America, and the Caribbean. Suddenly, we were publishing writings about the Rodney King beating and the riots that followed, pesticide poisoning and Chicano farmworkers, Chicana writers, Chicana herstorians, and Chicana artists. Puerto Rico and the Northeast also moved into *esto*, as contributors from Boston,

Brooklyn, Manhattan, and San Juan joined us. And many of the new con-
tributors brought new languages to *esto*—English and Spanish. We gave
Spanglish an official recognition in this issue's editorial. We wrote (in
Spanglish, here translated):

> Our policy is to publish articles in the language that they are submitted.
> We think we should leave it where people are at. Our Latina lesbian
> community includes women in the U.S. as well as in Latin America.
> We cannot say that English or Spanish is the "official" language of our
> community because this would exclude many. And if the question is
> being P.C., neither is more correct than the other; both are colonizing
> languages. In our daily conversations we usually mix both languages.
> Some things can only be expressed in English or in Spanish: How do
> you say "empowerment" in Spanish? How do you say "amar" in English?
> As Latinas from the U.S. and Latin America come together, we will
> naturally move towards speaking Spanglish. ¡Qué viva el Spanglish! (4)

It's from this issue onward, I think, that *esto* really rocks. Soon after,
we had the coolest covers—a photograph of two women in the nude,
one with her back to the camera, the other's pubic hair in full bloom
(volume 2, number 1); a handsome Cuban butch in a white guayabera
(this was Margarita) flirting with a high-heeled femme on a street corner
in South Beach (volume 2, number 2) (see fig. 2); Aztec lesbians bathed
in golden moonlight (volume 2, number 3); a Nuyorican salsera at the
Michigan Womyn's Music Festival (volume 2, number 4); and a cosmic
earth momma emerging from the trunk of a banyan tree (this was me)
(volume 3, number 1).

If you read *esto no tiene nombre*, you'll learn about a few of our icons
(Sor Juana Inés de la Cruz, Frida Kahlo); about some of our published
writers (Nancy Cárdenas, Rosamaria Roffiel, Terri de la Peña, Mariana
Romo-Carmona, Carmen de Monteflores, Cherríe Moraga, and Sara Levi
Calderón); and about our realities and concerns (identity, desire, politics,
international gatherings, building coalitions with women of color, fears,
feminism, language, and being in sisterhood with each other).

I have a few favorite pieces from all these pages. I dig Maria Cristina's
poem, "Pídeme tu hambre . . . en español" (ask me for your hunger . . . in
Spanish), an erotic play on the accents, diphthongs and peculiarities of the
Spanish language. Rosita Libre de Marulanda's "La niña, la puta y la Santa
María" (the girl, the whore, and the Santa Maria) analyzes Cristobal Colón's
journey to the Americas, concluding that the ship named *La Pinta* was really
a puta (whore) in disguise. Teresa Mendoza's poem, "She," honors butch

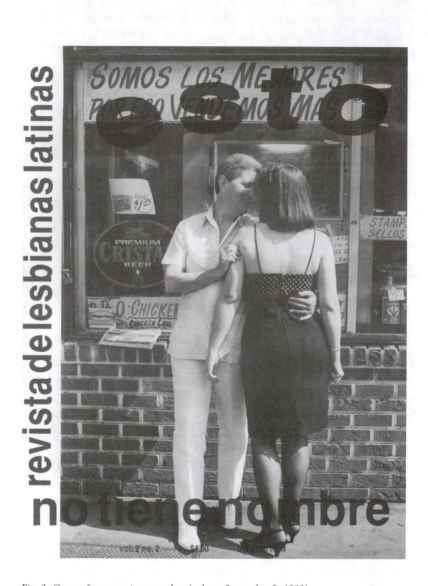

Fig. 2. Cover of esto no tiene nombre (*volume 2, number 2, 1993*).

masculinity in a way that only a femme can. There is an insightful interview of photographer Roberta Almerez, "A Mistaken Minority with a Wonder Bread Identity Tows [sic] the Thin Line Between Art, Pornography, and Living Happily Ever After," made all the more interesting by the fact that she interviewed herself (!) under a pseudonym. (We didn't know this at the time.) Rebecca García created some awesome cartoons of "la mujer ideal" (the ideal woman). I love Amy Santos's poem "Biology," and Margarita's poem "Fuiste mía en ese instante" (you belonged to me in that instant), and every single thing Vanessa ever wrote. I also like my mom's contribution, "El regalo" (the gift), about her acceptance and appreciation of being the mother of a lesbian. ("El regalo" was subsequently reprinted in other books and magazines, most recently in *Conversaciones*. See Restrepo 2001.)

Then there was a great compilation of news and gossip about groups, publications, individuals, and international political and cultural happenings that we published in each edition. Compiled by me and/or Patricia and/or Lori Cardona, this section was filled with many tiny bits of information about Latina lesbians and gays in the United States and in Latin America and Mexico. Valuable for reflecting the political climate and issues of the time, this section had a variety of incarnations and, thus, various names: "Estamos en todas partes" (we are everywhere); "Eventos, anuncios, noticias y publicaciones" (events, news, announcements, and publications); and "lesbianas y gays latinos pa'qui y pa'lla" (latina lesbians and gays over here and over there).

But my favorite thing about *esto no tiene nombre* is "Cuéntame, una charla anónima" (tell me, an anonymous interview). I love to do interviews; many of my earlier writings were features based on interviews. I like to dig in, to ask very personal questions about deep fears and desires, to expose humanity. The Cuéntame allowed this because it was anonymous—no one knew who I interviewed. I manipulated text to conceal the identity of the person interviewed. A few of these women were well known in their respective communities, and some were anonymous even to me. A few of the interviews were conducted via telephone and recorded with a tape recorder from Radio Shack, similar to the one Linda Tripp used to record Monica Lewinski (though *I* had permission).

I am amazed, to this day, that so many women trusted me with their intimacies. Each Cuéntame takes me back to each woman—the one who's married with children and always has a female lover on the side but won't call herself a lesbian; the one who allowed herself to come out with the help of booze and became an alcoholic; the one who hates herself for being fat; the burned-out suicidal activist; the 22-year-old virgin who was turned on by feminine women; the one who used a white woman for sex and then dumped her for a Latina as fast as you can burn a tortilla; the one who thinks lesbians dress poorly; the one who drives fast cars and is afraid of women; the one who can barely restrain herself from coming when she climbs on top of a woman. Perhaps these interviews say as much about me as they do about the women I interviewed, since it was my questions that led to their responses.

In any case, I think *esto* was pretty damn cool, and I know that I am not alone in this sentiment. We had a small but faithful audience of lesbians who subscribed and gave subscriptions to their friends. We received letters of appreciation and pleas for lesbian connections from all over, including Latin America, Mexico, Cuba, and Europe. We had national distribution via Inland and Fine Print as of the fifth issue. We had grant moneys that continued to flow in and support our vision. We had contributors on every coast. We were filling a void with *esto*; we were fulfilling our mission.

Hurricane Andrew and the Eye of the Storm

But it wasn't all rosy behind the scenes between those of us at the core of *esto no tiene nombre*. It was difficult work, we all had full-time jobs, and, worst of all, we were lovers. Each of us was volatile and passionate about publishing, and we differed in opinion on process and strategy. Even so, those were some of the greatest times in my life, because in between the disagreements there was a lot of love, respect, and a collective twisted sense of humor. But when Hurricane Andrew ravaged South Florida on 23 August 1992, we became part of the rubble. Vane and Patri were left homeless and moved to Miami Beach. Soon after, they separated, after eleven years of being together. My childhood house in Leisure City, where I still had a bedroom and many possessions, was destroyed, and my homeless family plus dog moved in with me. Margarita and I, already on shaky ground, broke up after she left me for a woman who had gotten her phone number from television, a result of my appearance on Telemundo. The four of us continued to publish *esto* even after our relationships fell all around us, but eventually, the beauty of publishing was not stronger than the hatred we came to have toward each other.

Hurricane Andrew hit right after Vane, Margarita, and I attended the Third Lesbian-Feminist Latin American and Caribbean Encuentro in

Puerto Rico. One moment we were making international lesbian connections, selling subscriptions, and conducting interviews, and then we were
in shock, our lives uprooted, the future uncertain. Although some of the
contents could be found strewn throughout the fields of South Dade,
Vanessa and Patricia's house literally disappeared, even the walls. Las
Salamandras gave a hand to some lesbians affected by the disaster, including Vanessa and Patricia, but bypassed me and my family. Along with much
of South Florida, we all went into a deep depression after Hurricane Andrew.
I lost the house that had been my home for twenty-one years, and I lost my
privacy and the home I had all to myself at the time of the disaster. We
wrote an editorial about the devastation, which was published (in Spanish) in the issue of *esto* that followed the storm:

> The hurricane buried our books and memories, destroyed our refrig-
> erator and sense of security, and drenched our mattresses and our souls.
> Andres left us unrecognizable pieces of our lives, destroyed our love
> and our nerves, stole our electricity, money, fine clothes, and the junk
> we had already forgotten about. He downed our telephone lines and
> our spirit, ripped out trees and roots. After Andrew we were ruined
> and miserable, with the heat of a summer without fans stifling our
> hopes. We looked at the rubble. We identified the photographs and
> porcelain figures that remained intact, the computer that still had its
> memory, the *estos* that remained dry, and the loves that remained in a
> state of transformation. We nourished ourselves with our own tears,
> hysteria, depression, bureaucracy, anger, and pain. Lesbian friends
> helped us. We bought beds, food, and underwear. Miraculously, *esto no
> tiene nombre*, revista de lesbianas latinas, takes shape again, inspires
> us. Life continues without being the same. We live knowing that walls
> crumble, that the illusion of security is history, and that we know noth-
> ing at all. (volume 2, number 1)

It wasn't just the hurricane that killed *esto no tiene nombre*. The end
was gradual, like a cancer diagnosed in its early stages that kills you just the
same. And we tried several times and in different ways to address the issues. In a nutshell, the problem was the combination of the workload required for producing *esto*, and the personalities of those of us at the core. I
was doing too much of the work, and I was a bitch, all business. My focus
was the end result, not the process. No one appreciated my badgering, and
no one worked fast, or hard or long enough as was necessary to keep up
with the production schedule. We tried bringing in people to work with
us, to smooth things out, such as Lori Cardona, but by then our cancer had
run amok. We were uncontrollable. Vanessa and Patricia finally pulled

out, and Margarita and I invited Amy Concepcion, who was Margarita's ex-lover, to join us. Amy was a wonderful co-editor, but then Margarita and I could not work together any longer.

Margarita wanted *esto* to end—she thought I was steering *esto* from our original mission because I was trying to make it too much like other national magazines. She didn't like my editing style. (True, Vanessa *was* a better editor.) She accused me of being too creative. Amy and I wanted to continue with *esto*; Margarita demanded that we cease publishing. She won.

conmoción, revista y red revolucionaria de lesbianas latinas

> **conmoción:** "commotion" (conmoción) and "with motion" (con moción), a powerful combination that alludes to social disturbances, earthly tremors, and all kinds of tumult. conmoción is a fury, a fervor, an endless fuck, a tempest you don't wanna tango with unless you're conmocionada, too!
>
> —de la tierra, "Las Sinvergüenzas"

That wasn't the end, though. Maybe I should have stopped, but I couldn't. By then, I was too obsessed, too invested. I had made too many connections, had gathered too much material, had raised too much money. Just as *esto* was in the process of reincarnating, we received the largest grant ever— $8,300 on 3 May 1994 from The Funding Exchange's Out, A Fund for Lesbian and Gay Liberation. We were also awarded another $2,500 from Astraea on 14 April 1994, and later, $2,000 from the Chicago Resource Center on 30 June 1995 and $1,000 from Mama Cash, from Amsterdam. If ever there was a time to think big, that was it. And think big I did.

The fine print in the editorial box reads in Spanglish, "*conmoción* is an international Latina lesbian vision that uses the published word to empower and terrorize, to destroy and create. we publish, support and develop any type of activity that leads to the betterment and greater visibility of Latina lesbians." And it lived up to its name. I was "la editora que echa humo" (the editor who emits smoke) and Amy Concepción, Cuban writer and good friend, was the associate editor. We formed a national editorial advisory board composed of Latina lesbian leaders and academics who helped us make connections within their community and solicit material, and who would be there should we run into glitches. We wrote grants and obtained the blessings, via letters of recommendation, from writers and academics who believed in our mission, including Cherríe Moraga, Luzmaría Umpierre, Lourdes Torres, Osa Hidalgo, Mariana Romo-Carmona, Marcia Ochoa, Terri de la Peña, Carmen Corrales, and Juana María Rodríguez. We circulated calls for submissions, signed contracts with eight distributors, doubled the print run, and took off. And we got Patri to do the graphics (this time, she got paid) and Margarita to contribute poetry and proofread in Spanish. Our base of support was possible because of *esto*. *Conmoción* was a continuation and expansion of *esto's* vision, pure and simple.

Besides being larger than *esto* and involving more people in the process, *conmoción* was constructed to have direct interaction with Latina lesbian groups and also with writers. La "cadena *conmoción*" focused on news about our groups and gatherings in América Latina and the United States. *La telaraña*, the Latina lesbian writers' web, was created as part of *conmoción*. Lesley Salas, from San Antonio, initially co-directed *La telaraña* with me. I edited a separate newsletter, *el telarañazo*, that supported emerging Latina lesbian writers. *El telarañazo* had information about where telarañeras were performing and publishing and gathering.

> **Telarañeras:** word weavers. Christened after fine and intricate spider webs as well as for "red," or "network." Those of us with a matrix of letters that squirm and squeal until they give birth to an urgent word. Those of us who envision text like sculpture, palabras like eagles, grammar like notas musicales, sentences like trains, paragraphs in the palm of our hands. Telarañeras, we prefer our words twisted and tongued and too too tough.
>
> —de la tierra, "Las Sinvergüenzas"

The first issue of *conmoción*, forty pages published in 1995, was devoted to activism. Carmelita Tropicana sings with a clenched fist on the cover (see fig. 3); Rosita Libre de Marulanda reveals childhood experiences that led her to founding La Liberación de la Teta (Titty Liberation) in New York City; Cherríe Moraga talks cultural activism; Achy Obejas is her writing-is-an-act-of-revenge self; Luzmaría Umpierre tells her story about homophobia in academia; Carmen Vazquez speaks of liberation; and I rant with my "a Latina lesbian activist's survival guide: o, mejor dicho, activism de-mystified, de-glorified & de-graded" (which was later published in *Latino Heretics*, de la tierra 1999b). There are also poetry, tributes to activists who've passed on, a lesbian journals, news about encuentros, reviews, essays, Cuéntame, a Spanish translation

Fig. 3. Cover of conmoción (*number 1, 1995*).

of "100 Simple Things You Can Do to End the Patriarchy" (which I had translated at the author's request, Nett Hart), and the beginnings of the *telaraña*. And then there's "La esquina de Erotiza Memaz," a perverted Dear Abby creation by Las Buenas Amigas from New York City that glorified lesbian sexuality.

The second issue of *conmoción* was forty-eight pages of erótica with Isabel Rosado's cuntal artwork on the front cover and Marcia Ochoa's bare-ass wonder photograph on the back. Inside you'll find Erika Lopez's strap-on cartoon, pics of breasts, vulvas, rear ends. There are writings and poetry on stripping for a living, dildos and feminism, sadomasochism, cybersex, and Doralisa Goitía's "The Colors of Transmission," which begins with a screaming statement, "PROMISCUITY IS A MOTHER-FUCKER AND THE RESULT IS HIV." There's vaginal poetry, cunt stories, love letters, Loana DP Valencia's lunar cuento, "Bajando la luna" (drawing down the moon, which subsequently won Best American Erotica of 1997), and omu's kinky "alfabeto incompleto" (incomplete alphabet). It was an openly sexual edition of *conmoción*, one that celebrated pleasure for the sake of pleasure.

The third issue of *conmoción*, which focused on identity, was published in 1996 (see fig. 4). It would be the last, as production and distribution costs had skyrocketed; several of our large distributors had filed for bankruptcy and, thus, never paid for issues of *esto* or *conmoción* sold in bookstores. And I was in poor health, fighting for my life. A group of lesbians from San Francisco were guest editors for the final issue. They selected and edited most of the material but they didn't make a magazine out of it. After my health crisis was over, I published the last issue, fifty-two pages of writings and art that directly spoke of who we are.

Virginia Benavides's photograph of a witchy woman dancing in dark waters extends across the front and back cover of the identity edition. Intriguing artwork reigns, including Dina Bursztyn's ceramic Totem Poles to Scare Lesbophobia, Laura Aguilar's powerful self-portraits, and a funky androgynous collage by Elisa Galdo. There are thought-provoking essays,such as Juana María Rodriguez's "Pensando en identidad" (thinking on identity), Theresa Becerril's autobiographical "Guns, Tetas & Me," Carmen Corrales's stunning "Amando a Cuba" (loving Cuba), and Patricia Meoño Picado's analysis of Latin soap operas. Also included in this issue is a conversation between three boricuas, Susana Cook's trans-lesbian poem "I Dress Therefore I Am," Maria de los Rios's story "The Language of Pain," and the "100% Latina Lesbian Checklist," which

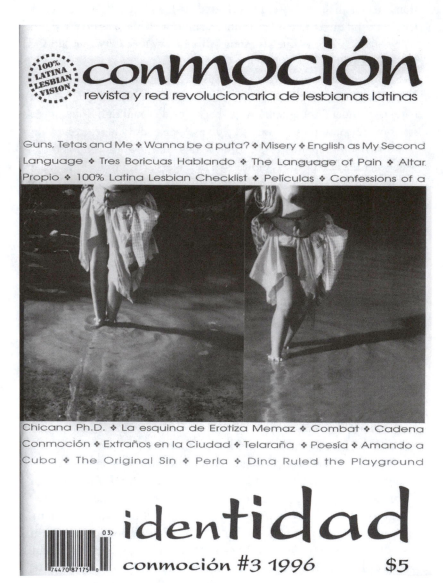

Fig. 4. Cover of conmoción (number 3, 1996).

poked fun at the red "100% Latina lesbian vision" logo on all the *conmoción* covers and made it impossible to be 100 percent anything.

Conmoción was just a magazine. What made it so special is that it was us on each page. It took 84 contributors from 38 cities to fill 140 pages. And gauging by subscriptions, sales in bookstores, and letters to the editor, lesbianas Latinas were grateful. Given that *conmoción* was distributed predominantly in the United States and Canada, we were surprised to receive correspondence from lesbians in Cuba, Guatemala, Chile, Mexico, Argentina, and Colombia. From the content of the letters it was clear that there was a need to connect with sisters across continents. And for Latinas living in the north, the impact was intense. As Brianna wrote in a letter to the editor published in the third edition, "The specific subject matter combined with such diverse writings evokes a feeling of sisterhood that gives me encouragement and hope in finding a community that I have been needing for a long time. You have shown me that my sisters are out there and that I am not alone in my experiences and feelings." In another letter published in the second edition, Ana Montero wrote that *conmoción* "shows that Latina lesbianas are coming out of the infamous closet to kick some ass with our own politics without waiting for the gringa dykes to give us space to speak our mind." *Conmoción* was a place where we could do the twist with our tongues and end up smiling regardless of the words exchanged.

It was impossible to continue publishing without money, though. In addition to the distributors that never paid for selling the magazines, grant proposals were rejected by foundations such as the Council of Literary Magazines, Ben and Jerry's, Digital Queers, The Sister Fund, National Association of Latina Lesbian and Gay Organizations, Womankind, and the Kimeta Society. We were also awarded funds by the Open Meadows Foundation, funds that we never received even after much badgering on my part. I tried to obtain funds for la telaraña in 1997, which had never received its own funding. But both Astraea and Chicago Resource Center rejected the proposals.

Besides running out of money for publication, I ran out of steam. I had been diagnosed with systemic lupus erythematosus in 1990. Mostly, I lived as I pleased. But I did have a life-threatening flare-up in 1995 that forced me to reconsider what I was doing with my life. Living on the edge had taken its toll. I loved publishing but it was a thankless job that I didn't get paid for. I was not surviving physically, economically, or even creatively. After much soul-searching, I decided to start anew—to break up with

Gloria, my Colombian lover, get away from Margarita, get away from my family, and end *conmoción*. I did all of the above and by 1999, I had my MFA in creative writing from the University of Texas at El Paso. Soon after, I was on my way to becoming a librarian at University at Buffalo (of the State University of New York).

And the Number Is? Shoddy Record Keeping

It's difficult to summarize the fruits *of esto no tiene nombre* and *conmoción* because, even after combing through the archives for weeks, the records are shoddy and incomplete.[4] Margarita kept track of the funds until 21 January 1994. The last subscriber she entered in the shorthand pad was #166. I know that there were more *esto* and *conmoción* subscribers. But with Lambda Community Center of Greater Miami, Inc. as our fiscal sponsor, our accounting was tricky. I gave Brian the receipts, and he gave us the money. I was not a consistent record keeper. The paper trail was all over the place—on pieces of paper jammed into folders, with *esto* records, with *conmoción* records, with Lambda Community Center records, in the computerized address list, (which "disappeared" several times due to electronic glitches), and who knows where else. I don't even know exactly how many subscribers we had. The mailing list had more than 2,000 names on it (not all paid subscribers). I recall mailing around 300 copies of *esto* (not all subscribers; there were many exchange subscriptions). From letters in the archives written by subscribers who didn't receive their issues, it's clear that our distribution was flawed.

Distribution was a nightmare, no matter how it was handled. I thought that if only we had Real Distribution, we would be sailing. We had been selling *esto* on consignment at a few bookstores and through a few individuals across the country. But in almost every single case, we were never paid, or we had to chase the bookstores down for a few bucks, and it wasn't even worth the phone calls. Inland Books became *esto's* first distributor in 1992, and Fine Print soon followed. *Conmoción* was distributed by a slew of companies, too many of them—Small Changes, Desert Moon, Fine Print, Golden Lee, Armadillo, Book People, RPM, and Doormouse (from Toronto). Most of them paid up; the largest ones didn't. I didn't even have the energy, in the end, to continue chasing after them all. Still, the distribution did result in *esto* and *conmoción* having national visibility. The magazines were in bookstores all over the country, and they sold well for "fringe" publications.

There was something worse than not getting paid, though. Our print run of *esto* was very small to begin with (200–500), so the issues were precious and I was guarded about sending them out. We had an agreement with Fine Print that unsold issues would be returned. At that point, Fine Print was the main distributor of *esto,* and they had what amounted to *esto*'s archives. They destroyed our archives. Today, there are very few original copies of *esto no tiene nombre* left; I do not even have an original set right now, although there are a few in storage in Miami that we plan to send to selected libraries and archives. Unfortunately, there are very few traces of *esto.* According to the WorldCat database, *esto* is only listed in the library catalogues of University of Arizona, University of Buffalo, and University of California at Berkeley.

Conmoción, though, is another story. By the time *conmoción* was published, the media and distribution machinery was already in place. And even though only three issues were published, *conmoción* had a print run of 1,000; most of the magazines were sent out to distributors. *Conmoción* just got around much more; there was more to go around. And *conmoción* had a bipad number—one of those computerized strings of numbers that you find in a bar code on products, issued on 29 December 1994 by the Council for Periodical Distributors Associations, bipad number 87175. Though it was not required, many distributors preferred titles with bar codes. It was part of playing the game Big. As a result, WorldCat lists nine lender libraries for *conmoción:* Cornell, New York Public Library, University of California at Riverside, California State University at San Bernadino, University of California at Santa Barbara, University of California at Berkeley, University of California at Santa Cruz, University of Buffalo, Michigan State University, University of Michigan Library, and University of Texas at Austin.

Traces of This, Which Has No Name

If one were to judge solely by the evidence from database and Internet searches, *esto* and *conmoción* barely ever existed. On Google, "'esto no tiene nombre' +latina +lesbians" results in ten hits and "conmocion +latina +lesbians" yields twenty hits. The listings lead to bibliographies, resource listings, syllabi, contributors, articles, and reviews. The scant results place *esto* and *conmoción* in the almost forgotten past, in the poetic days of snail mail. The online revolution happened without us. I didn't have e-mail until 1995 and I learned how to use the Internet, design web pages, and do research on academic databases just the other day in library school.[5]

173

I think Margarita was right—I was trying to do too much, thinking too big. I understand now the value of keeping a vision only as large as can be managed by those involved. *Conmoción* was too ambitious. It was practically a full-time job. It needed paid staff, a real office, high-tech equipment. The grant funds allowed *conmoción* to grow as it needed to, but they didn't go far enough.

Esto no tiene nombre and *conmoción* were tiny, unique publications, Latina lesbian megaphones. I feel fortunate to have been an integral part of their making. The early days of *esto no tiene nombre* were the happiest time in my life. I had a vision, I had hope, and I was not alone. There was a lot of love going around then—sexual love, spiritual love, friendship love, literature love, publishing love. Perfect love. I spoke with Patricia while writing this, to get her point of view, to help me fill in some blanks. While talking to her on the phone I thought of how much I still love her, how I wish we could still be doing it. *You can never go back.* My childhood home, intact in my mind's eye, was destroyed in the hurricane. *Esto* and *conmoción,* vivid and vibrant in my memory, are forever gone.

Of that era, Patri said, "It's a shame that moment didn't come at a time when we were more prepared, when we had more time to dedicate to it." And then she said, well, "everything is as it should be." Maybe. Today, Patricia is a science reference librarian at Florida International University and I am a reference and instruction librarian at University at Buffalo. I haven't spoken with Vanessa in years but I hear she is fine, working as a nutritionist in Miami. Margarita and I continue to love each other from a distance. Amy and I talk every once in a while. Gloria, the lover I broke up with, is a friend and a part of my family. Las Salamandras split up in 1994, before *conmoción* even began. I got an e-mail from one of them just the other day. I realize now, five years after cutting off family, friends, and magazines, that you can never truly free yourself from what you most love. Whenever I go to an event with Latina lesbian presence, *esto no tiene nombre* and *conmoción* are always riding on my shoulder.

Lovers and friends come and go, but magazines last forever.

27 de abril de 2000, Buffalo, Nueva York
revised 1 de noviembre de 2001, Buffalo, Nueva York

Notes

1. All translations from Spanish into English in this essay are my own.

2. Mari hit the clit right on. Turns out that I was a budding pornographer, but I didn't know that at the time. Much of my published writings to date are of the erotic variety. See de la tierra 2000.

3. Many of these phone interviews became quests for Latina lesbian herstory. Eventually, I researched Latina lesbian organizations in great detail and wrote about them. See de la tierra 1996.

4. After this writing, I found three more boxes of *esto* and *conmoción* materials in storage in Miami. The boxes contain an assortment of flyers, correspondence, fiscal papers, and copies of the magazines. Patri and I plan to send copies of *esto* and *conmoción* to selected libraries and archives with the intent of increasing public access to the magazines.

5. I became a librarian because I needed a survival mechanism and it seemed that I was already very "librarianish." I also wanted to find ways to use the tools and position of a librarian to continue with my brand of activism. I now work behind the scenes. Besides doing reference and bibliographic instruction, I examine subject headings for queer Latin texts, write book reviews, compile a comprehensive bibliography of Latin lesbian and gay materials, and scout out queer Latin titles in book fairs. I am also beginning to write and publish within the profession and hope to bring greater visibility to Latina lesbians and gays in this field. See de la tierra 2001.

Works Cited

Bathroom Sluts. 1991. Dykestyles series. Fatale Videos. Video–cassette.

Conmoción: revista y red revolucionaria de lesbianas latinas. 1995–1996. Miami Beach, FL: Lambda Community Center of Greater Miami.

de la tierra, tatiana. 2001. "Latina Lesbian Literary Herstory: From Sor Juana to *Days of Awe*." In *The Power of Language/El poder de la palabra: Selected Papers from the Second REFORMA National Conference*, ed. Lillian Castillo-Speed, 199-212. Englewood, CO: Libraries Unlimited.

———. 2000. "Dancing with Daisy" and "Celestial Bodies." In *Gynomite: Fearless Feminist Porn*, ed. Liz Belile, 30-42. New Orleans, LA: New Mouth from the Dirty South.

———. 1999a. "Jail Time for Beginners." *Tropic Miami Herald Sunday Magazine*, 8 March: 18–21. Reprinted in *Latino Heretics*, ed. Tony Diaz, 67-74. Normal, IL: Fiction Collective Two.

———. 1999b. "a latina lesbian activist's survival guide—o mejor dicho, activism de-mystified, de-glorified and de-graded." In *Latino Heretics*, ed. Tony Diaz, 64-66. Normal, IL: Fiction Collective Two.

———. 1999c. "Las Sinvergüenzas." Unpublished essay.

———. 1996. "Latina Lesbians in Motion." In *The New Our Right to Love: A Lesbian Resource Book*, ed. Ginny Vida, 225-229. New York: Touchstone.

———. 1994. Interview. "El Noticiero de las Siete." *Caracol Televisión*. Colombia.

———. 1988. "Latin American Lesbian-Feminists Together in Mexico." *Visibilities* (September/October): 8-11.

de la tierra, tatiana, and Margarita Castilla. 1993. Interview. "La ola lesbiana." *El Show de Marcia Morgado*. WCMQ AM Radio. Miami, Florida.

de la tierra, tatiana, and Fabiola Restrepo. 1992. Interview. "Cuando su hijo es gay." *Contacto*, Telemundo Televisión. Miami, Florida.

Dress Up for Daddy. 1991. Dykestyle series. Fatale Videos. Videocassette.

Esto no tiene nombre, revista de lesbianas latinas. 1991–1994. Miami Beach: Lambda Community Center of Greater Miami.

Moraga, Cherríe. 1983. *Loving in the War Years: Lo que nunca pasó por sus labios*. Boston: South End Press.

Moraga, Cherríe, and Gloria Anzaldúa, eds. 1981. *This Bridge Called My Back: Writings by Radical Women of Color*. New York: Kitchen Table.

Ramos, Juanita, ed. 1994. *Compañeras: Latina Lesbians, an Anthology*. New York: Latina Lesbian History Project, 1987. Reprinted, New York: Routledge.

Restrepo, Fabiola. 2001. "El regalo." In *Conversaciones: Relatos por padres y madres de hijas lesbianas e hijos gay*, ed. Mariana Romo-Carmona, 21-14. San Francisco: Cleis.

Shanahan, Gloria L. 1994. "tatiana no quiere que la amen a escondidas." *El Tiempo* 18 May: 1C+.

"Tatiana, la lesbiana." 1994. *Revista Semana* 11 October: 116. Unauthored article.

Trujillo, Carla, ed. 1991. *Chicana Lesbians: The Girls Our Mothers Warned Us About*. Berkeley: Third Woman.

Valencia, Loana DP. 1997. "Bajando la luna." In *Best American Erotica*, ed. Susie Bright. New York: Simon and Schuster.

Silencing Our Lady:
La Respuesta de Alma

Alma Lopez

In the beginning of a new millennium, *Our Lady* appeared in Santa Fe during Holy Week. Her appearance caused passionate discussions throughout the Americas. Hundreds met in a geographic space called Holy Faith to discuss and debate her contemporary apparition to a Chicana artist named Alma, a resident in the City of Angels. Thousands have also met, discussed, and debated *Our Lady*'s apparition in a space called Cyber in a world called the Wide Web.[1]

Before an Inquisition organized by the man, the priest, and the archbishop, Alma's Respuesta[2] is as follows:

I was born in Mexico and grew up in California. My family would visit our aunts, uncles, and cousins in Mexico at least once every two years. My parents felt it was important to nurture the relationship with our Mexican family, history, and culture. For these trips, my parents would save money for many months. On the morning of the trip we would pile up in the red Thunderbird and begin our long drive south at dawn.

In Mexico and in Los Angeles, the Virgen de Guadalupe was always in a special place in our homes. Sometimes she was a migrant Virgen. We always lived in overcrowded apartments and houses with two bedrooms at the most; one for my parents and the other one for all six kids. Often, when the house was too crowded and my mother needed to pray, she would take the Virgen and a candle into the restroom or sometimes a closet.

On 21 April, I participated in the Cesar Chavez Walkathon in East Los Angeles. We walked up Third Street past King Taco, around the Serbian Cemetery, and down Avenida Cesar Chavez to East Los Angeles City College. After the march, we drove west on Avenida Cesar Chavez past Soto Street to La Parrilla Restaurant for lunch. That day, I was in memory lane walking and driving past murals portraying the Virgen de Guadalupe and heroes such as Zapata, Aztec warriors, and now Cesar Chavez. I looked at some of these recently painted murals and saw that as Latinas we are still invisible. All of these murals neglected to portray female heroines such as UFW cofounder Dolores Huerta, poet Sor Juana Inez de la Cruz, Subcomandante Ramona, and Nobel Peace Prize winner Rigoberta Menchù.

The murals I grew up with rarely portrayed any strong Chicanas, except for the Judith Hernandez *La Adelita* in Ramona Gardens[3]. I remembered my childhood and thought of my eleven nieces, most of them quickly approaching their teens. I remembered that as an artist one of the reasons I focus on female images is to add to the visual history a more complex identity from our lived realities as Latinas.

I remembered that one of the first digital murals I produced, as a California Arts Council Artist in Residence in collaboration with Judith Baca's UCLA Cesar Chavez Center's digital mural course, was titled *Las Four* and installed in the new Estrada Courts Community Center in 1997. Soon after it was installed, the portable digital mural on vinyl portraying four young female residents of Estrada Courts Housing Project was slashed by young men.

At the time, I was most shocked by the violent attitude of the young men toward the young women. Referring to the young women as "hoodrats," they felt entitled to destroy the one image that featured their sisters. The excuse for the vandalism was that some of the young women portrayed had dated some of the young men in the neighborhood, and because the neighborhood was so small their dating possibilities were limited, so now one of the young women was dating someone outside of the neighborhood. The young women felt that the young men treated them as if they were neighborhood property. I also remembered how, at the request of one of the young women originally photographed on the front steps of their home, I replaced her, using Photoshop cut and paste techniques. She did not want to be part of the mural because she had a black eye her boyfriend had given her.

Currently, I feel like I am on trial. I am being forced to defend one of my digital prints in the *Cyber Arte: Tradition Meets Technology* exhibition at the Museum of International Folk Art in Santa Fe, New Mexico. The exhibition features four Chicana/Latina/Hispana artists who combine traditional cultural iconography with state-of-the-art technology. The artists

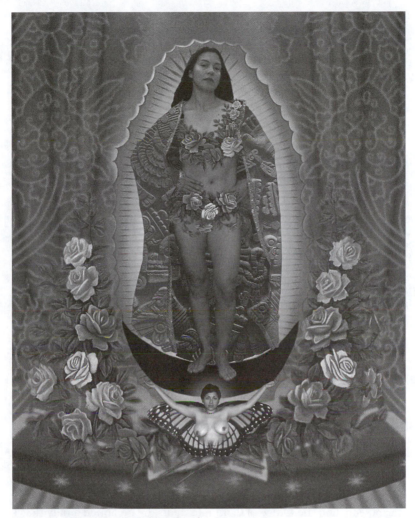

Fig. 1. Our Lady *(2000). Digital print by Alma Lopez.*

include Elena Baca (photographer), Marion Martinez (sculptor), Teresa Archuleta Sagel (weaver), and me, Alma Lopez. This exhibition was curated by Tey Marianna Nunn, a Latina scholar and art historian. Elena, Marion, Teresa, and Tey Marianna are Nuevo Mexicanas. The "offending" work titled *Our Lady* is a small photo-based digital print on exhibition in a museum (see fig. 1). It is not an object of devotion in a church.

Nowhere has there been such a strong response to my work as in Santa Fe. *Our Lady* has been exhibited in California, received a book cover award

179

for a book published by the University of Arizona Press, and was shown on ABC/Channel 7 Vista L.A. The *Lupe and Sirena* image was exhibited throughout California, in Chihuahua, Mexico, and on the cover of the journal *Aztlán*.

From this experience I have learned that as an artist I may have an intended meaning in the work I produce, but that once on exhibit, how it is interpreted depends on the experiences of the viewer. My intention as an artist was not disrespectful in any way. However, some people in Santa Fe feel offended. Who are those offended? Why do they feel more entitled to this cultural icon than the Chicana/Latina/Hispana women in the exhibition? Why are they unable to make a distinction between an image in a museum and an image in their church? Why is the church in New Mexico targeting this image when they have so many of their own issues?

The protest against my digital print *Our Lady* is organized and led by community activist Jose Villegas and Deacon Anthony Trujillo. New Mexico Archbishop Michael J. Sheehan has joined them, calling the artwork "sacrilegious" and "a tart." Mr. Villegas, Deacon Trujillo, and the archbishop see the *Our Lady* digital print with exposed legs, belly, and a female angel's breasts as "offensive." Yet I know that many churches, in Mexico and Europe and the United States house images of nude male angels and most prominently, a crucifixion practically naked except for a loincloth. On the internet, the most vicious attacks have come from Santa Fe artist Pedro Romero Sedeño and Berkeley-based Tonatiuh-Quinto Sol publisher Octavio Romano. Their faith and masculinity are threatened by my portrayal of the Virgen as a contemporary Latina.

On 17 March, I received an e-mail from Jose Villegas in which he described his upset feelings. He said that I have no right to express myself in regard to this particular cultural icon, and he threatened anyone who doesn't agree with his worldview. One week later, during a meeting with the museum and the Office of Cultural Affairs, he organized a rally that I saw on television.

On 4 April, at 10 A.M. at the museum complex, a meeting of 600 to 800 people was rescheduled to a larger venue to allow anyone who was interested to participate. At this meeting, almost half inside were supporters, and I know that some outside were also supporters. Supporters seem to be primarily Latinas, artists, writers, professors, and women. The protestors seem to be primarily men, priests, and older women who were transported via buses from the local churches. Villegas, about three men, and a priest dominated the conversation. As curator Tey Marianna Nunn was about to speak, she was interrupted and the meeting was rescheduled.

On Monday, 16 April, at 10 A.M. at Sweeney Center anywhere from 600 to 1,200 (reports vary, and some have told me that a smaller crowd gathered at this second meeting than were assembled at the first) met to discuss *Our Lady*. Unfortunately I was unable to attend this second meeting because of commitments to work, the cost of travel, anxiety about my physical safety, and because, at this point, I felt that if I was present I would be a target of discussion instead of participating in an open dialogue of concerns. When Elena and Marion, two artists featured in the exhibit, spoke in support of the exhibition, they were intimidated and harassed. Although this situation is very difficult and painful, I think that at some level there must be something positive about the dialogue it has prompted. This controversy must be about more than a small digital print. Among other issues, perhaps it's about local politics? Gentrification? Lack of opportunities for local artists? Fear of Latina women's liberation? Fear of change?

When I see *Our Lady* as well as the works portraying the Virgen by many Chicana artists, I see an alternative voice expressing the multiplicities of our lived realities. I see myself living a tradition of Chicanas who because of cultural and gender oppression have asserted our voice. I see Chicanas creating a deep and meaningful connection to this revolutionary cultural female image that appeared to an indigenous person at a time of genocide, and as an inspiration during liberation struggles such as the Mexican Revolution and the Chicano civil rights movement. I see Chicanas who understand faith.

Catholic or not, as Chicanas/Latinas/Hispanas, we all grew up with the ever-present image of the Virgen de Guadalupe. As an artist, I feel entitled to express my relationship to her in a way relevant to my own experiences. In doing so, I join many other visual, literary, and performance artists, such as Yolanda Lopez, Ester Hernandez, Santa Barraza, Delilah Montoya, Yreina Cervantez, Sandra Cisneros, and Raquel Salinas, all of whom have shared their own personal experiences in their works of the Virgen de Guadalupe.

More than twenty years ago, artists Yolanda Lopez and Ester Hernandez were threatened and attacked for portraying the Virgen in a feminist and liberating perspective. In 1978 Yolanda Lopez received bomb threats for her portrayal of the Virgen wearing low-heeled shoes. In this image the Virgen walks with her head bowed, hands clasped, wearing a dress below the knee. I think that people were upset because the Virgen was able to walk away, especially if she didn't care to listen to someone's prayers.

Our Lady features two of my friends: performance artist Raquel Salinas as a contemporary Virgen dressed in roses and cultural activist Raquel

Gutierrez as a nude butterfly angel. The two Raqueles and I grew up in Los Angeles with the image of the Virgen in our homes and community. The Virgen is everywhere. She's on tattoos, stickers, posters, air freshener cans, shirts, and corner store murals, as well as church walls. Many, including myself, feel that because she is everywhere there is nothing anyone can do to change how the original image of the Virgen de Guadalupe is generally perceived.

Our Lady was inspired by our own experiences; by Raquel Salinas's one-person performance titled *Heat Your Own*; Raquel Gutierrez's experiences in Catholic school; and by a Sandra Cisneros essay, Guadalupe the Sex Goddess. Sandra Cisneros writes: "She is a face for a god without a face, an indigena for a god without ethnicity, a female deity for a god who is genderless, but I also understand that for her to approach me, for me to finally open the door and accept her, she had to be a woman like me."

When Cisneros wonders if the Virgen has a dark Latina vagina and nipples underneath her dress, I imagined roses. Roses were the proof of her apparition to Juan Diego. Abstracted plants and flowers are imprinted on her dress. Amid the other symbolism in her depiction and apparition, flowers and roses connect her to us as natives. Xochitl is flower. Xochitlalpan is the flower earth place that can be translated as paradise or heaven. When I imagined the image of *Our Lady*, I saw a contemporary representation of a Latina woman covered with flowers.

Even if I look really hard at *Our Lady* and the works of many Chicana artists, I don't see what is so offensive. I see beautiful bodies: gifts from our creator. Maybe because my mother breastfed me as a baby, I see breasts as nurturing. Maybe because I love women, I see beauty and strength. I also see the true representation of Mary. Mary was an awesome woman and mother with a difficult task. She had a child who was not her husband's, she kept her son safe from a murderous king, she suffered her son's struggles and death, and most of all she raised her son to have love and compassion for everyone, including female prostitutes. I think Mary was a lot like some of our mothers.

I am forced to wonder how men like Mr. Villegas, Deacon Trujillo, and Archbishop Sheehan are looking at my work that the horrible words they use to describe it are "blasphemy, sacrilegious, the devil, a tart, a stripper." I am forced to wonder: how do they perceive women and our bodies? I wonder: why do they think that our bodies are inherently ugly and perverted that they cannot be portrayed in an art piece in a museum especially when nude or practically nude male bodies live in churches? I wonder:

where is their love and compassion for all men and women? I wonder: why are they attacking me for portraying my idea of a strong woman while protecting the sexual violence toward children and young women perpetrated by their own priests in their own churches in New Mexico? I wonder: will those priests ever be on public trial like I am today?[4]

This inquisition has been torturous. A few men self-righteously believe that they have the authority to dictate how a particular image should be interpreted. They believe they can tell me how to think. I am a woman who has grown up with the Virgen. Who are these men to tell me how to relate to her? Who are they to demand the censorship of an exhibition of four Latina artists curated by a Latina scholar? Who are they to believe that they hold the only and righteous worldview on this cultural icon? I wish they would realize that their perspective does not apply to everyone, not even all New Mexican Catholics. Not everyone is offended, and many more feel that the image should not be censored. E-mails, calls, and letters of support have included Catholics, Latinas/os, artists, educators, the governor and first lady of New Mexico, museum funders such as Neutrogena Corporation, free speech groups such as the New York based National Coalition Against Censorship, the ACLU, and various communities nationwide including Santa Fe. We all need to come to the conclusion that we can express our opinion, but no one has the right to silence anyone. I have the right to exhibit my work, and viewers have a right to voice their approval or disapproval.

I think that the museum and I are in a difficult situation and that the only fair solution to this issue would be to leave the work on exhibit. If the museum removes my work or makes it unavailable for the general audience in any way, they will be participating in censorship, acting against our first amendment rights, and losing credibility as a learning institution committed to present art that challenges and educates audiences. If I remove my work, I will be a Latina pushed to silence and invisibility. If my work is removed by the museum or by me, the message will be that I have no right to express myself as an artist and a woman. That, although all four artists and the curator are professionals in our fields, our work has no real merit and is unqualified unless it meets the approval of all. That the only voice that has value above everyone's including the museum, the artists in the exhibition, the curator, and people who expressed their support, is the voice of those who feel offended by my work.

I never thought that of necessity I would be siding with a museum since most of the time I feel extremely marginalized. In Los Angeles museums, Latino exhibitions are historical art phenomena. In the nearby city of Long Beach, the Museum of Latin American Art seems only to exhibit the art of non-U.S.-born Latinos. In the case of the Museum of International Folk Art, I feel that the museum has made an admirable effort to listen to everyone's concerns by organizing public community meetings with budgets exceeding the *Cyber Arte* exhibition budget. However, I am beginning to feel that while attempts are being made to listen and mediate this conflict, the voices of the artists on exhibit and their supporters may be overlooked or even ignored; essentially, that the voices of the men organizing for the removal of the work will carry more weight than the voices of the women in the exhibition.

Many opinions and recommendations compete to be heard concerning this issue, I would ask that in considering such recommendations that they also consider the following questions. How rare are museum exhibitions by a Latina curator featuring Latina artists? What will be the effects of this controversy on future exhibitions of Latina/o artists? Will artists be censored to avoid any future possible controversies? Will work be removed for any reason if someone doesn't like it? What happens to the rights of artists and curators to create and exhibit without censorship? Will audiences be accorded intellectual respect to visit museums and make their own conclusions?

Author's Note

Since completing this essay, the New Mexico Museum Committee on Sensitive Materials recommended that *Our Lady* digital print remain on exhibit. The committee came to this conclusion after reviewing the museum's policies, curatorial process, and community response. The Museum of International Folk Art also decided not to extend the exhibition to February 2002, so it closed as originally scheduled on 28 October 2001.

However, Jose L. Villegas and Deacon Anthony Trujillo filed appeals and lawsuits against the museum. Tom Wilson, director of the New Mexico Museums, denied their appeals. "Nowhere in your appeal do you recognize the rights of all points of views to be heard, the hallmark of a free and democratic society," wrote Wilson to Villegas and Trujillo.[5] "Nor do their requests address the importance of the museum as a place to present changing ideas and concepts, a mission shared with other museums accredited by the American Association of Museums and one that is central to the educational responsibility of museums in today's world," said Wilson. Mr. Villegas and Deacon Trujillo have filed their appeal to the Board of the New Mexico Museums, who will be having their regularly scheduled meeting in late September. Until the work is removed, Mr. Villegas and Deacon Trujillo are on a "holy fast" of breads and juices which they alternate weekly.

In May, New Mexican artists Pola Lopez and Delilah Montoya curated an exhibition of Nuevo Mexicana artists titled *Las Malcriadas* in Santa Fe in support of my work remaining on exhibit at the museum. They received very favorable press calling them "brave women." On Saturday 30 June approximately 300 protestors rallied, organized by America Needs Fatima, a Catholic organization based in Pennsylvania with origins in Brazil. That same day, Las Malcriadas hosted a closing party where local artists spoke about their art, poets read their work, and local playwright Sylvia Vergara read passages of a recent play she wrote on the entire *Our Lady* controversy. Due to numerous requests to host *Cyber Arte: Tradition meets Technology Exhibition*, the museum and artists are considering packaging the entire exhibit for travel nationwide.

Notes:

1. Please refer to www.almalopez.net for e-mails, news articles, and links specifically on *Our Lady*.

2. La Respuesta, literally translated in English as "The Answer", was the title of Sor Juana Ines de la Cruz's letter to the Catholic Church in her defense of pursuing writing and reading in seventeenth-century Mexico. She was a poet, scholar, and nun. She felt she would not be honoring her creator if she did not use the mind she was given to seek knowledge. Sor Juana Ines died a few years after the church took away her library and stopped her from writing.

3. *La Adelita*, painted in Ramona Gardens Public Housing Project in 1976, is signed by Los Four, and usually Carlos Almaraz is given credit for design. However, anyone who studies the artwork of Judith Hernandez, Carlos Almaraz, and Los Four must agree that the primary Adelita figure is rendered much like the women in Ms. Hernandez's work.

4. In 1993, when former Archbishop Robert F. Sánchez resigned after his own sexual improprieties came to light, he was replaced by Archbishop Michael J. Sheehan who publicly promised to stop the rampant sexual abuses by parish priests. Archbishop Sánchez covered up hundreds of sexual offenses by parish priests because, over the span of eighteen years, he had sexual relationships with eleven women who were all in their twenties. Since Sheehan took over the job

more than 150 claims have been settled. Over $3 million has been spent in an attempt to expiate this scandalous sin—not for victim counseling, but primarily on legal fees. The whereabouts of many of the perpetrators are currently unknown.

5. See Museum of New Mexico. 2001. "Museum Director Denies Appeal: Our Lady Stays." Press release.

Appendices: Las cartas

26 March 2001

Dr. Thomas Wilson, Director
Museum of New Mexico
P.O. Box 2087
Santa Fe, NM 87501

Dear Dr. Wilson,

I am writing to thank you for your continued support of Los Angeles Chicana artist Alma Lopez, among others, in the current show at the Museum of International Folk Art. I understand you have received a certain amount of protest to the exhibition, and I thank you for maintaining your support for the innovative and provocative work of the artists.

I am quite familiar with Ms. Lopez' artwork and the richness of expression she brings to both traditional and contemporary Chicana/o images and issues. From her public artwork on billboards and murals all over the L.A. area to her "digital" collections online, I find her artwork a unique contribution to an evolving Chicana feminist sensibility, with an altogether consistent and visionary spirituality.

I should also say that I am not at all surprised by some negative reaction to her portrayal of the Virgen de Guadalupe. Dismay and even anger are to be expected—indeed, may be crucial—in inviting viewers to think about the many layers of meaning latent in the Virgen's image and her ramifications for Chicana/o gender ideology as well as spirituality.

And as a scholar of Chicana/o and Religious Studies, I must point out that this is not the first time that Chicana artists seeking to reclaim and transform traditional religious imagery have been threatened and silenced. I'm sure you are familiar with the work of San Francisco Chicana artists Esther Hernandez and Yolanda Lopez, whose early work with the Virgen de Guadalupe received praise as well as various bomb threats, but is now widely recognized as a pivotal contribution to the Chicana and Chicano art "canon."

In closing, thank you again for your support of this amazing exhibition. Please do not hesitate to call if I can be of any assistance.

Sincerely,
Susana L. Gallardo, Ph.D. (ABD), Department of Religious Studies, Stanford University

April 2, 2001

Dr. Joyce Ice, Director
Museum of International Folk Art

Dr. Tey Marianna Nunn, Curator
Museum of International Folk Art
(Curator of the *Cyber Arte* exhibition)

Dear Dr. Ice and Dr. Nunn,

Hello, as a Nuevo Mexicano and someone who has worked in the arts community for over twenty years I wanted to offer my own thoughts on the issues surrounding Alma Lopez's work. Although I have been away from my beloved homeland for eleven years now I still very much consider myself a New Mexican.

Primarily what I wanted to say is that this experience, as scary and painful as it is (I have been through my own controversies as a curator and formerly a New Mexico Arts Division employee), can be a real opportunity for a true and meaningful dialogue and the further deepening of the relationship between the communities of New Mexico and the cultural institutions that represent them. Of course, for this to occur there needs to be respect, reflection, commitment, and passion, all basic Catholic values.

I believe that this specific event is not only about the piece by Alma Lopez but also about the historic layered tensions between the community and the cultural institutions in New Mexico. There has been a long history of neglect, racism, and exploitation of the cultural resources of New Mexico and its people, and only relatively recently has it begun to change for the better. So this specific event is like touching a wound on the psychic body of our people.

If one is not aware of the work by many Chicana and other artists that has led to this piece it can appear as a shocking and disrespectful image of the virgin, but in art, context is everything. If we look at art history there are many images that created scandal in their times that seem totally banal to our contemporary eyes. I would encourage you to do whatever it takes to further contextualize the work, through exhibitions, readings, slide shows, etc. Having been through the culture wars of the 1980s and 1990s I know one of the most effective tools used against artists and cultural institutions was the de or re-contextualizing of artwork.

It is my strong belief that there must be solutions other than whole-sale removal of the work. The solution is with the local community and the stewards of the institution. It would be a mistake to think that simply removing the piece would actually solve any of the deeper and long-term issues made manifest with this work.

I wish everyone there the strength, courage, and clarity of thought to struggle through this with dignity and respect. I will be in New Mexico the week before Easter and will come in to see the exhibit.

The very best regards,
Patricio Chávez
Artist, Community Activist

3 April 2001

Dr. Joyce Ice, Director
Museum of International Folk Art

Dr. Tey Marianna Nunn, Curator
Museum of International Folk Art
(Curator of the *CyberArte* exhibition)

Dear Dr. Ice and Dr. Nunn,

I am writing in support of Alma Lopez's image *Our Lady*, currently on exhibition in your CyberArte show at the Museum of International Folk

Art in Santa Fe, and especially in support of her right as an artist to produce this image and your right as museum professionals to exhibit it to the public. It has been with utter dismay and indignation that I have been following the controversy ignited by Mr. Jose Villegas and his demeaning interpretation of Alma's vision of *Our Lady*, and I am deeply disturbed not only by the egregious lack of historical and political awareness demonstrated by Mr. Villegas in his diatribes against a well-respected (and respectful) Chicana artist, but even more so, by the fact that your museum board is actually going to meet this Wednesday to decide whether or not to censor Alma's image from the exhibit. As a Chicana writer and cultural critic who works on Chicana/o art, as a professor of Chicana/o Studies who often invites Ms. Lopez to lecture in her classes at UCLA, I can only shudder at the fascistic connotations of that action. The repercussions for all artists and museum professionals who fail to conform to the patriarchal status quo are painfully clear.

Although the attack on artistic freedom and the threat of censorship are more than enough cause for alarm, I think a deeper issue at the heart of Mr. Villegas's critique is that it is women who are in positions of power here: in the directorship of this museum, the organization of this exhibition, and the production of this image. If that were not so, he would not be demanding your resignation, and he would not be targeting the work of a lesbian artist. Mr. Villegas does not have a right to threaten your careers any more than he has a right to perpetrate a modern-day witch hunt on Alma Lopez; and yet, he is getting exactly the response he seeks. That the archbishop has gotten involved only underscores the fallacy of artistic freedom in a society in which, as the NEA debacle taught us over a decade ago, art is held accountable to church and state. Why is it that, instead of catering to Mr. Villegas, instead of meeting to discuss the removal of *Our Lady* from your exhibition, you are not taking him to task for his offensive remarks and the way in which he is slandering the reputations of your museum and the artist? I sincerely hope the Museum of International Folk Art, a museum I have always enjoyed and respected, does not fall prey to these McCarthyist tactics. I ask you to refuse to participate in an action meant to undermine your constitutional rights, and those of the artist, and I beg you not to capitulate to the arrogant demands and colonized interpretations of men who dwell in the backwater of cultural and sexual politics.

Again, I want to reiterate in the strongest possible terms my unconditional support of and admiration for the revisionist work of Alma Lopez. Your institution would be most remiss if it were to permit her contribution to be censored.

Respectfully yours,
Alicia Gaspar de Alba, Ph.D.
Interim Director, LGBT Studies Program
Associate Professor of Chicana/Chicano Studies
UCLA

20 April 2001

Dear Alma,

I hope it is not too late to add my voice in support of your artwork. As you know, I have been an admirer of your work for many years, so please pass the following on to the museum.

I am a practicing, not just a cultural Catholic. My four children, including my three daughters, attend Catholic school and I have commissioned three santos from a New Mexico santero. I personally believe in the power of the Virgen to be a healer and a source of inspiration and comfort to me and my family. I took my children to the Basilica for the first time this past summer so that they too would know of her place in their Catholic, Mexican and Chicano history. (I am not unmindful of the controversies regarding her appearance, etc.)

But the issue today is not my personal beliefs, or those of any other viewer; the issue is our tolerance of your artistic vision, and the failure of the board to defend your right to that artistic vision against those who would for various reasons seek to deny you this right. I happen to love the image, but even if I didn't, I do, and Mr. Villegas should, respect that right, whether he agrees with it or not.

The museum's failing thus far seems to be that it has opened the door for a discussion of whether the piece should be removed. Enter the likes of Mr. Villegas. As others have already commented, where will the intolerance end? Will the Board allow Mr. Villegas, the archbishop, or anyone else, for that matter, to come to the museum and summarily order the removal of any other works, because they are sacrilegious, offensive, in bad taste, historically incorrect, badly composed, oddly dimensioned, or too big or too small? While the question may seem ludicrous, the answer seems to be yes, if enough people, especially the well connected, or of the threatening kind, say so.

Therefore, the museum should establish a standard. I recommend a ballot box at the entrance. Visitors may then vote on which, if any, pieces

should be removed. If a piece receives enough votes, regardless of the reason, it will be removed. Of course that practice should be applied to all exhibitions at the museum, including those of folk,
contemporary, conceptual, video, and other art forms. The board will be saving itself the trouble of calling special meetings whenever there are enough malcontents to warrant a review of the artistic vision of its invited artists or the curatorial prerogatives of its professional staff.

In short, this controversy is not your problem, Alma. And I hope it will not dissuade you from continuing to create works that question and inspire, not only aficionados like me, but especially young women like my daughters who need to interpret for themselves what their role in society is and need artists like you to help them do so.

Afectuosamente,
Armando Durón
Lawyer
Member, Chicano Art Collectors Anonymous

11 May 2001

Alma and Raquel,

I have been following up on the course of events of the "controversy" over Alma's art piece in which Raquel so beautifully represents *Our Lady*. The first time I saw it, I smiled and thought to myself, "Yeah, that's what our lady is all about." I mean really, that's what I have imagined her to be since I became an adult. She's chingona like that and proud, and causes controversy the way you are.

Since, I was a little girl, I have felt the oppression imposed on mujeres in society. Actually, when I was little, there was a period of time, where unaware of anatomy, I wondered what exactly made me different from little boys, and how did I know I was a girl. At four years old, I began my study of what made me different, what made me a girl. Not knowing that the difference is that boys have pee pees and girls don't, my first observation of difference was that girls had long hair and they couldn't go outside and play with pelotas or pretend to be in war. That's what made me a girl. My mom dressed me up in frilly little things and sat me down with a doll, and said sit there and stay clean. "Niñas like you, se sientan silensitas, you play quietly." That was my next observation, women were quiet, never yelled or spoke out; they sat silent with eyes on the ground (como la Virgen) or looking out to nowhere. When they yelled they were irrational and emotional. Asi son las mujeres. . . . Disregarded either way.

Today, I am still suffering and my heart still bleeds from all the quiet that has been imposed on me and the quiet I see imposed on my sisters (mujeres in general). I was molested for several years by a family member, and I have been quiet. Don't share my anger, it's not ladylike. I've been feeling so angry at the quiet that we have to carry as mujeres. Worse than a cross, we carry an anvil on our back. For the sake of FAMILIA, we endure some of the worst tortures. I told my mom two years ago, she cried and felt bad, probably guilty, but she asked me not to tell. It would be too hard for the family. They wouldn't understand. My cousin would be hurt that it was her brother, maybe she wouldn't come over. No le digas a tu papa, she said. It would hurt him too much. Don't tell your boyfriend, he might think you come from a bad family. Don't tell. Don't tell. Don't tell. So when he comes over, I smile and I act cordial. Like a lady. But inside . . . inside . . . it's not quiet. It's all noise, earthquake and all the fire from hell. It's inside, so nobody gets hurt.

Pero yo, que? Me pudro?

The one thing that has made me strong is my mission to end the cycle of quiet, and the noise I hear from mujeres, artists like yourselves, que no se dejan. You give the voiceless and unimportant like me a voice. I'm an artist myself and fascinated by the archetype of Guadalupe/Tonanztin, who in my eyes is all woman with fire and pride in her eyes, just like you, Raquel. Not complacency. She's a warrior and carries a machete and she's beautiful and brown and strong the way you are. Funny coincidence, but I had been working on some sketches to do a portrait of a naked and pregnant Guadalupe. So when I read the stories and different points of view, I couldn't help but think, I love mi raza, but sometimes we are just as tapados as anyone else

I guess what I'm trying to say by writing this e-mail is, Thank You. Muchisimas gracias for creating empowering images of mujeres where we could see our reflection. It all begins there. We need to change the images that have controlled and kept us down for so long. Your work communicates the urgency in the need for us to love our bodies brown and round the way they are. It also communicates to me the need for us to keep our head up with our gaze always aflame, always watchful, and always aware, our souls ready to fight. The quiet has killed us for too long. I'm still a youngster and still learning how to yell. I'm trying not to let the anger eat me up. It's hard to live ashamed. But in the meantime thank you for speaking out for mujeres como yo. Your work saves us and our souls. The fact that you are willing to stand up for that is an inspiration to me. I hope I could one day follow your example of courage. So, no se dejen. Keep on talking, keep on painting, keep on yelling, just keep on.

Gracias con todisísimo el corazon,
Adriana
Santa Ana, Califas

Breaking Down Glass Walls

Ruben Ochoa

¡Q-vo! In 1943, U.S. bona fide sailors and service men roamed the barrios of East Los Angeles. They were not there for the culture and nightlife. They were there to dispose of an enemy. They were there for reprisal after a group of sailors declared they were attacked. The enemy could not be the Japanese; they were serving time in "relocation centers" throughout unknown deserts, unknown to themselves and their families. There was an additional enemy to fill the racial paranoid void lurking in the minds of Southern California's hysteria. This enemy did not tiptoe after hours and attempt to conceal their identities. They thumped and tapped their Stacy Adam's as they Pachuco Hopped throughout the nightclubs of *East Los*, allowing them to be quite visible in their intentions to not conform to American standards. This put them in a space of contention with over two hundred sailors mobilized to confront them, which resulted in the Zoot Suit Riots.

By not succumbing to American assimilation those Mexican-Americans ended up paying a heavy price for their defiance. Retribution, usually carried out by death, took the form of humiliation as well as dehumanization. One by one the pachucos were disconnected from reality and transported back in time to a sacrificial re-enactment for the Amerindian deity Xipe Totec. Absolutely not in the manner of being bludgeoned to death in the ritualistic fashion of drinking the blood of one's first kill. On the contrary, pachuco's skin became the prop for Xipe Totec's ceremonial use of skin, placing it over one's own body to signify renovation through death to insure the continuation of life. The pachucos were stripped and flayed of their visible markers, *sus trapos*, their zoot suits, their second skin, and left naked, jailed, and humiliated. All the while the press hailed the servicemen as heroes for stemming the spreading of corruption and contamination to others by pachucos.

Carrying this weight of historical fragility over my shoulders, my arms, my head, and my shoes, *Pachuco a la Vidrio* enters another space known for contention toward non-Anglicized artists, "The White Cube." The photos formally taken to serve as documentation only, depicts the glass encrusted zoot suit out of action. An aspect lost is the guerilla performance that disrupted the walls and minds of art patrons at the Escondido Center for the Arts, Museum. A Museum filled mostly by Anglo patrons and Anglo artists. The only hint of Latino artists was the ploy of using an international Latino artist annually to fulfill a "diverse" quota—a strategy used by many Museum institutions. However, the work on display at the moment was a glass blown art-for-art's sake exhibition, a calling card for an apolitical audience.

Just as the pachuco's clothes of the 1940s made meaning with their bodies, hateful and desirable, my suit acted in the same manner. The

Fig. 1. *Ruben Ochoa and Joey Azul at the Escondido Center for the Arts Museum. Photo by Pasha E. Turley.*

friction of glass resonated, this audible vibrancy of crashing glass, throughout the entire institution. The noise startled, disrupted, and yet enchanted the audience. Staff members, docents, and gallery attendees alike were shocked, alerting the security guards into action. But I had total agency. I strategically entered through the service entrance as an employee of the institution. I knew the space and they knew my face. I painted those white walls and installed those very works of glass on the pedestals with my own hands. But my appearance were no longer that of a laborer. I literally transformed and metaphorically jumped off a pedestal as a walking art piece subverting the institution. Thus forcing the museum to become my personal artist space.

Fig. 2-3. Details from Pachuca a la Vidrio (1999) by Ruben Ochoa. Glass and zoot suit; 5'8", US size 10, and 240 pounds minus 60 pounds for trapos. Photography by Patrick Miller.

Yet I did not act alone. I had an accomplice, Joey Azul. Azul appeared as one of them but was recognized as the Other. Emphatically reading and pronouncing Azul's name and visually seeing Azul takes you beyond boundaries, genders, and ethnicities. Upon confrontation, one clearly sees that Azul is neither male nor a recipient of the Spanish surname by birth or marriage. This conscious and sadistic positioning is intentional. Causing a conundrum with her verbal name and blond haired, blue-eyed physical appearance. Especially effective when read on paper, her names signifies several other connotations.

As we continued to roam the halls of the museum, no one dared to strip us of our actions and glass suits. They physically could not without causing direct harm to themselves by handling raw shards of glass. This was the new improved *tacuche* zoot suit. I had the choice to shed my own skin and placed it onto others, not empowering them but myself. Audience members and patrons were allowed to wear my *trapo*, my coat, and *tando*, my brimmed hat. They animated themselves through fear and excitement by being encrusted in a glass zoot suit and becoming part of a pachuco aesthetic. The empowerment took place briefly right afterwards, when the audience member wanted to return to normalcy. Through fear of getting cut, they could not remove the *garras*, the suit, by themselves. I took on the position of Xipe Totec and flayed this added second skin. Orale!

Note

I would like to give special thanks to Joey Azul, for her performance collaboration; Ray Estrella from El Pachuco Zoot Suits, located in Fullerton, CA, for donating the zoot suit; Harry Gamboa Jr., for his video collaboration; Cam La, for her immeasurable support; Patrick Miller, for his photography; Therman Statom, for donating the glass shards; and Pasha E. Turley, for her photography.

Field Reports

Turning Sunshine into Noir and Fantasy into Reality:

Los Angeles in the Classroom

Alvina E. Quintana

David Reiff opens *L.A.: Capital of the Third World* with a series of L.A. jokes that his friends and acquaintances shared with him before he left New York to relocate to Los Angeles:

> "Their idea of reading is a long personalized license plate." "Don't forget to buy that beachfront property in Nevada while it's still affordable." "L.A.'s only contribution to civilization is being able to make a right turn on a red light." [An Annie Hall appropriation that Reiff describes as "life imitating kitsch."] "Just be sure to peek behind those facades every so often. Everything in L.A. is a stage set, up to and including the mountains. Those Santa Ana winds they all complain about are probably produced by a huge wind machine out at the Paramount sky lot." "Wasn't it Los Angeles that Gertrude Stein had in mind when she made that crack about there being 'no there there?'" . . . How are you going to know when you've gotten there, anyway? The whole place is just a hundred suburbs masquerading as a city." (1991, 17–18)

My first reaction to the jokes in Reiff's prologue was one of déjà vu. Struck by a series of powerful recollections, I was forced to reconsider some of the provincial attitudes I had encountered after leaving Santa Barbara, California, to relocate to the East Coast.

When I first heard comments about the laziness or stupidity of the average "laid back" Californian, whose primary concern in life was supposedly New-Age fanaticism or a narcissistic obsession with physical perfection (a preoccupation most commonly characterized as the "cult of the bod"), I was not only shocked but deeply offended. Over time, though, my defensive reaction began to shift from indignation to tolerance as I allowed myself to listen to the attitudes expressed by the inhabitants of my new and somewhat alien community. I began to understand how relocation had liberated me and fostered an awareness of the cultural baggage I carry with my native Californian status. Others' facile perceptions coerced me into reassessing my own assumptions and made me aware of individual's innocent but problematic tendency to turn a critical eye on unfamiliar terrain and self-righteously pass judgements that evoke the imaginary more then the real. Reiff's collection of L.A. jokes, which disregard the rampant social inequality and exploitation in Los Angeles, reduces the city to a vicinity overrun by the kind of carte blanche and frivolous sensibility that generally only flourishes with class privilege. Misleading as this portrait may be, a multi-million dollar movie industry produces and maintains this illusion of L.A.

Although Reiff's brief survey reveals unquestionably problematic perspectives, his geographically based humor enables him to confront a series of provincial reactions; namely, for people living outside of Southern California, the name Los Angeles does not refer to a city any more than the name Hollywood refers to a neighborhood within that city. Rather, when speaking of L.A, the public seems to unconsciously summon cinematic recollections. L.A. is a place that exists outside of reality, a place inhabited with superhumans or myths rather than real people. It is interesting, though not surprising, that New York wit represents Los Angeles as a haven of whites, "superficiality," and entitlement—the L.A. depicted in vintage cinema, the land of Hollywood and Vine, Lana Turner, tight sweaters, and dizzy, platinum blondes. But we must concede that regional ignorance is neither unusual nor limited to East Coast misconceptions about the American West. For the most part, Americans live as exiles within their own country; they are limited by provincial attitudes that encourage competitive views about geographic, racial, and ethnic difference. Ironically in this technologically advanced society, where many people have used the Internet to explore the dry and desolate terrain of Mars, Americans remain marginally informed about American geography and racial, ethnic, or cultural difference(s).

I am a native of San Francisco and well aware of the way people in the Southwest conceive of the East Coast. The reaction of my best friend upon learning that I might accept a tenure-track appointment at the University of Delaware comes to mind: "You'll hate it, Alvina, the only tortillas they sell are in cans!" Aside from inspiring cultural anxiety about leaving the West, this comment tainted my arrival with a sense of panic that eventually dispatched at least twenty concerned members of the English Department in pursuit of fresh tortillas and cilantro for their new Chicana "multiculturalist."

Yet, my relocation to Delaware has enabled me to modify my provincial attitudes about the East Coast and my California chauvinism. I remember my surprise when first exposed to Delawarean pride in their first-state status, a position to which I had never given much thought. The best I could do was muster a vague recollection of an early American portrait of George Washington crossing the Delaware River. And even that reference proved to be faulty, for as one of my colleagues pointed out, the painting depicts the Delaware river not the state! Today I recognize that my regional illiteracy was a consequence of my socialization to believe the many early explorers who described California as the "promised land," "beautiful," and "golden." I understand that, like other Americans, my concept of self and nation has been greatly influenced, or better yet, overdetermined by the prevailing attitudes of my homeland.[1]

Far from uncommon, geographical biases are indicative of the regional and cultural prejudices on which this country was founded. Even a cursory survey of American pioneering shows how Manifest Destiny was used to justify the distribution of territory away from indigenous peoples and excuse their dislocation or exile. The unsettling narratives of urban renewal and white flight from racially diverse suburban communities testify that, even as we approach the twenty-first century, many Anglo Americans continue to inflect their cultural, racial, and regional biases by positioning themselves in opposition to racialized or ethnic groups they deem socially inferior. The "our forefathers" concept of the American Dream can be more realistically likened to the American Horror film, as Ed Guerrero suggests, where "the social construction and representation of race, otherness, and nonwhiteness is an ongoing process, working itself out in many symbolic, cinematic forms of expression, but particularly in the abundant racialized metaphors and allegories of the fantasy, sci-fi, and horror" (1993, 56). Guerrero's analysis of film and Reiff's depiction of humor unveil a quintessential American ideology that naturalizes, through its social constructions, the marginalized, invisible, or inferior status of ethnic/racial difference (Hall 1996).[2]

The misconceptions revealed in Reiff's prologue are valuable because they underscore one of America's most haunting problems and thus provide a useful point of entry for addressing the fear that continues to augment social barriers and instill contempt. In fact, I was so impressed with David Reiff's book that in the spring semester of 1993 I decided to use it as a model for a course that would use the magic and allure of Hollywood to deepen student interest in and awareness of America. My course "L.A.: City of the Angels" had broad campus appeal because of its promise for California dreaming while satisfying the university's "multicultural" requirement.[3]

In order to accomplish my goal of deepening student awareness about American diversity, I developed an interdisciplinary approach that emphasized history, political theory, film studies, and literature and enabled me to move my students from fantasy to actuality by introducing them to the Los Angeles recognized by the ordinary California resident. (One of my colleagues, without realizing it, provided the final push for this project when she suggested that in Delaware, diversity means "white" students from New Jersey, Pennsylvania, or New York.) My syllabus described the course in the following way:

> According to Ryzard Kapuscinski's report in *New Perspectives Quarterly*, "Los Angeles is the premonition of a new civilization. Linked more to the Third World and Asia than to the Europe of America's racial and cultural roots, Los Angeles will enter the 21st century as a multiracial and multicultural society." With this thesis in mind, the course will focus on Los Angeles as a center for multicultural production. We will study a variety of representations of L.A. reading, listening, and viewing. Our reading will feature contemporary writing produced by African Americans, Chicano/Latinos, Asian Americans, as well as Euro-Americans. In addition, we will examine a number of Hollywood films, considering how commercial film is shaped by cultural forces.

The reading list for the course included Mike Davis's *City of Quartz*, Ruben Martinez's *The Other Side/El Otro Lado*, Helen Hunt Jackson's *Ramona*, Chester Himes's *If He Hollers Let Him Go*, Ron Arias's *The Road to Tamuzunchale*, John Rechy's *The Miraculous Day of Amalia Gomez*, Michael Tolkin's *The Player*, Hisaye Yamamoto's *Seventeen Syllables and Other Stories*, and the edited volume *Invocation L.A.*

My hope was to challenge the East Coast students' stereotypic assessment of Southern California by considering the interconnections between regionalism and cultural/racial prejudice. The course experimented with notions of self-imposed exile in that I forced students to distance themselves from what they perceived to be their native understanding of

Los Angeles, to deconstruct the way they, with the assistance of the Hollywood apparatus, had fabricated an "imagined community." I was working very deliberately to create a feeling of discomfort and unfamiliarity, a foreign sensibility that would challenge the student's preconceived ideas about the city. In many ways this teacherly structuring or planning compelled me to become theoretically cognizant of the way my own relocation to the East Coast disassociated me from many of the beliefs of my native land, challenging me to reassess my territorial attitudes about myself and my country.

The cinematic screenings enabled me to reproduce the apprehension that results from being thrust into a foreign environment. As a class, we viewed *L.A. Story, Chinatown, Colors, Bladerunner, El Norte, Zoot Suit, American Me,* and *The Player.* I was operating under the assumption that most of my students were aware of and probably had, for that matter, already seen *Boyz in the Hood.*[4] I selected the films screened in class with the intention of facilitating a sense of difference that would lead "mainstream" students into a process of self-discovery. Beginning with the familiarity of the comedic/stereotypic as depicted in Steve Martin's *L.A. Story,* I asked students to write an essay that looked critically at the film, discussing whether it represented an L.A. of "Sunshine or Noir," in Mike Davis's terms (1992, 15-88).

In response to this assignment, one student opened his paper with the following quote from the film's leading character, a wacky TV weatherman (Steve Martin) who is trying to sort out his life:

> "Sitting there at that moment, I thought of something else Shakespeare said, 'Hey, life is pretty stupid with lots of hubbub to keep you busy, but really not amounting to much.'"

Without commenting on the insipid, trend-conscious sensibility of Martin's character, who exhibits no intellectual sophistication, my student launched into his analysis, stating that throughout *City of Quartz:*

> Davis exposes Los Angeles's myriad of woes, and offers little hope of remedy. Yet, this alone does not make Los Angeles noir. Steve Martin's romantic comedy *L.A. Story* demonstrates that, indeed, Los Angeles need not be considered in purely negative terms. Rather, Martin depicts a city that, though culturally vapid, possesses an underlying charm. Like *City of Quartz, L.A. Story* considers Los Angeles in a dualistic fashion. *L.A. Story* is both "sunshine," characterized by a light, playful atmosphere, and *noir,* characterized by an equally lighthearted rendering of a deeper, darker truth.

It was this "deeper, darker truth" that began to emerge as the course evolved. As we interrogated the "lighthearted" comfort of the comedic form, students began to enhance their awareness about multicultural concerns and the dystopic representations in *Bladerunner* and Ruben Martinez's *El Otro Lado*. Reflecting on three of the featured films, another student addressed the racial implications set forth by cinematic representation:

> *L.A. Story* perpetuates the stereotypical, relegating minorities to service roles. The only "person of color" in the film, excluding Iman, is a waiter who relays the menu in rap. Even though the film is categorized as a comedy, full of slapstick humor, it is not immune from the kind of negative patterns of representation which are more blatant in such films as *Colors* and *Bladerunner*.

Overall, the students' responses to my writing assignments echoed the above examples, employing either a romantic sense of optimism (reflected in an acknowledgement of difference that self-consciously depicts both sides of the equation) or developing an oppositional perspective that challenged the narrative's representational practices.

The quotes from student papers are also useful because they serve as a template for understanding some common reactions that surface when students are faced with the task of interrogating a text in order to identify its "political unconscious." The first assignment provided the class with the opportunity to engage in a dialectical analysis that considered Los Angeles within the binary set of the Sunshine/Noir opposition. Students were thus motivated to understand the consequence of privilege, to discover that one person's sunshine is, more often that not, founded and sustained by another's darkness. Interestingly, some students responded by structuring arguments based on the ideology of romance and sentimentalism, while others offered critiques marked by their resistance and opposition to demeaning cultural representations.

The course readings and films during the early weeks of the term engaged students to the point where they began to follow Davis's example, reading literature, cinema, and current events critically, considering the relationship between dominant ideology and popular culture. During the final weeks, students were able to rigorously assess their course of study and reflect on cultural production as a means for articulating some of L.A.'s social concerns. Contemplating the 1992 L.A. Rebellion, one student agreed with many political critics who suggest that "in reality" the "riots" should have been viewed as the first tremor of the social earthquake that is to come unless actions are taken to remedy ethnic/cultural unrest. Her final paper on the Community Arts Movement in Los Angeles argued that artistic communication leads to harmony and understanding. As supporting evidence, she cited Michael Newton, President of the Performing Arts Council of the Music Center of Los Angeles County:

> "What the arts can do is release us from a state of being alone and remind us of our dependence on others and their dependence on us. The arts remind us that man can only fulfill his private passions, ideas, and dreams by sharing them with others."

It seems opportune to conclude this segment of my discussion concerning student reflections with a passage that summarizes the final sentiment of the class. In a paper entitled "Los Angeles's Burning Streets: Where Poetry and Rap Music Converge," the student suggested that:

> Along the brutal streets of Los Angeles, the poet and the rapper are one. Ice Cube, Kid Frost, Naomi Quinonez, and Wanda Coleman are the prophets of the modern urban nightmare. . . . Their words are as angry and violent as their world. It is a world that methodically stalks them, all the while threatening to destroy them. Somewhere, along a side street, another victim of Los Angeles dies, and close by these poets pronounce their frustration to a deaf world.

Although the course proved successful because the students developed a deeper appreciation for American diversity, it was for me an extremely difficult and challenging episode. Of my thirty students, only two were not white. For individuals unfamiliar with issues surrounding ethnic/racial diversity, multicultural studies courses run the risk of being reduced to consciousness raising groups wherein students want to discuss themselves; that is, their guilt, their anger, their frustrations, their prejudices, rather than the issues that the featured cultural producers raise.

I am reminded of the "classic example" Gloria Anzaldúa provides in the introduction to *Haciendo Caras*. Describing the dynamics in the U.S. Women-of-Color class she taught at U.C. Santa Cruz, she reports:

> Two of the goals I had were for the 120 students to identify and interpret instances of Racism ("internalized dominance") and to both recognize their internalized Racism and oppression and to develop strategies against them. . . . I wanted to call attention to the dynamic of avoidance among us, of not acknowledging each other—an act of dehumanizing people like ourselves. Yet another goal was to encourage them to emerge from "blank-outness" and openly combat the dominant groups denial

207

> and erasure of ethnic subjectivity by allowing the students a relatively safe space to speak up and "expose" their feelings. At first, what erupted in class was anger—anger from mujeres of color, anger and guilt from whites, anger, frustration and mixed feelings by Jewish women who were caught in the middle (being white but often sympathizing with colored), and anger and frustration on my part from having to mediate between all these groups. Soon my body became a vessel for all the tensions and anger, and I dreaded going to class. Some of my students dreaded going to class. (1990, xix-xx)

As the "multiculturalist" in our department, I develop and teach courses like the one Anzaldúa describes above. Generally, I come away from the experience exhausted, extremely tempted to limit my future teaching endeavors to the "traditional" American literary canon. Teaching the canon would afford the opportunity to make a choice I do not have as a multiculturalist—the option of either emphasizing the aesthetic, rather than the political context that shaped it, or selectively explicating the text by limiting the analysis to formalistic concerns.

But I continue to avoid the easy path provided by apolitical approaches because my teaching experiences have made me realize that with the discomfort and tension, the anger, guilt, fear, and frustration, comes the opportunity for personal development and social change. In the end, my students, regardless of their East or West Coast status, have consistently come away from a demanding educational ordeal renewed and motivated to discover more about diversity, more about the so-called "other." This was certainly the case with the "L.A.: City of the Angels" course. If I were to teach this class again, I would revise the reading requirements and course emphasis so that they could be used to illuminate today's cultural predicament.[5] In Mike Davis's terms, studying L.A. provides a method for "excavating the future." For instance, in a recent review of Quentin Tarantino's *Jackie Brown*, Joseph Giovannini alludes to the material and mythic importance of L.A.:

> Some people may believe there is no there there in Los Angeles, but ever since film noir of the 1940s and cinematic monuments like "Sunset Boulevard," the industry has known otherwise. Especially after "Shampoo," "Chinatown," and this year's "L.A. Confidential," the city has increasingly emerged as a character in movies.

On the last day of class, one of my students shared the following insight with me: "I can't wait to visit L.A., only now I know I've got to take lots of money." How's that for moving from fantasy to reality!

Notes

1. A recent double issue of *The New Yorker* (Feb. 23 & Mar. 2, 1998), subtitled the "California Issue," featured a number of articles that represented the state in general and L.A. in particular as the model for the future. With essays like "L.A. Glows: Why Southern California Doesn't Look Like Any Place Else," "Annals of Enterprise—The Comeback," and "Annals of Architecture—Desert Cool," the magic and allure of the place is packaged for East Coast/American consumption.

2. Speaking of difference and contestation, Stuart Hall explains that, "The play of identity and difference which constructs racism is powered not only by the positioning of blacks as the inferior species but also, and at the same time, by an inexpressible envy and desire; and this is something the recognition of which fundamentally *displaces* many of our hitherto stable political categories, since it implies a process of identification and otherness which is more complex than we had hitherto imagined" (1996, 167, emphasis in the original).

3. The University of Delaware requires all undergraduates to take three units stressing multicultural, ethnic, and/or gender related content. The requirement provides students with some awareness of and sensitivity to cultural pluralism, which the university views as necessary for educated persons in a diverse world.

4. *Poetic Justice* and *Menace II Society*, also relevant as examples of the gang genre and the overall course focus, had not yet been released.

5. Future courses might include films such as *To Sleep With Anger*, *Falling Down*, *South Central*, *Strange Days*, *Mi Vida Loca*, *L.A. Confidential*, *Devil in a Blue Dress*, *Jackie Brown*, *Bullworth*, and a variety of multicultural texts including but not limited to Karen Tei Yamashita's *The Tropic of Orange*, Cynthia Kadohata's *In The Heart of the Valley of Love*, Sanyika Shakur's *Monster: The Autobiography of an L.A. Gang Member*, Luis J. Rodriguez's *Always Running*.

Works Cited

Anzaldúa, Gloria. 1990. *Haciendo Caras*. San Francisco: Aunt Lute Press.

Arias, Ron. 1987. *The Road to Tamuzunchale*. Tempe, AZ: Bilingual Press.

Clinton, Michelle T., Sesshu Foster, and Naomi Quiñonez, eds. 1989. *Invocation L.A.: Urban Multicultural Poetry*. Albuquerque, NM: West End Press.

Davis, Mike. 1992. *City of Quartz*. New York: Vintage Press.

Giovannini, Joseph. 1997. "Tarantino's Los Angeles: Roadside Noir." *New York Times* 147 (December 30): B1.

Guerrero, Ed. 1993. *Framing Blackness: The African American Image in Film*. Philadelphia: Temple University Press.

Hall, Stuart. 1996. "New Ethnicities." In *Black British Cultural Studies*, ed. Houston Baker, Manthia Diawara, and Ruth Lindeborg. Chicago: University of Chicago Press.

Himes, Chester. 1947. *If He Hollers Let Him Go*. New York: Thunder's Mouth Press.

Jackson, Helen Hunt. 1988. *Ramona*. New York: Penguin.

Kadohata, Cynthia. 1992. *In the Heart of the Valley of Love*. New York: Penguin Books.

Martinez, Ruben. 1992. *The Other Side/El Otro Lado*. New York: Vintage.

Rechy, John. 1993. *The Miraculous Day of Amalia Gomez*. Boston: Arcade Publishers.

Reiff, David. 1991. *L.A.: Capital of the Third World*. New York: Touchstone Press.

Rodriguez, Luis J. 1993. *Always Running*. New York: Touchstone Press.

Shakur, Sanyika. 1993. *Monster: The Autobiography of an L.A. Gang Member*. New York: Penguin.

Tolkin, Michael. 1995. *The Player*. Emerville, CA: Publishers Group West.

Yamamoto, Hisaye. 1988. *Seventeen Syllables and Other Stories*. Latham, NY: Kitchen Table Press.

Yamashita, Karen Tei. 1997. *The Tropic of Orange*. Minneapolis, MN: Coffee House Press.

Ethnicity, Fieldwork, and the Cultural Capital that Gets Us There:
Reflections from U.S. Hispanic Marketing

Arlene Dávila

With global culture industries localizing their operations and targeting cultural differences, how are race, ethnicity, and cultural differences structured into their own workings and operations? Moreover, how do our own ethnicities, backgrounds, and identities as researchers mediate our access to and understanding of such processes? In what follows I explore these issues through an examination of my fieldwork experience, particularly my level of access to the corporate staff and the workings of the U.S. Hispanic marketing industry during recently completed ethnographic research. Specifically, I want to call attention to the challenges posed to fieldwork and ethnography by the processes of globalization, in this case by the global integration and market segmentation of the advertising industry, in order to contend that our access or lack of access to such global industries is as revealing of their current operations as it is of the challenges and possibilities for contemporary fieldwork.

My argument addresses recent rethinking of anthropological fieldwork and, in particular, of the "field" as the place, space, and location where fieldwork is done. As Gupta and Ferguson note, anthropologists have long engaged in critical assessments of the concept of culture, the politics and practice of ethnography and ethnographic writing, and even the relationship between writers and their subjects, but less emphasis has been given to probing and deconstructing the field as the space of ethnographic work (1997). As a result, though increasingly self-critical, anthropological analyses have continued to privilege a space and location, fixity, and authority, recycling the same canonical assumptions that we have criticized so much about the concept of culture and about the anthropological endeavor. A face-to-face encounter with an informant and direct participant observation is still given more ethnographic validity and authority than any alternative method, just as fieldwork in the most exotic places abroad is still assumed to be the most valuable and authentic. Such hierarchies of scholarly validation have led to various exclusions, most notably the continued devaluation of work by women, who are more likely to encounter difficulties accessing "exotic" locations, and the familiar disregard of U.S.-based anthropological work.[1] But what new problems and hierarchies of scholarly knowledge are created when our fieldwork sites disband, being no longer containable in one location or temporal moment, and when we are unable to access the multiple "sites" where the global phenomena that concern us take place?

Obviously, problems of access are not new to ethnographers studying institutions of power. Already in 1969, Laura Nader identified access as the most powerful obstacle to "studying up," while excessive bureaucracy and concerns over privacy have long been recognized as central variables affecting the study of formal organizations, such as private industries and corporations (Nader 1999 [1969]; Schwartzman 1993). Today, however, the growing segmentation of culture industries across different transnational spaces and their growing embeddedness in the logics of private capital, which are generally antagonistic to the rules of full disclosure and critical inquiry, further complicate our access and understanding of such spaces and call us to rethink approaches to their study (Calabrese 1999; Miller 1999). Against this background, anthropologists have rightfully called for new methods with which to expand our research imaginary, and pointed to the need to reformulate the ways research is conceived if we are to understand the multiple implications of cultural phenomena in the contemporary globalized and mass mediated world. Hence Gupta and Ferguson (1997) suggest that we are better off seeking to gain "situated knowledges" about processes and situations, without fetishising the field per se. In a similar vein, Marcus (1998) has advanced multiple recommendations for reshaping "fieldwork" spaces, such as by going beyond a particular space and instead following the thing, the person, or the event; while Hannerz (1998) and Foster (1999b) propose that we break from the possessive association of author and research and be more open to collective projects that allow us to supersede the challenges of time and space presented by the study of such global phenomena as contemporary advertising.

My discussion is located at the intersection of these debates; however, my aim is not to provide alternatives to the methodological challenges posed by globalization to the "ways" and "hows" of contemporary field-work, but rather to suggest that there is much to be learned from exploring the predicaments involved in accessing fieldwork sites and locations. What I call for is not so much a rethinking of fieldwork sites, or an end to the confining emphasis on fixity and location, as it is a critical engagement with the forces that mediate our entry into the very real spaces where globalization takes place, such as the closed quarters of a corporate board-room or a New York City advertising agency. In particular, I am concerned with ethnicity, not because I am oblivious to the many other factors affect-ing the ethnographic study of formal organizations such as global advertis-ing, but because I want to emphasize the structuring of ethnicity within contemporary global culture industries. Specifically, I seek to call atten-tion to how such industries are increasingly tapping into cultural and eth-nic differences and similarly incorporating such variables into their own operations. Finally, my analysis is also reflexive and speaks to the always present, though not always pursued, anthropological concern with how our subjectivities, backgrounds, and racial, ethnic, and social identities intersect with our ethnographic research.[2] My emphasis, however, will be in using this reflexive examination as a tool to analyze how ethnicity bears on the working of global culture industries such as advertising, and how, in turn, it may affect our ability to study their operations.

Before proceeding I should mention that I am a Latina born and raised in Puerto Rico, and now based in the United States, whose research has primarily revolved around analysis of Puerto Rican and U.S. Latino cul-tural politics and commercial culture. This makes me a so-called "native anthropologist" insofar as the focus of my research is generally considered to be "my own group" and "my own culture," although I neither subscribe to the authenticating premises of this concept nor seek to comment here on the debate about the nature and authenticity of research by native an-thropologists. It has already been amply noted that such works are oftentimes vested with greater authenticity as representative of the researcher's "own group," but are simultaneously considered a lesser type of anthropology given the discipline's continued emphasis on the putative distance between informant and researchers, who must deploy supposedly unique anthropological research skills.[3] Instead, in identifying myself as a Latina working in the marketing and commodification of U.S. Latino cul-ture, I seek to establish some of the factors that shaped my interest in probing how ethnicity and cultural backgrounds mediate our access and ability to conduct research on global cultural industries in a context where ethnicity and culture have become prominent marketing variables.

Contemporary U.S. Hispanic marketing, a culturally specific and rapidly growing segment of U.S. marketing, presents an interesting instance of these dynamics. As I discuss later, not only does this industry function as an intermediary between Anglo corporate America and U.S. Latinos, but it also maintains close transnational linkages with Latin America, and the nationalities and backgrounds of those employed in the industry are important in its workings and organization. In this context, my background was both a help and a hindrance in gaining access to the different levels and processes of this industry. It is what such issues of access reveal about this industry's organization around ethnic lines that is the main concern of this work.

My discussion draws from my previous ethnographic research on Puerto Rico's marketing industry (1993–95) and on U.S. Hispanic marketing agencies primarily in New York City (1998–99).[4] I start by reviewing my research experiences in Puerto Rico in order to contrast the access I received there to my experience in New York City agencies, and to suggest that my informants' reception of my work was indicative of the role and position of marketing in these different locations. I then devote the rest of the discussion to the U.S. Hispanic marketing industry. In particular, I discuss how cultural differences among U.S. Hispanic marketing staff—such as those of language use, nationality, and ethnic background—are incorporated into this industry in ways that maximize its ability to target its market constituency. I conclude by considering how these factors mediated my entrance to and understanding of this industry andhow they suggest the place of cultural differences in the operations of contemporary culture industries.

The Marketing Context: Perspectives from Puerto Rico and the United States

Whether I would be granted access to U.S. Hispanic marketing agencies in New York City was always an issue as I started to think about conducting ethnographic fieldwork on this industry and on its impact on the public definition and projection of U.S. *latinidad*. Prior research and experience working with advertising agencies in Puerto Rico had introduced me to the secrecy that characterizes the marketing industry, to the bureaucracy involved in setting up meetings with informants, and to the difficulty involved in gaining access to strategic planning meetings with corporate clients. What I was surprised to learn, however, was the extent to which such issues would be directly tied to and revealing of the different contexts in which this industry operates in the States and on the island.

In Puerto Rico, though directly tied to transnational advertising networks, the industry operates as a national industry, an intrinsically Puerto Rican operation, whose production is geared to addressing the distinctiveness of the Puerto Rican consumer. This is not unique to Puerto Rico, but is a documented aspect of transnational advertising which, insofar as it operates in national terms—addressing a territorially and culturally distinct constituency and hiring local staff and personnel—sees and projects itself in a similar fashion irrespective of its direct connections with global advertising networks (Miller 1997). In fact, it is this self-presentation that feeds its profitability in local contexts, where advertisers can make connections with local elites and use the idiom of cultural distinctiveness to justify the development of new campaigns directed at the preferences of local consumers. It is also this stance that has prompted scholars to study marketing as a vector of cultural formation (Foster 1999a; O'Barr 1989; Wilk 1995). And indeed, in Puerto Rico, though most agencies are directly involved with global advertising networks, it is Puerto Ricans, construed as a nationally homogeneous constituency, who provide the sole consumer base, while the existence of any other type of consumer is never an issue.

At the time of my research, carried out in postindustrial and "postwork" Puerto Rican society (López 1994), the service industry was on a rapid rise, employing the brightest, most connected, and best-looking *blanquitos*, a popular appellate for the middle- and upper-class, highly educated, light-skinned Puerto Ricans on the island. They made up a privileged sector of the Puerto Rican economy, and one that was difficult to access. Specifically, in contrast to my informants working in U.S. Hispanic marketing, whom I will consider later, those in Puerto Rico seemed to care little if they had already canceled or failed to appear for previous interviews at the arranged time and place. Talking with an anthropologist seemed to be the least of their priorities.

My research in Puerto Rico was not limited to this industry but revolved around larger issues of cultural politics and local cultural production, which arguably could have contributed to marketers' seeming disinterest in my work. After all, I was not exclusively focused on their work and operations, and never gained the level of familiarity and involvement as I later did with U.S. Hispanic marketers. At the same time, the enthusiasm with which U.S. Hispanic marketers greeted me from the inception of my research suggests that other factors, which I will consider later, were also at play. In any event, given that I was primarily concerned with how corporate marketing strategies impacted on local cultural politics, my research was not affected by my restricted access to the marketing industry. My interviews with the advertising staff and marketing representatives for some of the most heavily advertised U.S. brands on the island provided enough information about how marketing strategies affected the island's status debate, their advertising both drawing from and fueling the island's cultural nationalism (Dávila 1997). Brands such as Clorox, Budweiser, and Winston had all become associated with Puerto Rican culture in one way or another, while advertising agencies like Lopito, Ileana, and Howie had become known for their pro–Puerto Rican stance in their product campaigns. And these were no small matters in Puerto Rico, a commonwealth of the United States where expressions of national pride have historically been viewed as suspect and subversive. Thus, poignantly, transnational marketing and advertising were not conceived as a threat to Puerto Rican culture, but rather had been popularly recognized even by island's elites and cultural nationalists as an important institution helping to fuel local cultural production. This stance was vividly reflected in the comment of one informant that "there are no gringos anywhere," emphasizing the marketing industry's autonomy from its corporate clients, as well as in the many nationalist intellectuals working at ad agencies where they saw themselves and their work as promoting and disseminating the value of Puerto Rican culture.

These were the types of issues that triggered my subsequent interest in the U.S. Hispanic marketing industry and its role in the construction and public dissemination of a U.S. Latino/a identity. I was particularly concerned with how the ethnic marketing industry was contributing to the current popularization of U.S. latinidad, to the "salsa beats ketchup" phenomenon, and the seeming Latinization of U.S. popular and mainstream culture. Because this industry's profitability is directly predicated on the existence of Latinos as an undifferentiated people and a market, it was my premise that marketing was greatly responsible for fueling the growing popularization of a common category of identification for the highly diverse peoples of Latin American background in the United States.

I was afraid that U.S. marketers would likely be just as inaccessible as their Puerto Rican counterparts or even more so, in what I anticipated to be a more bureaucratic marketing environment. But to my surprise, my hunches were wrong. After placing random calls to Hispanic ad agencies in New York City to gauge the type of resistance my research was likely to encounter, I soon found someone who showed enthusiasm about my interest in the industry, who assured me that everyone would want to talk to me and that it would be an "important work." Most importantly, this person proceeded to give me names and numbers of people at other agencies I should contact to do my research—all of this over the phone! Obtained a year before I was ready to begin my research, the contacts he gave me meant little to me until later, when I learned that he had provided me with some of the actual founding figures of Hispanic marketing. They included people such as Castor Fernandes, Alicia Conill, and Daisy Exposito, founders of Castor Advertising N.Y., Conill Advertising N.Y., and The Bravo Group N.Y. respectively. These people did indeed require countless phone calls, letters, and pleas before they would talk to me, though this time I was pleased to have meetings canceled by agency founders and directors rather than by account executives at the bottom of an agency's hierarchy. These experiences confronted me early on with the difference that context could make both in the industry and in my ability to study its operations. Specifically, it was soon evident that for most U.S. Hispanic marketers I encountered I was not a nuisance but a likely ally: someone who could potentially validate their work and their market, for whatever I wrote would be "publicity."

I was now an assistant professor, not a graduate student pursuing doctoral research, though this new status was not solely responsible for the more welcoming stance of U.S. Hispanic marketers toward my work. Instead, I soon realized that it was the marginal position of the Hispanic marketing industry and of its prospective base of consumers—U.S. Latinos—within corporate America that was behind it. That is, in contrast to the Puerto Rican marketers interviewed three years earlier, U.S. Hispanic marketers were faced with the challenge not only of selling ideas and ad campaigns to their clients, but, more importantly, with the challenge of proving the existence and viability of "Hispanics" as a targetable market. As one noted: "We Hispanic marketers work twice as hard as do people in the general market. Not only are we in the business of selling marketing ideas but we are also selling our consumer, our market. We are constantly giving people lessons in Hispanic 101." Indeed, the U.S. Hispanic market is not territorially contained as are Puerto Ricans on the island, but rather concerns an ethnic minority on U.S. soil comprising over twenty-seven nationalities and a myriad of differences in variables such as language use, class, politics, ethnicity, and race. Latinos in the United States thus represented a diverse and phantom audience that many corporate clients found difficult to understand and address through advertisements. Moreover, U.S. Hispanic marketers were particularly frustrated to find that their consumer market was often considered an advertising-unworthy audience by corporate clients, most of whom were Anglos with little knowledge of the U.S. Latino consumer and stereotypes of all Latinos as destitute and poor. The specter of Latinos' minority status loomed large in marketers' efforts; they needed to thoroughly prove the advertising worthiness of this population by emphasizing those qualities that rendered them a commercially viable population.

During my research, evidence of the second-class status of the Hispanic consumer included a 1998 memo by Katz Radio Group containing derogatory remarks about blacks and Latinos and implying that advertising for these audiences was appealing to "suspects, not prospects"; it became the subject of great controversy in the industry and public at large (Hispanic Market Weekly 1998). Further evidence came from the lagging advertising expenditures in this market. In 1999, in the midst of the so-called "Latin boom" in U.S. popular culture, the Association of Hispanic Advertising Agencies estimated that Hispanic marketing received only 1 percent of all advertising spending in the United States. This was so even though Latinos made up 11.6 percent of the U.S. population and were supposedly in vogue (Larmer 1999; Riley 2000).

Such disparities make U.S. Hispanic marketers defensive and vulnerable and in greater need of validation of their industry and the viability of their market. Such conditions explain why, unlike their counterparts in Puerto Rico, many U.S. marketers saw in my work a validation and recognition of their own efforts. This was so even when my work was ultimately critical of the essentialist definitions of Latinos so promoted by their commercial representations. In fact, in order to protect their market, the industry has oftentimes resorted to aggressive marketing appeals, and in particular, to images that homogenize Latinos' language use, media habits, values, and disposition in order to give the impression of a unified and sizeable market. The result is the pervasive picture of the Spanish-dominant, traditional, brand-loyal Latino, a faithful watcher of Spanish-language television—a stereotypical and patronizing portrayal of U.S. Latinos.[5] In these constructions, the Spanish language is construed as the paramount basis of U.S. latinidad, as evident in the industry's common designation of

"Hispanic marketing" and "Hispanic-driven media." Indeed, this industry's premise and rationale for existence is not only that there are basic differences between Latinos and other consumers that need to be addressed through culture- and language-specific marketing, but also that there is a continuous influx into the United States of Spanish-speaking people who would not be reached by advertising were it not for this type of marketing.

Access to U.S. Hispanic marketers was additionally assisted by the fact that I am an educated, Spanish-speaking, light-skinned Latina, who presented no threat to their normative ideal of latinidad. This image of the Spanish-speaking, light-complexioned, upward mobile Latino is one they themselves have cultivated and maintained as a means of proving to their clients the worthiness of what is generally considered a marginalized and destitute consumer. And in fact, just like the Puerto Rican marketers mentioned earlier, U.S. Hispanic marketers are mostly from middle-class and upwardly mobile backgrounds, and most significantly, are Spanish-dominant. This, as I discuss later, is a pivotal trait in an industry predicated on the supposed language distinctiveness of Latinos, the greatest rationale for the development of customized campaigns for the U.S. Latino/a consumer.

Yet as the staff at a Los Angeles marketing agency put it, U.S. Hispanic marketing is ultimately "about corporate America, not corporate Hispanic America." Far from an isolated phenomenon, it is an ancillary segment of U.S. marketing and corporate America, and the agencies' productions always depend on their clients' approval. Most of these are Anglo firms representing the local and transnational interests of corporations, adding to the interests screening and affecting the production of commercial representations of Latinos, and most significantly for the purposes of this work, requiring constant interaction between Anglo and Latino personnel in the creation of the ads. This structure in turn has contributed to an ethnic and linguistic division of labor within the industry that also mediated the level of my involvement and ability to study its operations. It is to these dynamics that I now turn.

U.S. Hispanic Marketing and Its Ethnic Division of Cultural Labor

Hispanic marketing now spans a network of more than eighty advertising agencies operating in every U.S. city with a sizable Latino population. Yet only thirty years ago, this industry consisted of little more than a couple of recently arrived Cuban expatriates who were intent on convincing a skeptical corporate America of the existence and profitability of a culturally specific market. Behind this growth were three interdependent and parallel developments: the federal designation in the 1970s of any person of Spanish descent in this country as "Hispanic"; the growing interest on the part of marketers in segmented and targeted campaigns;[6] and the immigration of Cuban expatriates, who had been active in transnational advertising agencies in Cuba and had the expertise and contacts to establish their own agencies in New York, Miami, and later Los Angeles. Today, however, it is not solely these early Cuban entrepreneurs who are marketing to Latino populations but hundreds of self-identified "Latinos" or "Hispanics" attracted to the business opportunity offered by what is now considered one of the fastest growing segments within U.S. marketing.

As a result, U.S. Hispanic marketing is not a homogenous industry but consists of staff who differ in, among other variables, their nationality, race, class, and language use (being Spanish or English dominant). Moreover, the industry's operations and profitability are predicated on this diversity to such an extent that it informs the location of different staff within different sectors of the industry. Specifically, the central place of the Spanish language in this linguistically distinct industry has led to a linguistic division of labor whereby Latin American professionals, who have kept their grammatically correct Spanish language skills, dominate in the creation and dissemination of "Hispanic" images. These are people who have relocated to the United States as adults, often to pursue advanced studies; many have had previous experience in the advertising and marketing industries of some of the major Latin American markets for U.S. brands, such as Mexico and Puerto Rico. Recent imports are particularly common in creative departments, where demands for "perfect language skills" bar most U.S.-born Latinos. For creative jobs, a "pure Latin American" coming from one of the major transnational advertising conglomerates in Latin America is the most favored due to his or her "fresh" and untainted language skills.

Indeed, more than one agency I encountered had just hired someone directly from South America to run their creative departments. Consider the three Mexican creatives who at one point worked at New York City's Castor Advertising. Rodolfo, who joined Castor after working in Ferrer Publicidad in Mexico, explained that he had been hired at Castor only because his CV landed in the hands of his friend Sergio who already worked there. Sergio, in turn, had gotten his job in New York through yet another friend he met in the Dominican Republic where he was sent on assignment by Mexico's Leo Burnett Advertising. When that friend migrated to the United States, Sergio came too, and through him, Rodolfo. In between, Sergio had worked in production in Venezuela where he met Roberto Alcazar who, through his assistance, was eventually hired by Castor Advertising. Rodolfo, a former anthropology major at the University Metropolitana in Mexico, even drew me a kinship chart to explain the multiple connections spanning transnationally to Latin America, and in particular to countries with strong U.S. advertising affiliates such as Mexico, Venezuela, and Puerto Rico.

Meanwhile, Latinos born and/or raised in the United States are more prevalent in production, client services, and research departments. These areas require what was described to me as "more Americanized" skills to handle corporate clients or negotiate with other segments of the industry. The industry craves highly educated bilingual Hispanics whose ethnicity does not present a problem to Anglo clients and who can accurately represent and translate Spanish creative concepts for Anglo clients. These are typically what writers, following Rubén Rumbaut, have called the "one- and one-half generation": individuals who were born in Latin America but were educated and came of age in the United States (Rodríguez 1999, 5). This provides them a simultaneous insider and outsider perspective into both U.S. Hispanics and corporate America.

The inequalities embedded in this ethnic division are evident when we consider that within the advertising industry at large, creatives, that is, the staff who conceive an ad's creative strategy, generally gain more visibility and prestige than any personnel who deal with research, accounts, or clients. It is the creative who wins prizes and name recognition, what Dornfeld (1998) has called "career capital," distinctions stemming from Bourdieu's (1993) discussion of the anti-economic logic that predominates, to various degrees, in different fields of cultural production. It is this form of capital that over and above financial compensation provides an employee with prestige and connections in the industry, which will allow him to found his own agency at a later time. I say "him" purposefully because there is a gender disparity alongside this ethnic division of labor. While women have attained positions of power within the industry, the most renowned creatives I encountered during the course of my research (such as Tony Dieste, Roberto Alcazar, Luis Miguel Messiano, Sergio Alcocer, and Jorge Moya) were all Latin American–born men, as were most agency directors.

These are some of the distinctions that render the label of "Hispanic marketers" not a homogenous construct, just as "Latino" and "Hispanic" do not represent a unique identity. Therefore, contrary to the prevailing view of the relative advantages of native anthropologists, my background did not provide me an unqualified connection with my informants on the basis of a common identity. It did, however, contribute to my research by functioning as a conduit and trigger to conversations about the importance of culture, ethnicity, and national background in the workings and operations of this industry. For one, as documented in other contexts, evaluations of my insider status as a Latina served to reveal the "content" of a given identity, that is, the criteria participants associated with group membership (Lomba de Andrade 2000). Similarly, discussions about our respective accents, speech mannerisms, and fluency (or lack thereof) in Spanish pointed to their emphasis on Spanish as one of the primary defining variables of Latino/a identity. Most revealing, their own and my own background almost always surfaced during conversations, and it was clear that they saw me not as a Latina but as a Puerto Rican, just as they see themselves not as Hispanics or Latinos but rather as members of particular nationalities; these perceptions pointed to the distinctions along lines of nationality and language use that were commonly made by participants and their significance to members of this industry. As previously mentioned, these distinctions are not value neutral, but inform the hierarchical placement of Latino marketers within different sectors of the industry.

Nonetheless, in this industry Hispanic marketers function mostly as "cultural brokers" (Astroff 1997), people who provide the cultural know-how for addressing the Latino consumer but are not the ultimate decisive force in ad creation. Instead, such power is exerted by American investors of Anglo background, who have bought many of the Hispanic ad agencies, or else by the corporate clients who are always in charge of approving and validating the agencies' creations. And suggestively, for my research this became a coveted and inaccessible sector, not because clients were ever given the opportunity to reject me, but rather because my access to them was restricted by Latino marketers themselves who subserviently took to heart the industry's paramount concern with the protection of its clients.

Deference to clients is, of course, not unique to Hispanic marketers but is a common trait in the advertising industry; yet Hispanic marketers' dealings with their clients were additionally shaped by this industry's subordinate position. If I was given a contact on the client's side, it was usually a Latino or Latina working as a corporate representative or ethnic marketing director; these were contacts with whom agency staff had close relations and sometimes friendships, but who were peripheral to the companies' decision-making structures. Anglo personnel at client firms, in contrast, seemed to be omnipresent figures in the minds of the marketers, people they had to defer to and negotiate with but with whom they had few personal relations.

Once again, ethnicity played a role in the maintenance of such a distance, as suggestively expressed in Hispanic marketers' use of "gringos," "Americanos" and "Anglos" almost interchangeably to define their clients. This pointed to their general assumption and awareness that larger corporate America is white and that they saw themselves in opposition to a white Anglo-Protestant ideal, devoid of Blacks, Latinos, or other "ethnics." Within this discursive opposition between "Anglo client" and "Latino marketer," I was a temporary member of their Hispanic marketing community, someone who, like them, was peripheral and subordinate to the corporate client. The following statement from one marketer illustrates how they tended to assimilate me into the "Hispanic" category and how this category was, in turn, defined in opposition to "the Anglo":

> The Hispanic is a very particular race. It has 50 percent of similarities, in that we are all the same: *You and I are attached to our families, we love our families, we respect our ancestors and are proud of them, unlike the American.* We are proud of our roots and keep eating rice and beans. But we are 50 percent different in that the Cuban is different from the Argentinean and he in turn from the Colombian ... What we seek is to tap into that 50 percent that makes us all the same (emphasis added).

I eventually made some contacts with corporate clients, but given that my ethnographic focus was the agencies and their staff, I was happy to limit my research into the corporate side of the business to attending marketing workshops and seminars and reading the trade literature. In exchange, I learned much about the business from the perspective of Hispanic marketers. The latter I found particularly open about their frustrations with corporate clients and other difficult topics, such as the extent to which race and racism permeated the industry and the relationships between the Latino agency staff and their Anglo clients. Perhaps they were even more open than they would have been if I had contacted or identified with their clients. Still, I was unable to access meetings with clients, the real spaces where the commodification of Latino culture takes place.

By calling attention to how ethnicity comes to bear in these culture industries and to its potential role in mediating our access to global industries, I am not proposing that we draw facile assumptions regarding who, on the basis of his/her racial, ethnic, or cultural background, is more likely to have comprehensive access to particular culture industries. Within the study of contemporary global industries—so segmentally organized around ethnicity, as evidenced in the case of Hispanic marketing and my two aforementioned studies—it is increasingly difficult and even irrelevant to distinguish who "belongs" more or less to the "people" one studies when our research concerns not groups or cultures but rather processes and institutional structures impacting the production of cultural representation within global industries. This is why I insisted on deconstructing my own and my informants' Latino/a identity and noted how this putative identity was helpful in some but not other contexts of my study. What I am proposing instead is that engaging these issues is not only essential but in fact may help us probe the operations of global culture industries such as advertising. For, insofar as global culture industries are structuring cultural differences into their own workings and operations—such as by localizing their staff and customizing their creations in ethnic and culturally specific ways— we are more than ever summoned to inquire into the place of ethnicity in the operations of these industries and in their reorganization to address such different constituencies.

Investigating how and in what ways our own identities and backgrounds affect our access to such processes points us to the structuring of race, ethnicity, gender, and nationality within these coveted spaces of globalization. In the case of Hispanic marketing, for instance, my informants' understanding of me as a Latina simultaneously suggested their views about the place of Latinos in the marketing industry and highlighted the pervasive distinctions between Latino marketers and Anglo clients informing their work and advertising creations. Their reception of my work also suggested the structural isolation of Hispanic marketing relative to other sectors of contemporary global marketing, and the active role that ethnicity may play in this position and in our ability to study some marketing sectors in all of their complexity. In this way, our background, as perceived by our informants, can translate to more or less access to different sectors and stages of cultural production. Whether we are seen according to our professional identity, that is, as anthropologists, sociologists, or ethnographers, orin terms of our ethnicity, nationality, or gender—conveys particular allowances or barriers thatcan reveal much about the manners in which ethnicity factors into the hierarchical organization of global marketing. Awareness of these issues does not guarantee access to all of the different levels of cultural production within contemporary global culture industries, but it is certainly more likely to point us toward a closer understanding of the nuanced place of "culture" in their current operations.

Notes

Arlene Dávila's recent book on this topic, *Latinos, Inc.: The Marketing and Making of a People*, was reviewed in *Aztlán: A Journal of Chicano Studies*, 27, no. 2 (fall 2002).

1. See Dell Hymes 1999 for a revealing assessment of changes and continuities in the discipline as a result of the changing contexts of and critical challenges to its premises and operations since the 1970s.

2. Indeed, while such issues have been amply discussed in the anthropological and ethnographic literature, they often take the form of methodological and theoretical considerations, and are less often reflected in the ethnographic record itself. See Abu-Lughod 2000 for a discussion of the need to further study what she calls the "politics of location" and how it affects research and writing. The ongoing gaps between theory and practice in the ethnographic record are discussed by, among others, Willis and Trondman (2000).

3. The location of "native anthropologists" in relation to the discipline is a long-standing issue that has been debated widely and is beyond the scope of this work. Readers may consult Limón 1991, Abu-Lughod 1991, and Jones 1970, among others.

4. My research in Puerto Rico included twenty-two interviews with members of the advertising and marketing industry, focusing primarily on those working on the campaigns of Bacardi, R. J. Reynolds, and Anheuser-Busch. The outcome of this research appears in Dávila 1997. My research in U.S. Hispanic marketing was more extensive and included more than sixty interviews with different advertising staff at sixteen agencies, most of them in New York City, as well as participant observations of their meetings and conventions and other informal discussions in 1997–99. This information was supplemented by content analysis of their advertising disseminated in both the print and broadcast media, and monitoring of major developments in the Hispanic/Latino–oriented and general market industry in trade magazines and ethnic-specific media. See Dávila 2001.

5. In order to adhere to the primary concerns of this work, I will not delve here into the characteristics of the dominant commercial portrayal of Latinos. These issues are discussed in greater detail in Dávila 2001.

6. On this issue see Turow 1997.

Works Cited

Abu-Lughod, Lila. 2000. "Locating Ethnography." *Ethnography* 1, no. 2: 291–98.
———. 1991. "Writing Against Culture." In *Recapturing Anthropology: Working in the Present,* 137–62. Santa Fe, NM: School of American Research.

Astroff, Roberta. 1997. "Capital's Cultural Study: Marketing Popular Ethnography of US Latino Culture." In *Buy this Book: Studies in Advertising and Consumption,* ed. Mica Nava, Andrew Blake, Iain MacRury, and Barry Richards, 120–138. London: Routledge.

Bourdieu, Pierre. 1993. *The Field of Cultural Production.* New York: Columbia University Press.

Calabrese, Andrew. 1999. "The Welfare State, the Information Society, and the Ambivalence of Social Movements." In *Communication, Citizenship, and Social Policy: Rethinking the Limits of the Welfare State,* ed. Andrew Calabrese and Jean-Claude Burgelman, 259–78. Lanham, MD: Rowman and Littlefield.

Dávila, Arlene. 2001. *Latinos, Inc.: The Marketing and Making of a People.* Berkeley and Los Angeles: University of California Press.
———. 1997. *Sponsored Identities: Cultural Politics in Puerto Rico.* Philadelphia: Temple University Press.

Dornfeld, Barry. 1998. *Producing Public Television.* Princeton, NJ: Princeton University Press.

Foster, Robert. 1999a. "The Commercial Construction of 'New Nations.'" *Journal of Material Culture* 4, no. 3: 263–82.
———. 1999b. "Globalization: A Soft Drink Perspective." Work in progress presented in the Anthropology Department, Syracuse University, October.

Gupta, Akhil, and James Ferguson, eds. 1997. *Anthropological Locations: Boundaries of a Field Science.* Berkeley and Los Angeles: University of California Press.

Hannerz, Ulf. 1998. "Transnational Research." In *Handbook of Methods in Cultural Anthropology,* ed. Russell Bernard, 235–58. Walnut Creek, CA: AltaMira.

Hispanic Market Weekly. 1998. "Oops." *Hispanic Market Weekly* 20 (18 May).

Hymes, Dell. 1999. *Reinventing Anthropology.* Ann Arbor: University of Michigan Press.

Jones, Delmos. 1970. "Towards a Native Anthropology." *Human Organization* 29, no. 4: 251–59.

Larmer, Brook. 1999. "Latino America." *Newsweek* (12 July): 50–58.

Limón, Jose. 1991. "Representation, Ethnicity and the Precursory Ethnography: Notes of a Native Anthropologist." In *Recapturing Anthropology: Working in the Present,* 115–36. Santa Fe, NM: School of American Research.

Lomba de Andrade, Lelia. 2000. "Negotiating from the Inside: Constructing Racial and Ethnic Identity in Qualitative Research." *Journal of Contemporary Ethnography* 29, no. 3: 268–90.

López, Milagros. 1994. "Post Work Selves and Entitlement 'Attitude' in Peripheral Postindustrial Puerto Rico." *Social Text* 38: 111–34.

Marcus, George. 1998. *Ethnography Through Thick and Thin.* Princeton, NJ: Princeton University Press.

Miller, Daniel. 1997. *Capitalism: An Ethnographic Approach*. Oxford: Berg.

Miller, Toby. 1999. "Television and Citizenship: A New International Division of Cultural Labor?" In *Communication, Citizenship, and Social Policy: Rethinking the Limits of the Welfare State*, ed. Andrew Calabrese and Jean-Claude Burgelman, 279–92. Lanham, MD: Rowman and Littlefield.

Nader, Laura. 1999 [1969]. "Up the Anthropologist—Perspectives Gained From Studying Up." In *Reinventing Anthropology*, 284–311. Ann Arbor: University of Michigan Press.

O'Barr, William. 1989. "The Airbrushing of Culture: An Insider Looks at Global Advertising." *Public Culture* 2, no. 1: 1–19.

Riley, Jennifer. 2000. "AHAA: Creating a Bridge Between Corporate America and the Hispanic Media." *Hispanic Magazine* (June): 40–46.

Rodríguez, America. 1999. *Making Latino News, Race, Language, Class*. Thousand Oaks, CA: Sage.

Schwartzman, Helen. 1993. *Ethnography in Organizations*. Newbury Park, CA: Sage.

Turow, Joseph. 1997. *Breaking Up America: Advertisers and the New Media World*. Chicago: University of Chicago Press.

Wilk, Richard. 1995. "Learning to Be Local in Belize: Global Systems of Common Difference." In *Worlds Apart: Modernity Through the Prism of the Local*, ed. Daniel Miller, 110–33. London: Routledge.

Willis, Paul, and Mats Trondman. 2000. "Manifesto for Ethnography." *Ethnography* 1, no. 1: 5–17.

Bibliography

Bibliography of Chicana/o Autobiography and Personal Essays in Spanish and English

Primary Literature

Books

Acosta, Oscar Zeta. 1972. *The Autobiography of a Brown Buffalo*. San Francisco: Straight Arrow Books.

———. 1973. *The Revolt of the Cockroach People*. San Francisco: Straight Arrow Books.

Anaya, Rudolpho A. 1986. *A Chicano in China*. Albuquerque: University of New Mexico Press.

Arteaga, A. 1997. *House with the Blue Bed*. San Francisco: Mercury House.

Baca, Jimmy Santiago. 1992. *Working in the Dark: Reflections of a Poet of the Barrio*. Santa Fe, NM: Red Crane Books.

Barrera, Aída. 2001. *Looking for Carrascolendas: from a Child's World to Award-Winning Television*. Austin: University of Texas Press.

Campobello, Nellie. 1988. *Cartucho; and, My Mother's Hands*. Austin: University of Texas Press.

Chacón, R., and J. Meketa. 1986. *Legacy of Honor: The Life of Rafael Chacón, a Nineteenth-Century New Mexican*. Albuquerque: University of New Mexico Press.

Corona, Bert. 1994. *Memories of Chicano History: The Life and Narrative of Bert Corona*, ed. Mario T. García. Berkeley: University of California Press.

Corral, Jesús C. 1984. *Caro Amigo: The Autobiography of Jesús C. Corral*. Tucson, AZ: Westernlore Press.

Demarco, T. 2000. *Vinny Castilla*. Childs, MD: Mitchell Lane Publishers.

Elizondo, Virgilio P. 1988. *The Future Is Mestizo: Life Where Cultures Meet*. Oak Park, IL: Meyer-Stone Books.

Frías, G. 1982. *Barrio Warriors: Homeboys of Peace*. Los Angeles: Díaz.

———. 1989. *Barrio Patriots: Killing and Dying for America*. [Los Angeles?, S.N.].

Fuente, Mario de la, and Baye de Mente. 1972. *I Like You, Gringo—But!* Phoenix, AZ: Phoenix Books.

231

Galarza, Ernesto. 1971. *Barrio Boy*. Notre Dame, IN: University of Notre Dame Press.

Galindo, R., and E. Marcus. 1997. *Icebreaker: The Autobiography of Rudy Galindo*. New York: Pocket Books.

Galvan, Jesse. 1992. *The Way Back: The Autobiography of Jesse Galvan, Jr.: Businessman, Comedian, Federal Employee*. San Antonio, Texas: Watercress Press.

García, Lionel G. 1994. *I Can Hear the Cowbells Ring*. Houston, Texas: Arte Público Press.

García, Mario T. 2000. *Luis Leal: An Auto/Biography*. Austin: University of Texas Press.

García, Ricardo L. 2001. *Coal Camp Days: A Boy's Remembrance*. Albuquerque: University of New Mexico Press.

Gilbert, Fabiola Cabeza de Baca. 1989, 1954. *We Fed Them Cactus*. Albuquerque: University of New Mexico Press.

Gonzales, George L. 1987. *The Other Side of the Coin*. Ogden, Utah: N. P.

Gonzales, Ray. 1993. *Memory Fever: A Journey Beyond El Paso del Norte*. Seattle, WA: Broken Moon Press.

Guerrero, Salvador. *Memorias, a West Texas Life*. Lubbock: Texas Tech. University Press, 1991.

Hart, E. T. 1999. *Barefoot Heart: Stories of a Migrant Child*. Tempe, AZ: Bilingual Press/Editorial Bilingüe.

Herrera, Jess Robert. 1992. *Memories of My Life*. San Francisco: J. R. Herrera.

Herrera, Juan Felipe. 1997. *Mayan Drifter: Chicano Poet in the Lowlands of America*. Philadelphia: Temple University Press.

Jaramillo, Cleofas M. 1941. *Shadows of the Past (Sombras del pasado)*. Santa Fe, NM: Seton Village Press. Reprinted Albuquerque: University of New Mexico Press, 2000.

———. 1955. *Romance of a Little Village Girl*. San Antonio, Texas: Naylor Co. Reprinted Albuquerque: University of New Mexico Press, 2000.

Jiménez, Francisco. 1997. *The Circuit: Stories from the Life of a Migrant Child*. Boston: Houghton Mifflin.

Johnson, Kevin. R. 1999. *How Did You Get to Be Mexican?: A White/Brown Man's Search for Identity*. Philadelphia, PA: Temple University Press.

López, Alma. 2001. *Silencing Our Lady: La respuesta de Alma*. Aztlán: A Journal of Chicano Studies 26, no. 2 (Fall): 249–267.

López, Arcadia H. 1992. *Barrio Teacher*. Houston, Texas: Arte Público Press.

López Tijerina, Reies. 2000. *They Called Me 'King Tiger': My Struggle for the Land and Our Rights*, trans., ed. José Angel Gutierrez. Houston, Texas: Arte Público Press.

Lucas, María Elena. 1993. *Forged Under the Sun: The Life of Maria Elena Lucas*. Ann Arbor: University of Michigan Press.

Marichal, Juan, with Charles Einstein. 1967. *A Pitcher's Story*. Garden City, NY: Doubleday.

Maril, Robert Lee. 1992. *Living on the Edge of America: At Home on the Texas-Mexico Border*. College Station: Texas A & M University Press.

Martin, Patricia Preciado. 1983. *Images and Conversations: Mexican Americans Recall a Southwestern Past*. Tucson: University of Arizona Press.

Martínez, Adrian. 1986. *Adrian: An Autobiography*. Written with Felix Garcia. Austin, Texas: Morgan Printing and Publishing.

Martínez, José. 1970. *A Foot in Two Worlds*. Chicago: Children's Press.

Martínez, Rubén. 2001. *Crossing Over: A Mexican Family on the Migrant Trail*. New York: Metropolitan Books.

Martínez, Víctor. 1996. *Parrot in the Oven: Mi Vida: A Novel*. New York: HarperCollins.

Mendoza, Lydia. 1993. *Lydia Mendoza: A Family Autobiography*. Houston, Texas: Arte Público Press.

Mora, Pat. 1993. *Napantla: Essays from the Land in the Middle*. Albuquerque: University of New Mexico Press.

Moraga, Cherríe. 1983. *Loving in the War Years: Lo Que Nunca Paso Por Sus Labios*. Cambridge, MA: South End Press.

Morales, Dionicio. 1997. *Dionicio Morales: A Life in Two Cultures*. Houston, Texas: Piñata Books.

Nava, Julián. 2002. *Julian Nava: My Mexican-American Journey*. Houston, Texas: Arte Público Press.

Navarrette, Rubén. 1993. *A Darker Shade of Crimson: Odyssey of a Harvard Chicano*. New York: Bantam Books.

Núñez Cabeza de Vaca, Alvar. 1993. *The Account: Alvar Núñez Cabeza de Vaca's Relación*. Houston, Texas: Arte Público Press.

Ochoa, Rubén. 2003. Breaking Down Glass Walls. *Aztlán: A Journal of Chicano Studies* 28, no. 1 (Spring): 175–178.

Osío, Antonio María. 1996. *The History of Alta California: A Memoir of Mexican California*. Madison: University of Wisconsin Press.

Pérez, Ramón Tianguis. 1991. *Diary of an Undocumented Immigrant*. Houston, Texas: Arte Público Press.

Ponce, Mary Helen. 1993. *Hoyt Street: An Autobiography*. Albuquerque: University of New Mexico Press.

Prieto, Jorge. 1989. *Harvest of Hope: The Pilgrimage of a Mexican-American Physician*. Notre Dame, IN: University of Notre Dame Press.

Ramos, J. 2002. *Atravesando Fronteras: La autobiografía de un periodista en busca de su lugar en el mundo*. New York: Rayo.

———. 2003. *No Borders: A Journalist's Search for Home*. New York: Rayo.

Recinos, Harold J. 1989. *Hear the Cry!: A Latino Pastor Challenges the Church*. Louisville, KY: Westminster/John Knox Press.

Ríos, Alberto. 1999. *Capirotada: A Nogales Memoir*. Albuquerque: University of New Mexico Press.

Rivas, R. A. 1977. *Survival: My Life in Love and War*. Hicksville, NY: Exposition Press.

Rodríguez, Luis J. 1994. *Always Running: La Vida Loca, Gang Days in L.A.* New York: Simon and Schuster.

Rodríguez, Richard. 1983. *Hunger of Memory: The Education of Richard Rodríguez: An Autobiography*. New York: Bantam Books.

————. 1992. *Days of Obligation: An Argument with My Mexican Father*. New York: Viking.

————. 2002. *Brown: The Last Discovery of America*. New York: Viking.

Romano-V., Octavio Ignacio. 1990. *Geriatric Fu: My First Sixty Five Years in the United States*. Berkeley, CA: TQS Publications.

Roque Hernández, Lamberto. 2002. *Cartas a Crispina*. Oaxaca, Mexico: Carteles Editores.

Ruiz, D. V. 1981. *A Soul in Exile: A Chicano Lost in Occupied Land*. New York: Vantage Press.

Ruiz, R. E. 2003. *Memories of a Hyphenated Man*. Tucson: University of Arizona Press.

Salas, Floyd. 1992. *Buffalo Nickel*. Houston, Texas: Arte Público Press.

Sanabria, R. 2001. *Stewing in the Melting Pot: The Memoir of a Real American*. Sterling, VA: Capital Books.

Santos, John Phillip. 1999. *Places Left Unfinished at the Time of Creation*. New York: Viking.

Soto, Gary. 1985. *Living Up the Street: Narrative Recollections*. San Francisco: Strawberry Hill Press.

————. 1986. *Small Faces*. Houston, Texas: Arte Público Press.

————. 1988. *Lesser Evils: Ten Quartets*. Houston, Texas: Arte Público Press.

————. 1990. *A Summer Life*. Hanover, NH: University of New England.

————. 1992. *Living Up the Street: Narrative Recollections*. New York: Dell.

Taylor, Sheila Ortiz. 1996. *Imaginary Parents: A Memoir*. Albuquerque: University of New Mexico Press.

Tierra, Tatiana de la. 2002. Activist Latina Lesbian Publishing: esto no tiene nombre and conmoción. *Aztlán: A Journal of Chicano Studies* 27, no. 1 (Spring): 139–178.

Torres, Olga Beatriz. 1994. *Memorias de Mi Viaje: Recollections of My Trip*. Albuquerque: University of New Mexico Press.

Treviño, J. S. 2001. *Eyewitness: A Filmmaker's Memoir of the Chicano Movement*. Houston, Texas: Arte Público Press.

Trujillo, Charley, ed. 1990. *Soldados: Chicanos in Viet Nam*. San Jose, CA: Chusma House.

Tywoniak, Frances Esquibel, and Mario T. García. 2000. *Migrant Daughter:: Coming of Age as a Mexican American Woman*. Berkeley: University of California Press.

Urrea, Luis Alberto. 1998. *Nobody's Son: Notes from an American Life*. Tucson: University of Arizona Press.

————. 1999. *Wandering Times: Western Notebooks*. Tucson: University of Arizona Press.

Villegas de Magnon, Leonor. 1993. *The Rebel*. Houston, Texas: Arte Público Press.

Villaseñor, Victor Edmund. 1991. *Rain of Gold*. Houston, Texas: Arte Público Press.

————. 1994. *Walking Stars: Stories of Magic and Power*. Houston, Texas: Piñata Books.

————. 2001. *Thirteen Senses: A Memoir*. New York: Rayo.

Zúñiga, José. 1994. *Soldier of the Year*. New York: Pocket Books.

Anthologies with Chicano Autobiographies

Anzaldúa, Gloria A. 1990. *Making Face, Making Soul: Haciendo Caras: Creative and Critical Perspectives by Women of Color*. San Francisco: Aunt Lute Foundation Books.

Augenbraum, Harold., ed. 1993. *Growing Up Latino*. Boston: Houghton Mifflin.

Augenbraum, Harold, and Margarite Fernandez Olmos, eds. 1997. *The Latino Reader: An American Literary Tradition from 1542 to the Present*. Boston: Houghton Mifflin.

Binder, Wolfgang, ed. 1985. *Partial Autobiographies: Interviews with Twenty Chicano Poets*. Erlangen, W. Germany: Verlag Palm and Enke.

Cortez, Jaime, ed. 1999. *Virgins, Guerrillas and Locas: Gay Latinos Writing on Love*. San Francisco: Cleis Press.

Delgado, Richard, and J. Stefancic, eds. 1998. *The Latino/a Condition: A Critical Reader*. New York: New York University Press.

Fernández, Roberta, ed. 1994. *In Other Words*. Houston, Texas: Arte Público Press.

González, Ray, ed. 1994. *Currents from the Dancing River*. New York: Harcourt Brace.

Heide, Rich, ed. 2002. *Under the Fifth Sun: Latino Literature from California*. Santa Clara, CA: Santa Clara University.

Hernández-Gutiérrez, Manuel de Jesús, and David William Foster, eds. 1997. *Literatura Chicana, 1965–1995: An Anthology in Spanish, English, and Calo*. New York: Garland Pub.

Horno-Delgado, Asunción., eds. 1989. *Breaking Boundaries: Latina Writing and Critical Readings*. Amherst, MA: University of Massachusetts Press.

Kanellos, Nicolás, ed. 1995. *Hispanic American Literature: A Brief Introduction and Anthology*. New York: Longman.

Ludwig, Ed, and James Santibanez, eds. 1971. *The Chicanos: Mexican American Voices*. Baltimore, MD: Penguin Books.

Noriega, Chon A. and Wendy Belcher, eds. 2004. *I Am Aztlán: The Personal Essay in Chicano Studies*. Los Angeles: UCLA Chicano Studies Research Center Press.

Payne, James Robert, ed. 1992. *Multicultural Autobiography: American Lives*. Knoxville, TN: University of Tennessee Press.

Ramos, Juanita, ed. 1994. *Compañeras: Latina Lesbians: An Anthology*. New York: Routledge.

Siems, Larry, ed. 1992. *Between the Lines: Letters between Undocumented Mexican and Central American Immigrants and Their Families and Friends*. Hopewell, NJ: Ecco Press.

Tatum, Charles M., ed. 1992. *New Chicana/Chicano Writing*. Tucson: University of Arizona Press.

Vázquez, Francisco H., and Rodolfo Torres, eds. 2003. *Latino/a Thought: Culture, Politics, and Society*. Lanham: Rowman and Littlefield.

Personal Essays

Acosta, Oscar Zeta. 1996. Autobiographical Essay. In *Oscar "Zeta" Acosta: The Uncollected Works*, ed. Oscar Zeta Acosta and Ilan Stavans, 3–15. Houston, Texas: Arte Público Press.

———. 1998. Life in the Trenches. In *The Latino/a Condition: A Critical Reader*, ed. Richard Delgado and J. Stefancic, 332–338. New York: New York University Press.

Alvarez, Jorge. 1970. Autobiography in Maize. *El Grito* 3, no. 2 (Winter): 44.

———. Autobiography in Maize. 1972. In *El Espejo-The Mirror: Selected Chicano Literature*, ed. Octavio Ignacio Romano-V. and Herminio Ríos C., 248. Berkeley, CA: Quinto Sol Publications.

———. 1973. Autobiography in Maize. In *From the Belly of the Shark*, ed. Walter Lowenfels, 82–83. New York: Vintage Books.

Alvarez, Julia. 1997. An Unlikely Beginning for a Writer. In *Mascaras*, ed. Lucha Corpi, 188–199. Berkeley, CA: Third Woman Press.

Anaya, Rudolfo A. 1990. Rudolfo A. Anaya: An Autobiography. In *Rudolfo A. Anaya: Focus on Criticism*, ed. César A. González-T., 359–389. La Jolla, CA: Lalo Press.

Anonymous. 1994. Hombre de Palabra (Oral History). In *Compañeras: Latina Lesbians: An Anthology*, ed. Juanita Ramos. New York: Routledge.

Anonymous. 1994. Homofobia: el miedo de una sociedad (Oral History). In *Compañeras: Latina Lesbians: An Anthology*, ed. Juanita Ramos, 44–53. New York: Routledge.

Anonymous. 1994. It Took Everything I Had (Oral History). In *Compañeras: Latina Lesbians: An Anthology*, ed. Juanita Ramos, 44–53. New York: Routledge.

Anzaldúa, Gloria A. 1981. La Prieta. In *This Bridge Called My Back*, ed. Cherríe Moraga, Gloria A. Anzaldúa, and Toni Cade Bambara, 198–204. Watertown, MA: Persephone Press.

———. 1997. Movimientos de rebeldía y las culturas que traicionan. In *Latinos and Education: A Critical Reader*, ed. Antonia Darder , 259–265. New York: Routledge.

Archambeau, Ernest R. Spanish Sheepmen on the Canadian at Old Tascosa. *Panhandle-Plains Historical Review* (1946): 45–73.

Baca, Jimmy Santiago. 1994. Imagine My Life. In *Currents from the Dancing River*, ed. Ray Gonzalez, 514–521. New York: Harcourt Brace.

Baez, Joan. 1971. Thoughts on a Sunday Afternoon. In *The Chicanos: Mexican American Voices*, ed. Ed Ludwig and James Santibanez, 255–260. Baltimore, MD: Penguin Books.

Barraza, Santa C. 2001. The Maguey: Coming Home. *Aztlán: A Journal of Chicano Studies* 26:1 (Spring): 199–202.

Barrera, Nancy. 1984. Mi Sueño. *Revista Mujeres* 1, no. 2 (June): 13–14.

Benavídez, Max. 1997. Subterranean Homesick Blues. *Aztlán: A Journal of Chicano Studies* 22, no. 2 (Fall): 139–149.

Brinson-Piñeda, Barbara. 1985. [Interview With] Barbara Brinson-Piñeda. In *Partial Autobiographies: Interviews with Twenty Chicano Poets*, ed. Wolfgang Binder, 16–27. Erlangen, W. Germany: Verlag Palm and Enke.

Brito, Mónica. 1990. An Autobiography. *Llueve Tlaloc* no. 17: 35.

Bruce-Novoa, Juan. 1990. Mexico in Chicano Literature. In *Retrospace: Collected Essays on Chicano Literature Theory and History*, Juan Bruce-Novoa, 52–62. Houston, Texas: Arte Público Press.

Calvillo, Daniel. 1991. Mi Diario (Segmentos). *Llueve Tlaloc* no. 18: 1–6.

Cancio, Sinsi Mercedes Hernandez. 1990. To Tell One's Story: Women's Self-Definition in Latino Male/Female Relationships. *Latino Studies Journal* 1, no. 2 (May): 74–93.

Canon, James. 1999. My Lessons with Felipe. In *Virgins, Guerrillas and Locas: Gay Latinos Writing on Love*, ed. Jaime Cortez, 65–80. San Francisco: Cleis Press.

Castillo, Ana. 1985. [Interview With] Ana Castillo. In *Partial Autobiographies: Interviews with Twenty Chicano Poets*, ed. Wolfgang Binder, 28–38. Erlangen, W. Germany: Verlag Palm and Enke.

Cervantes, Lorna Dee. 1985. [Interview With] Lorna Dee Cervantes. In *Partial Autobiographies: Interviews with Twenty Chicano Poets*, ed. Wolfgang Binder, 39–53. Erlangen, W. Germany: Verlag Palm and Enke.

Chávez, César E. 1966. The Organizer's Tale. *Ramparts* 5, no. 2 (July): 43–50.

———. 1969. Nonviolence Still Works. *Look Magazine* (April 1): 3.

———. 1973. The Organizer's Tale. In *Chicano: The Evolution of a People*. Compiled by Renato Rosaldo, Robert A. Calvert, Gustav L. Seligmann, 297–302. Minneapolis, MN: Winston Press.

———. 2002. From 'The Organizer's Tale'. In *Under the Fifth Sun: Latino Literature from California*, ed. Rich Heide, 291–296. Santa Clara, CA: Santa Clara University; Berkeley, CA: Heyday Books.

Chávez, Denise. 1989. Heat and Rain (Testimonio). In *Breaking Boundaries: Latina Writing and Critical Readings*, ed. Asuncion Horno-Delgado, 27–32. Amherst, MA: University of Massachusetts Press.

Cisneros, Sandra. 1985. [Interview With] Sandra Cisneros. In *Partial Autobiographies: Interviews with Twenty Chicano Poets*, ed. Wolfgang Binder, 54–74. Erlangen, W. Germany: Verlag Palm and Enke.

Cisneros, Sandra. 1986. Living as a Writer: Choice and Circumstance. *Revista Mujeres* 3, no. 2 (June): 68–72.

———. 1987a. Do You Know Me?: I Wrote The House On Mango Street. *The Americas Review* 15, no. 1 (Spring): 77–79.

———. 1987b. Ghosts and Voices: Writing from Obsession. *The Americas Review* 15, no. 1 (Spring): 69–73.

———. 1987c. Notes to a Young(er) Writer. *The Americas Review* 15, no. 1 (Spring): 74–76.

———. 1990. Only Daughter. *Glamour* (November): 256, 285.

———. 1995a. Ghosts and Voices: Writing from Obsession. In *Hispanic American Literature: A Brief Introduction and Anthology*, ed. Nicolas Kanellos, 45–49. New York: Longman.

————. 1995b. Notes to a Young(er) Writer. In *Hispanic American Literature: A Brief Introduction and Anthology*, ed. Nicolas Kanellos, 50–52. New York: Longman.

————. 1997. Only Daughter. In *Mascaras*, ed. Lucha Corpi, 118–123. Berkeley, CA: Third Woman Press.

Coronado, Raúl, Jr. 1999. Dallas, Summer 1986. In *Virgins, Guerrillas and Locas: Gay Latinos Writing on Love*, ed. Jaime Cortez, 47–51. San Francisco: Cleis Press.

Coronel, Antonio Franco. 1994. De cosas ce California de Antonio Franco Coronel. *Crítica* (Spring): 123–136.

Corpi, Lucha. 1985. [Interview With] Lucha Corpi. In *Partial Autobiographies: Interviews with Twenty Chicano Poets*, ed. Wolfgang Binder, 75–85. Erlangen, W. Germany: Verlag Palm and Enke.

Crawford, John F. 1990. Jimmy Santiago Baca: Interview. In *This Is About Vision: Interviews with Southwestern Writers*, William Balassi, 180–193. Albuquerque: University of New Mexico Press.

————. 1990. Rudolfo Anaya: Interview. In *This Is About Vision: Interviews with Southwestern Writers*, William Balassi, 82–93. Albuquerque: University of New Mexico Press.

Cruz, George Xavier. 1988. Being Hispanic in Houston, TX: From the "Barrio" and Back Again. *The Americas Review* 16, no. 1 (Spring): 53–64.

Cuadros, Gil. 2002. Indulgences. In *Under the Fifth Sun: Latino Literature from California*, ed. Rich Heide, 488–494. Santa Clara, CA: Santa Clara University; Berkeley, CA: Heyday Books.

Cunningham, Veronica. 1985. [Interview With] Veronica Cunningham. In *Partial Autobiographies: Interviews with Twenty Chicano Poets*, ed. Wolfgang Binder, 86–92. Erlangen, W. Germany: Verlag Palm and Enke.

Dávila, Arlene. 2003. Ethnicity, Fieldwork, and the Cultural Capital That Gets Us There: Reflections from U.S. Hispanic Marketing. *Aztlán: A Journal of Chicano Studies* 28, no. 1 (Spring): 145–161.

de Hoyos, Angela. 1985. [Interview With] Angela de Hoyos. In *Partial Autobiographies: Interviews with Twenty Chicano Poets*, ed. Wolfgang Binder, 109–116. Erlangen, W. Germany: Verlag Palm and Enke.

de Leon, Eduardo S. 1996. El Chicano y el Joto. *Latino Studies Journal* 7, no. 3 (Fall): 26–42.

Eysturoy, Annie O. 1990. Denise Chavez: Interview. In *This Is About Vision: Interviews with Southwestern Writers*, William Balassi, 156–169. Albuquerque: University of New Mexico Press.

Franco, Jean. 1990. Joseph Sommers: A Personal Memoir. *Crítica* 2, no. 2 (Fall): 16–18.

Franco, Juan Roberto. 1978. Name Frames II: The Nomenclature of an Autobiography. *Nuestro* 2, no. 8 (August): 36–37.

Gallegos, Magdalena. 1985. The Swallowtail Butterfly. *Colorado Heritage* no. 2: 21–26.

Gamboa Jr., Harry. 1997. Phantoms in Urban Exile. *Aztlán: A Journal of Chicano Studies* 22:2 (Fall): 197–203.

Garcia, Jerry. 2004. The Measure of a Cock: Mexican Cockfighting, Culture, and Masculinity. In *I Am Aztlán: The Personal Essay in Chicano Studies*, ed. Chon A. Noriega and Wendy Belcher. Los Angeles: UCLA Chicano Studies Research Center Press.

Gil, Carlos B. 1989. Washington's Hispano American Communities. In *Peoples of Washington: Perspectives On Cultural Diversity*, ed. Sid White and S.E. Solberg, 159–193. Pullman: Washington State University Press.

Gilbert, Elliot. 1994. An Interview with Luis Valdez. *Low Rider Magazine* 16, no. 11 (November): 22, 27.

Gómez-Peña, Guillermo. 1991. El performance como peregrinación binacional. In *Visual Arts on the U.S./Mexican Border*, ed. Harry Polkinhorn, 73–95. Calexico, CA: Binational Press.

González, Michelle. 1986. Reflexiones de una estudiante chicana. *Fem* 10, no. 48 (October-November): 40–41.

Gonzales, Rebecca. 1985. [Interview With] Rebecca Gonzales. In *Partial Autobiographies: Interviews with Twenty Chicano Poets*, ed. Wolfgang Binder, 93–94. Erlangen, W. Germany: Verlag Palm and Enke.

Groth, Gary. 1989. The Hernandez Bros. Interview. *The Comics Journal* (January): 60–111.

Guerra, Erasmo. 1999. Sexmoneylove. In *Virgins, Guerrillas and Locas: Gay Latinos Writing on Love*, ed. Jaime Cortez, 93–98. San Francisco: Cleis Press.

Guerra de Ord, Angustias de la. 1994. Del testimonio de Doña Angustias de la Guerra de Ord: Ocurrencias en California, relatadas a Thomas Savage en Santa Barbara, 1878. *Crítica* (Spring): 68–74.

Herrera, Juan Felipe. 1989. Memoir: Checker-Piece. In *Best New Chicano Literature*, ed. Julian Palley, 83–87. Tempe, AZ: Bilingual Press.

———. 1991. Mission Street Manifesto: Circa 1959–1982. *Guadalupe Review* no. 1 (October): 175–216.

———. 1992. Blowfish: An Autobiography. In *New Chicana/Chicano Writing 1*, ed. Charles M. Tatum, 119–141. Tucson: University of Arizona Press.

Huerta, Dolores. 1972. Dolores Huerta Talks. *La Voz Del Pueblo* 3, no. 8 (November-December): 8–10, 22.

Lichty-Uribe, Pat. 1994. I Had a Choice. In *Compañeras: Latina Lesbians: An Anthology*, ed. Juanita Ramos, 28–34. New York: Routledge.

López, Enrique Hank. 1971. Back to Bachimba. In *The Chicanos: Mexican American Voices*, ed. Ed Ludwig and James Santibanez, 261–270. Baltimore, MD: Penguin Books.

Lorenzana, Apolinaria. 1994. Memorias de Doña Apolinaria Lorenzana "La Beata" dictadas por ella en Santa Barbara en Marzo de 1878 a Thomas Savage, Bancroft Library 1878. *Crítica* (Spring): 1–14.

Lorenzo, Orestes. 1993. Power of Love. *Hispanic* (May): 50, 52, 54.

Luna, Jesús. 1973. Luna's Abe Lincoln Story. In *Chicano: The Evolution of a People*, ed. Renato Rosaldo, Robert A. Calvert, Gustav L. Seligmann, 347–355. Minneapolis, MN: Winston Press.

Machado de Ridington (Wrightington), Juana. 1994. Los tiempos pasados de la alta California: Recuerdos de la Sra. Doña Juana Machado de Ridington, Bancroft Library 1878. *Crítica* (Spring): 15–29.

Martínez, Elisa A. 1983. Sharing Her Tiny Pieces of the Past. *Nuestro* 7, no. 7 (September): 51–52.

Martínez, Jesús. 1993. National Identity and Binational Migration: An Autobiography. *San Jose Studies* [San Jose State University] 19, no. 1 (Winter): 89–103.

Martínez, Oscar. 1993. Gregorio Hernandez Moreno: Diary of an Undocumented Worker. *Journal of Borderlands Studies* 8, no. 2 (Fall): 59–72.

Mendoza, Lupe. 1984. ¿Porque lo podemos hacer—a poco no? *Revista Mujeres* 1, no. 2 (June): 33–37.

Mohr, Nicholasa. 1986. On Being Authentic. *The Americas Review* 14, no. 3–4 (Fall-Winter): 106–109.

Molleur, Suzanne. 1974. A Chicano Bishop Looks At His Church: An Interview with Bishop Flores. *Saint Anthony Messenger* 82, no. 5 (October): 37.

Montoya, Margaret E. 1998. Masks and Acculturation. In *The Latino/a Condition: A Critical Reader*, ed. Richard Delgado and J. Stefancic, 435–441. New York: New York University Press.

———. 1998. Masks and Identity. In *The Latino/a Condition: A Critical Reader*, ed. Richard Delgado and J. Stefancic, 37–43. New York: New York University Press.

Moraga, Cherríe. 1981. La Güera. In *This Bridge Called My Back*, ed. Cherríe Moraga, Gloria A. Anzaldúa, and Toni Cade Bambara, 27–34. Watertown, MA: Persephone Press.

———. 2003. Queer Aztlán: The Re-Formation of Chicano Tribe. In *Latino/a Thought: Culture, Politics, and Society*, ed. Francisco H. Vázquez and Rodolfo Torres, 258–274. Lanham, MD: Rowman and Littlefield.

Morales, Tomás. 1985. Entering the "New World" of College. *Nuestro* 9, no. 9 (November): 48.

Negrón-Muntaner, Frances. 1999. Beyond the Cinema of the Other or Toward Another Cinema. *Aztlán: A Journal of Chicano Studies* 24, no. 2 (Fall): 149–154.

Nericcio, William Anthony. 1988. Autobiographies at La Frontera: The Quest for Mexican-American Narrative. *The Americas Review* 16, no. 3–4 (Fall-Winter): 165–187.

Noriega, Chon A. 2002. Research Note. *Aztlán: A Journal of Chicano Studies* 27, no. 2 (Fall): 1–8.

Olivas, Michael A. 1990. The Chronicles, My Grandfather's Stories, and Immigration Law: The Slave Trader's Chronicle as Racial History. *Saint Louis University Law Journal* 34, no. 3 (Spring): 425–441.

———. 1998. "Breaking the Law" on Principle. In *The Latino/a Condition: A Critical Reader*, ed. Richard Delgado and J. Stefancic, 320–331. New York: New York University Press.

Osuna de Marrón, Felipa. 1994. Recuerdos de Doña Felipa Osuna de Marrón natural de San Diego donde vive actualmente con varios papeles originales pertenecientes al archivo particular de la misma señora, que los obsequio a la Bancroft Library 1878. *Crítica* (Spring): 45–53.

P., Terry de la. 1991. Beyond el Camino Real. In *Chicana Lesbians: The Girls Our Mothers Warned Us About*, ed. Carla Trujillo. Berkeley, CA: Third Woman Press.

Paredes, Américo. 1993. The Hammon and the Beans. In *Growing Up Latino*, ed. Harold Augenbraum, 159–164. Boston: Houghton Mifflin.

Pérez, Emma. 1991. Gulf Dreams. In *Chicana Lesbians: The Girls Our Mothers Warned Us About*, ed. Carla Trujillo. Berkeley, CA: Third Woman Press.

Pérez, Eulalia. 1994. Eulalia Perez, una vieja y sus recuerdos dictados a la edad avanzada de 139 anos, San Gabriel, California, 1877. *Crítica* (Spring): 31–44.

———. 1997. An Old Woman Remembers. In *The Latino Reader: An American Literary Tradition from 1542 to the Present*, ed. Harold Augenbraum and Margarite Fernandez Olmos, 72–80. Boston: Houghton Mifflin.

Pérez, Vincent. 1999. Heroes and Orphans of the Hacienda: Narratives of a Mexican American Family. *Aztlán: A Journal of Chicano Studies* 24, no. 1 (Spring): 33–106.

Pesqueira, Randy. 1999. Daddycakes. In *Virgins, Guerrillas and Locas: Gay Latinos Writing on Love*, ed. Jaime Cortez, 53–57. San Francisco: Cleis Press.

Pico, María Inocenta. 1994. Cosas de California contadas a Thomas Savage en Avila y San Luis Obispo por Doña Maria Inocenta Pico, viuda de Don Miguel Avila, 1878 Bancroft Library. *Crítica* (Spring): 57–66.

Pineda, Cecile. 1997. Deracinated: The Writer Re-Invents Her Sources. In *Mascaras*, ed. Lucha Corpi, 56–70. Berkeley, CA: Third Woman Press.

Ponce, Mary Helen. 1983. El jabon de Doña Chonita. *Nuestro* 7, no. 10 (December): 44–45.

———. 1994. The Day Rito Died. In *Currents from the Dancing River*, ed. Ray Gonzalez, 197–203. New York: Harcourt Brace.

———. 1997. On Language. In *Mascaras*, ed. Lucha Corpi, 110–117. Berkeley, CA: Third Woman Press.

Prado, José M. 1994. From Farm Work to a Washington Fellowship. *The Hispanic Outlook in Higher Education* 4, no. 12 (April 15): 6–7.

Prida, Dolores. 1989. The Show Goes On (Testimonio). In *Breaking Boundaries: Latina Writing and Critical Readings*, ed. Asuncion Horno-Delgado, 181–188. Amherst, MA: University of Massachusetts Press.

Quinn, Manuela (Nellie). 2002. From the Original Sin. In *Under the Fifth Sun: Latino Literature from California*, ed. Rich Heide, 229–236. Santa Clara, CA: Santa Clara University; Berkeley, CA: Heyday Books.

Quintana, Alvina E. 1998. Turning Sunshine into Noir and Fantasy into Reality: Los Angeles in the Classroom. *Aztlán: A Journal of Chicano Studies* 23, no. 2 (Fall): 179–189.

Ramírez, Walter C. 1993. Diary of a Madman. In *New Chicana/Chicano Writing 3*, ed. Charles M. Tatum, 115–140. Tucson: University of Arizona Press.

Rebolledo, Tey Diana. 1990. Pat Mora: Interview. In *This Is About Vision: Interviews with Southwestern Writers*, William Balassi, 128–139. Albuquerque: University of New Mexico Press.

Reynoso, Cruz. 2002. Brief Remembrances: My Appointment and Service on the California Court of Appeal and Supreme Court, 1976–1987. *Berkeley La Raza Law Journal* 13, no. 1 (Spring): 15–27.

Rips, Geoffrey. 1983. Living History: Emma Tenayuca Tells Her Story. *Texas Observer* (October, 28): 7–15.

Rivera, Edward. 1993. First Communion. In *Growing Up Latino*, ed. Harold Augenbraum, 211–249. Boston: Houghton Mifflin.

Rodríguez, Richard. 1974. Going Home Again: The New American Scholarship Boy. *American Scholar* 44, no. 1: 15–28.

———. 1989. An American Writer. In *The Invention of Ethnicity*, ed. Werner Sollors, 3–13. New York: Oxford University Press.

———. 1993. Aria. In *Growing Up Latino*, ed. Harold Augenbraum, 305–328. Boston: Houghton Mifflin.

———. 1997. Prologue: Middle-Class Pastoral. In *Literatura Chicana, 1965–1995: An Anthology in Spanish, English, and Calo*, ed. Manuel de Jesús Hernández-Gutiérrez and David William Foster, 62–65. New York: Garland Pub.

———. 1998. A Scholarship Boy. In *The Latino/a Condition: A Critical Reader*, ed. Richard Delgado and J. Stefancic, 419–420. New York: New York University Press.

Romo, Ricardo. 1986. A Westside Story. *Texas Observer* 78, no. 25 (December): 10–12.

Roque Ramírez, Horacio N. 1999. El Sereno. In *Virgins, Guerrillas and Locas: Gay Latinos Writing on Love*, ed. Jaime Cortez, 5–12. San Francisco: Cleis Press.

Ruelas, J. Oshi. 1987. Moments of Change. *Revista* Mujeres 4, no. 1 (January): 23–33.

Sandoval, Anna. 1999–2000. Building Up Our Resistance: Chicanas in Academia. *Frontiers: A Journal of Women Studies* 20, no. 1: 86–92.

Sandoval, Lito. 1999. I Love You Also. In *Virgins, Guerrillas and Locas: Gay Latinos Writing on Love*, ed. Jaime Cortez, 27–30. San Francisco: Cleis Press.

Schirra, Roger. 1999. News of Your Country. In *Virgins, Guerrillas and Locas: Gay Latinos Writing on Love*, ed. Jaime Cortez, 83–92. San Francisco: Cleis Press.

Seguín, John N. 2003. The Making of a Tejano: The Personal Memoirs of John N. Seguín. In *Latino/a Thought: Culture, Politics, and Society*, ed. Francisco H. Vazquez and Rodolfo Torres, 102–121. Lanham, MD: Rowman and Littlefield.

Sierra, Rubén. 1979. [Untitled Autobiography]. *Metamorfosis* 2, no. 1–2 (Summer): 5.

Small, Mario. 1996. West Indian Latino. *Latino Studies Journal* 7, no. 3 (Fall): 43–47.

Smith, Norman. 1986. Buffalos and Cockroaches: Acosta's Siege at Aztlán. In *Contemporary Chicano Fiction: A Critical Survey*, ed. Vernon E. Lattin, 82–93. Binghamton, NY: Bilingual Press/Editorial Bilingüe.

Solís, Manuel. 1996. Growing Up Tejano. *Latino Studies Journal* 7, no. 3 (Fall): 17–25.

Soriano, Diane H. 1984. "Ni he tenido tiempo para mi": Entrevista con Gabriella S. Mejia. *Revista Mujeres* 1, no. 2 (June): 38–41.

Sosa, Maribel. 1999. Sense and Responsibility. *Frontiers: A Journal of Women Studies* 20, no. 1: 97–104.

Soto, Gary. 1993. Being Mean. In *Growing Up Latino*, ed. Harold Augenbraum, 274–279. Boston: Houghton Mifflin.

Thomas, Raul. 1999. They Say I'm One of Those: Excerpts from Dicen Que Soy. In *Virgins, Guerrillas and Locas: Gay Latinos Writing on Love*, ed. Jaime Cortez, 33–45. San Francisco: Cleis Press.

Thwaites, Jeanne. 1992. The Use of Irony in Oscar Zeta Acosta's *The Autobiography of a Brown Buffalo*. *The Americas Review* 20, no. 1 (Spring): 73–82.

Tijerina, Aleticia. 1994. I Am the Lost Daughter of My Mama's House (Oral History). In *Compañeras: Latina Lesbians: An Anthology*, ed. Juanita Ramos. New York: Routledge.

Trujillo, Carla. 1992. Confessions of a Chicana PhD: On Lesbians, Class, and Interracial Relationships. *Out/Look* (Winter): 23–27.

Urrea, Luis Alberto. 1994. Father's Day. In *Currents from the Dancing River*, ed. Ray Gonzalez, 198–111. New York: Harcourt Brace.

Vallejo, Manuel Salvador. 1994. De notas históricas sobre California de Jose Manuel Salvador Vallejo, Sonoma, California, 1874. *Crítica* (Spring): 91–104.

Vallejo, Platón Mariano Guadalupe. 1994. From Memoirs of the Vallejos. *Crítica* (Spring): 106–122.

Vela, Richard R. 1978. Autobiography with Horses. *De Colores* 4, no. 1–2: 52.

———. 1978. Poetry. *De Colores* 4, no. 1–2: 50–52.

Vicioso, Sherezada (Chiqui). 1989. An Oral History (Testimonio). In *Breaking Boundaries: Latina Writing and Critical Readings*, ed. Asuncion Horno-Delgado, 229–234. Amherst, MA: University of Massachusetts Press.

Villalón, Joel Antonio. Boots. 1999. In *Virgins, Guerrillas and Locas: Gay Latinos Writing on Love*, ed. Jaime Cortez, 13–25. San Francisco: Cleis Press.

Villanueva, Alma Luz. 1985. [Interview With] Alma Villanueva. In *Partial Autobiographies: Interviews with Twenty Chicano Poets*, ed. Wolfgang Binder, 201–202. Erlangen, W. Germany: Verlag Palm and Enke.

———. 1997. Abundance. In *Mascaras*, ed. Lucha Corpi, 36–55. Berkeley, CA: Third Woman Press.

Villegas, Ygnacio. 2002. From Boyhood Days. In *Under the Fifth Sun: Latino Literature from California*, ed. Rich Heide, 8–10. Santa Clara, CA: Santa Clara University; Berkeley, CA: Heyday Books.

Viramontes, Helena María. 1989. "Nopalitos": The Making of Fiction. In *Breaking Boundaries: Latina Writing and Critical Readings*, ed. Asuncion Horno-Delgado, 33–38. Amherst: University of Massachusetts Press.

———. 1990. "Nopalitos": The Making of Fiction. In *Making Face, Making Soul: Haciendo Caras: Creative and Critical Perspectives by Women of Color*, ed. Gloria Anzaldúa, 291–294. San Francisco: Aunt Lute Foundation Books.

Williams, Norma. 1988. A Mexican American Woman Encounters Sociology: An Autobiographical Perspective. *American Sociologist* 19, no. 4 (Winter): 340–346.

Zamora, Bernice. 1985. [Interview With] Bernice Zamora. In *Partial Autobiographies: Interviews with Twenty Chicano Poets*, ed. Wolfgang Binder, 221–229. Erlangen, W. Germany: Verlag Palm and Enke.

————. 1997. Silence at Bay. In *Mascaras*, ed. Lucha Corpi, 20–34. Berkeley, CA: Third Woman Press.

Zamora, Rodolfo. 1999. The Lost City. In *Virgins, Guerrillas and Locas: Gay Latinos Writing on Love*, ed. Jaime Cortez, 59–63. San Francisco: Cleis Press.

Secondary Literature

Adams, Timothy Dow. 2001. "Heightened by Life" vs. "Paralyzed by Fact": Photography and Autobiography in Norma Cantu's Canicula. *Biography* 24, no. 1 (Winter): 57.

Alvarez, Francisco R. 1993. *The Autobiography of a Brown Buffalo* de Oscar Zeta Acosta: Escritura, ser e ideología en la autobiografía chicana de los 70. *Monographic Review*: 162–175.

Bell, Michael Davitt. 1982. Fitting into a Tradition of Autobiography. *Change* 14, no. 7 (October): 36–39.

Bello, Ruth T. 1988. Being Hispanic in Houston, TX: A Matter of Identity. *The Americas Review* 16, no. 1 (Spring): 31–43.

Bellver, Pilar. 1999. La historia oral como autobiografía cultural: dos ejemplos chicanos. *Aztlán: A Journal of Chicano Studies* 24, no. 2 (Fall): 49–72.

Bruce-Novoa, Juan. 1985. Mexico en la literatura chicana (II). *La Comunidad* no. 268 (September 8): 14–15.

————. 1986. Homosexuality and the Chicano Novel. *Confluencia* 2, no. 1 (Fall): 69–77.

————. 1990. Mexico in Chicano Literature. In *Retrospace: Collected Essays On Chicano Literature Theory and History*, ed. Juan Bruce-Novoa, 52–62. Houston, Texas: Arte Público Press.

————. 1995–1996. The U.S.-Mexican Border in Chicano Testimonial Writing: A Topological Approach to Four Hundred and Fifty Years of Writing the Border. *Discourse* [Berkeley, CA] 18, no. 1–2 (Fall-Winter): 32–53.

Cancio, Sinsi Mercedes Hernández. 1990. To Tell One's Story: Women's Self-Definition in Latino Male/Female Relationships. *Latino Studies Journal* 1, no. 2 (May): 74–93.

Christopher, Renny. 2002. Rags to Riches to Suicide: Unhappy Narratives of Upward Mobility: Martin Eden, Bread Givers, Delia's Song, and Hunger of Memory. *College Literature* 29, no. 4 (Fall): 79–109.

Davis, Rocío G. 2002. Metanarrative in Ethnic Autobiography for Children: Laurence Yep's *The Lost Garden* and Judith Ortiz Cofer's *Silent Dancing*. *MELUS: Multi-Ethnic Literature of the United States* 27, no. 2 (Summer): 139–156.

Fachinger, Petra. 2001. Lost in Nostalgia: The Autobiographies of Eva Hoffman and Richard Rodriguez. *MELUS: Multi-Ethnic Literature of the United States* 26, no. 2 (Summer): 111–127.

Fernández, Roberta. 1997. Depicting Women's Culture in Intaglio: A Novel in Six Stories. In *Mascaras*, ed. Lucha Corpi, 72–96. Berkeley, CA: Third Woman Press.

Fischer, Michael M. J. 1986. Ethnicity and the Post-Modern Arts of Memory. In *Writing Culture: The Poetics and Politics of Ethnography*, ed. James Clifford and George E. Marcus, 194–233. Berkeley: University of California Press.

Flores, Lauro. 1990. Chicano Autobiography: Culture, Ideology and the Self. *The Americas Review* 18, no. 2 (Summer): 80–91.

Gamio, Manuel. 1980. Señora Flores de Andrade. In *Mexican Women in the United States: Struggles Past and Present*, Magdalena Mora and Adelaida del Castillo, 189–192. Los Angeles: UCLA Chicano Studies Research Center.

Herrera-Sobek, María. 1997. Geography of Despair: The Mean Streets of L.A. of Luis Rodriguez's *Always Running*. *Latino Studies Journal* 8, no. 2 (Spring): 56–67.

Hunsaker, Alan C. 1990. Book Review of *The Autobiography of a Brown Buffalo* and *the Revolt of the Cockroach People*. *Hispanic Journal of Behavioral Sciences* 12, no. 3 (August): 328–334.

Iwabuchi, D. S., and R. Stuhr-Rommereim. 2003. *Autobiographies by Americans of Color, 1995–2000: An Annotated Bibliography*. Albany, NY: Whitston Publishing Co.

Kowalczyk, Kimberly A. 1988. Oscar Zeta Acosta: The Brown Buffalo and His Search for Identity. *The Americas Review* 16, no. 3–4 (Fall-Winter): 198–209.

Marinic, S. 1996. *Contemporary Autobiography in the Mexican American Borderland: Richard Rodriguez in Perspective*. Austria: University of Salzburg.

Márquez, Antonio C. 1984. Richard Rodriguez's Hunger of Memory and the Poetics of Experience. *Arizona Quarterly* 40, no. 2 (Summer): 130–141.

———. 1987–1988. Self and Culture: Autobiography as Cultural Narrative. *Bilingual Review* 14, no. 3 (September-December): 57–64.

———. 1990. Self and Culture: Autobiography as Cultural Narrative. *Discurso literario: Revista de temas hispanicos* 7, no. 1: 51–66.

McKenna, Teresa. 1997. *Migrant Song: Politics and Process in Contemporary Chicano Literature*. Austin: University of Texas Press.

Murray, David. 1988. Authenticity and Text in American Indian, Hispanic and Asian Autobiography. In *First Person Singular: Studies in American Autobiography*, ed. A. Robert Lee, 177–197. New York: St. Martin's Press.

Nericcio, William Anthony. 1988. Autobiographies at La Frontera: The Quest for Mexican-American Narrative. *The Americas Review* 16, no. 3–4 (Fall-Winter): 165–187.

Neumaier, Diane. 1990. Judy Baca: Our People Are the Internal Exiles. In *Making Face, Making Soul: Haciendo Caras: Creative and Critical Perspectives by Women of Color*, ed. Gloria Anzaldúa, 256–270. San Francisco: Aunt Lute Foundation Books.

Nuiry, Octavio Emilio. 1993. Book Review of *Growing Up Latino. Hispanic* (August): 62.

Olazagasti-Segovia, Elena. 2000. The Mother Figure. *Latino(a) Research Review* 4, no. 3 (Winter): 40–42.

Padilla, Amado M. 2003. The Origins of the Hispanic Journal of Behavioral Sciences: A Personal Memoir. *Hispanic Journal of Behavioral Sciences* 25, no. 1 (February): 3–12.

Padilla, Genaro M. 1984. The Self as Cultural Metaphor in Acosta's *The Autobiography of a Brown Buffalo. The Journal of General Education* 35, no. 4: 242–258.

———. 1988. The Recovery of Chicano Nineteenth-Century Autobiography. *American Quarterly* 40, no. 3 (September): 286–307.

———. 1988. "Yo Sola Aprendi": Contra-Patriarchal Containment in Women's Nineteenth- Century California Personal Narratives. *The Americas Review* 16, no. 3–4 (Fall-Winter): 91–109.

———. 1991. Imprisoned Narrative? or Lies, Secrets, and Silence in New Mexico Women's Autobiography. In *Criticism in the Borderlands: Studies in Chicano Literature, Culture, and Ideology*, ed. Héctor Calderón and José David Saldívar, 43–60. Durham, NC: Duke University Press.

———. 1993. Discontinuous Continuities: Remapping the Terrain of Spanish Colonial Narrative. In *Reconstructing a Chicano/a Literary Heritage*, ed. Maria Herrera-Sobek, 24–36. Tucson: University of Arizona Press.

———. 1993. *My History, Not Yours: The Formation of Mexican American Autobiography*. Madison: University of Wisconsin Press.

Paredes, Raymund A. 1992. Autobiography and Ethnic Politics: Richard Rodriguez's *Hunger of Memory*. In *Multicultural Autobiography: American Lives*, ed. James Robert Payne, 280–296. Knoxville: University of Tennessee Press.

Pines, Paul. 1992. Book Review of *Working in the Dark. Multicultural* Review 1, no. 3 (July): 48.

Portales, Marco A. 1998. Book Review of *From Labor to Letters: A Novel Autobiography. MELUS: Multi-Ethnic Literature of the United States* 23, no. 1 (Spring): 177–181. 50

Ramírez, Arthur. 1975. Book Review of *The Autobiography of a Brown Buffalo* and *The Revolt of the Cockroach People. Revista Chicano-Riquena* 3, no. 3 (Summer): 46–53.

Randolph, Donald A. 1988. Autobiography as Pain: Anthony Quinn's *The Original Sin. The Americas Review* 16, no. 3–4 (Fall-Winter): 144–164.

Rivera, Tomás. 1984. Richard Rodriguez's *Hunger of Memory* as a Humanistic Antithesis. *MELUS: Multi-Ethnic Literature of the United States* 11, no. 4 (Winter): 5–13.

Rockwell, Susan L. 1994. Book Review of *My History, Not Yours: The Formation of Mexican American Autobiography. Explorations in Sights and Sounds* no. 14 (Summer): 62–64. 1994: 6–7.

Rodríguez, Luis J. 1991. Literacy and the Writer's Spirit. *Guadalupe Review* no. 1 (October): 277–280.

Rodríguez, Randy A. 1998. Richard Rodríguez Reconsidered: Queering the Sissy (Ethnic) Subject. *Texas Studies in Literature and Language* 40, no. 4 (Winter): 396–424.

Romero, Lora. 1993. "When Something Goes Queer": Familiarity, Formalism, and Minority Intellectuals in the 1980s. *The Yale Journal of Criticism* 6, no. 1 (Spring): 121–42.

Romero, Osvaldo. 1974. Book Review of *The Autobiography of a Brown Buffalo*. *Oester* 4, no. 2 (April): 141.

Rose, Shirley K. 1987. Metaphors and Myths of Cross-Cultural Literacy: Autobiographical Narratives by Maxine Hong Kingston, Richard Rodriguez and Malcolm X. *MELUS: Multi-Ethnic Literature of the United States* 14, no. 1 (Spring): 3–15.

Sabat-Rivers, Georgina. 1983. Book Review of *A Woman of Genius: The Intellectual Autobiography of Sor Juana Inés de la Cruz*. *Nuestro* 7, no. 6 (August): 62–64.

Saldívar, José David. 1992. The School of Caliban: Pan-American Autobiography. In *Multicultural Autobiography: American Lives*, ed. James Robert Payne, 297–325. Knoxville: University of Tennessee Press.

Saldívar, Ramón. 1985. Ideologies of the Self: Chicano Autobiography. *Diacritics* 15, no. 3 (Fall): 25–34.

———. 1990. *Narrative: The Dialectics of Difference*. Madison: University of Wisconsin Press.

Sánchez, Rosaura. 1995. *Telling Identities: The Californio Testimonios*. Madison: University of Wisconsin Press.

Schilt, Paige. 1998. Anti-Pastoral and Guilty Vision in Richard Rodriguez's *Days of Obligation*. *Texas Studies in Literature and Language* 40, no. 4 (Winter): 424–432.

Scotto, Barbara. 1990. Book Review of *A Summer Life*. *Wilson Library Bulletin* 65, no. 3 (November): 142–143.

Shirley, Carl R. 1988. *Understanding Chicano Literature*. Columbia: University of South Carolina Press.

Smith, Norman. 1986. Buffalos and Cockroaches: Acosta's Siege at Aztlán. In *Contemporary Chicano Fiction: A Critical Survey*, ed. Vernon E. Lattin, 82–93. Binghamton, NY: Bilingual Press/Editorial Bilingüe.

Staten, Henry. 1998. Ethnic Authenticity, Class, and Autobiography: The Case of Hunger of Memory. *PMLA* 113, no. 1 (January): 103–117.

Stuhr-Rommereim, Rebecca. 1997. *Autobiographies by Americans of Color 1980–1994: An Annotated Bibliography*. Troy, NY: Whiston Publishing Co.

Torres, Héctor A. 1992. Chicano Narrative: The Dialectics of Difference. *College Literature* 19, no. 3 (Oct-Feb): 265–70.

Torres, Lourdes. 1991. The Construction of the Self in U.S. Latina Autobiographies. In *Third World Women and the Politics of Feminism*, ed. Chandra Talpade Mohanty, 272–287. Bloomington: Indiana University Press.

Trouve, Maria del Carmen. 1997. La mujer en la negociación de la identidad chicana: *The Autobiography of a Brown Buffalo*, de Oscar Zeta Acosta. In *Jornadas de la asociación argentina de estudios americanos: ponencias*, ed. Rolando Costa Picazo, 377–386. [Rio Cuarto, Argentina]: Editorial de La Fundación, Universidad Nacional de Rio Cuarto.

Velasco, Juan. 1995. *Los laberintos de la mexicanidad: la construcción de la identidad en la autobiografía chicana contemporánea.* Ph.D. diss., University of California, Los Angeles.

Woods, Richard D. 1988. *Mexican Autobiography: An Annotated Bibliography [La autobiografía Mexicana: Una bibliografía razonada].* New York: Greenwood Press.

Zavala, Iris M. 1982. Ideologías y autobiografías: Perspectivas femeninas. *Third Woman* 1, no. 2: 35–39.

Index

Boldface locators indicate photographs, tables, and illustrations.

A

Absalom, Absalom! (Faulkner), 53
acculturation, selective, 121
acquired speech, 6
advertising. *see* U.S. Hispanic marketing
Afro-Puerto Ricans, 35
agricultural laborers, 60–61
agricultural workers' strike, 1936, 61
Aguascalientes, Valley of, 68
Aguilar, Antonio, 26, 29
AIDS in Puerto Rican film, 36–37
AIDS in the Barrio (film, 1989), 33, 36, 37
Almarez, Carlos, 185 n3
Almerez, Roberta, 163
American Dream, 203
American ideology, ethnic/racial difference in, 203–204
Americans as exiles, 202
American Southwest
   cockfighting, 110, 112, 115
   "critical mass" of Mexicans in, 202
   hacienda (rancho) system, 51
   Mexican immigration into, 8
   Mexican Revolution's impact on, 99 n15
   nineteenth century, 54
   perception of East Coast, 202
A Mistaken Minority with a Wonder Bread Identity Tows the Thin Line Between Art, Pornography and Living Happily Ever After (Almarex), 163
Anglo American attitudes toward Mexicans, 125, 203
Anglo American biases, 124, 203–204

Anglo American cockfighting, 117, 126. *see also* cockfighting in the Pacific Northwest; cockfighting in the United States
Anglo American colonialism, 45, 64
Anglo American conquest, 45
Anglo American culture
   bicultural identity in, 101
   Mexican American identity and, 57, 59, 60, 92, 101
   racism, 203
Anglo American hegemony
   cause of alienation, 101
   influence on Mexican American foundational narratives, 45
   Mexican American cultural identity, 45, 50, 90
   sociocultural regime, 57, 59, 60
Anglo Americans
   in art world, 196
   experience of masculinity compared to Mexicans, 119
   life in Texas, 123
   Mexican attitudes towards, 8, 101 n21, 100 n20–101 n20, 144
   Mexican, Mexican American alienation from, 100 n20–101 n20, 144
   in U.S. Hispanic Marketing, 214, 218–219, 221–223
Anglo and Miami Lesbian communities compared, 143–144
antemadres, 19
antepadres, 19
anthropology. *see* ethnography
Anzaldúa, Gloria, 21, 97 n7, 207–208
Arango, Doroteo. *see* Villa, Francisco "Pancho"

Archuleta Sagel, Teresa, 178–179
art
    for art's sake, 196
    establishment of identity through, 3
    Latin American, 184
    public, x
    reestablishment of past through, 3
    as witness, 9–10
    women as subjects of, 182–183
ASCO (East L.A. art group), 8
assimilation
    cockfighting as buffer, 134
    markers of, 133–134
    and Mexican self, 9, 53
    pressures of, 221
    from Puerto Rican to Hispanic, 223
    "resistance masculinity," 133
    of Róbles Pérez progeny, 93
    in workplace, 121
Association of Hispanic Advertising
    Agencies, 218
Astraea, National Lesbian Action
    Foundation, 156–157, 166
Augustine, Saint, 111
authenticity of place, 38
autobiographical voice
    in *Aztlán: A Journal of Chicano Studies*, vi
    Barrio Boy, viii
    of Chicano, Latino scholar, x–xi
    in Chicano scholarship, vii–viii
    Córdova, Gilbert Benito, vi–vii
    in non-Chicano scholarship, vii
    in social stories, viii
autobiography, intersection of personal and
    historical in, viii, ix–x
autobiography studies
    current trends, 102 n26–103n26
    poststructuralist critiques, 102 n26–
    103n26
    structuralist critiques, 102 n26–103n26
Awatovi (Hopi site), 7
Aztecs
    blood sport among, 112
    effect of Spanish brutality on, 118
    gladiatorial sacrifice among, 112
    relationship with maguey, 20–21
Aztlán: A Journal of Chicano Studies, v–vi
Azul, Joey, **196, 198**

B
Baca, Elena, 178–179
Balinese cockfighting, 117, 122, 130, 136 n8
Bali shadow puppet theater, 10

Bancroft, Hubert H, 42
Barraza, Santa C., ix
Barrera, Mario, 59
Barrio Boy (Galarza), 48, 73, 80
Basques, 66
Becker, A. I., 10
Beltrán, Lola, 29
*Beyond the Cinema of the Other or Toward
    Another Cinema*, 33
black male expression, 120
blacks, racism towards, 209 n2
Bladerunner (film), 205, 206
blood sport, 111, 112
borderlands
    Chicana metaphor, 21
    concept of identity, 21, 100 n19–101 n20
    cultural space, 51, 101
    paradigm, 51
    South Texas, 21
"borderlessness," 121
borders, changing concept of, 121
border, U.S.-Mexico
    concept of, 121
    crossing, 29, 58, 60, 100
    cultural center of Mexicanness, 121
    Mexicans on both sides of, 121
    as symbol, 59, 70, 97, 121
braceros, Mexican, 125
The Bravo Group, N.Y., 217
Brincando el charco (film), 33–35, 37
Buenas Amigas, Las, 169
Bufa, La (mountain), 65, 66, 68, 85, 104
"butch" masculinity, 161–162

C
Cabeza de Vaca, Álvar Nuñez, 100 n18
cacicazgo
    hacienda society and, 85
    Madero Revolution and, 86
caciquismo, identification with hacienda
    system, 51
California
    class, gender contradictions, 45
    early Mexican American autobiography
    in, 45, 47, 60
    hacienda life in Mexican, 47, 63, 104
    labor unrest, 62
    Lopez, Alma, childhood in, 177–178
    misconceptions about, 201–203, 203
    Our Lady (Lopez) in, 179–180
    pre-1848 "alta," 45
    racism, 195
    stereotypes of, 203, 204, 209

U.S. annexation of, 45
Virgen de Guadalupe in, 177–178
California (Hispano) texts, 60
California (Mexican) society, pre-1848, 47
Californian stereotyped, 201–202
California *testimonios,* 48, 91, 99 n14, 104
n32
Californio narratives, 90
Cantú, Lionel, 119
Casas, Pancho, 94
Cash, Johnny, 28
Castellanos, Mari, 150, 153
Castilla, Margarita
conmoción, 167
esto no tiene nombre, 148–149, 150, 152,
154–156
relationship with tatiana de la tierra,
164–165, 166, 167, 172
Castor Advertising, NY, 217, 220
Catholic attitudes towards our Lady (Lopez),
183, 185
Catholic Church
de la Cruz, Sor Juana Inés, 185 n2
Lopez, Alma *respuesta* to, 10
sexual misconduct, 185–186
Catholicism
Chicanas, 181, 182
patriarchal authority, 181–182
Cerro de la Bufa, 65. *see also* La Bufa
(mountain)
Cervantes, Trinidad, 84
Chicago Resource Center, 166
Chicana artists
in *esto no tiene nombre: revista lesbianas
latinas en Miami,* 161
exhbited in *CyberArte Meets Technology,*
178–179
Lopez, Alma, 177–193
portrayal of the Virgen, 181–182
Chicana feminist writing
Chicano/Mexicano patriarchy in, 48
in *esto no tiene nombre, revista lesbianas
latinas en Miami,* 160
on history, culture, 97 n7
ideological contradictions in, 98 n7
Mexican homeland in, 97 n7
Chicana Lesbians (Trujillo), 144
Chicanas
connections to the Virgen, 181
faith, 181, 182
identity struggles, 21
images, 178, 2178
invisibility, 178

Nepantla as space of, 21
position in patriarchal society, 97
Chicano
as distinctive language and culture, 101
n20
Jerry Garcia as, 135
Chicano art
gothic, 8–10
Los Angeles, 9–10
themes, 8–10
transformative nature of, 9
Chicano artists, 8
Chicano cinema, 25
Chicano family history, 48
Chicano historical studies, 83, 98 n12–99
n12
Chicano literary studies, 83
Chicano literary theory, 97 n2
Chicano literature, 41
Chicano masculinity compared to Latin
American masculinity, 119
Chicano Men and Masculinity (Baca Zinn),
118–119
Chicano/Mexicano patriarchy, in Chicana
writing, 48
Chicano renunciation of Mexican history,
52–53–54
Chicano resistance, *corrido* as, 25
Chicanos in Pacific Northwest, 109–139
"Chicano voice," vi
Chichimeca Indians, 57, 66
chismes, 5
cinema. *see* film
cinema of the other, 36
City of Quartz (Davis), 205, 206
class. *see also* lower class; middle class; upper
class
alliances in 19th Century, 36
biases, 56
conflicts in *Memorias* (Róbles Pérez), 36
in Róbles family narrative, 36
class and gender discourses in California
testimonios, 48
class conflict in Mexican hacienda society,
42, 89
class contradictions in Mexican hacienda
society, 45
class privileges in Los Angeles, 36
Coahuila (State of), 86
cockfighting, British, 110, 113
cockfighting in American Southwest, 115
cockfighting in Bali, 115–116, 130

cockfighting in the Pacific Northwest. *see also* Mexican American cockfighting, cockfighting in the United States
  Anglo participation in, 115, 126
  British, 110
  concept of cultural borders in, 121
  early, 115
  effect of Mexican immigration on, 126
  gaff in, 115
  Mexican contrasted with Mexican American, 120
  Mexican dominance in, 110, 130, 136 n2
  place in Mexican American world of, 121
  relation to U.S.-Mexico border region, 120
  resources on, 110, 136 n2
cockfighting in the United States. *see also* cockfighting in the Pacific Northwest; Mexican American cockfighting
  Anglo participation in, 126
  legal history of, 115
  objections to, 115
  origins of, 114
cockfighting in Venezuela, 113
cockfighting, Saint Augustine on, 111
cockfighting, Spanish, 113
cockpit in cockfighting, 117
cocks
  fighting (*see* fighting cocks)
  men's relationship with, 122
Cocks and Bulls in Caracas (Briceño), 113
Colombia media, tatiana de la tierra in, 158–159
colonialism
  concept, 37
  effects, 38
  legacy, 56
colonialism, Anglo American
  Mexican social elite and, 45
  social erasure by, 64
colonial *vs.* "colonial," 100 n17
Colors (film), 205, 206
communal vision of hacienda society, 70
community
  creation, 35
  and homelessness, 35
Community Arts Movement (Los Angeles), 207
Compañeras (Ramos), 144
Concepción, Amy, 165, 166
concept of self, 3, 203
Conill Advertising, N.Y., 217
Conill, Alicia, 217

conmoción (periodical)
  activism in, 167–168
  creation of, 166–167
  decline of, 171–172
  distribution of, 172–173
  erótica in, 167–168
  La esquina de Erotiza Memaz, 169
  first edition, 167–169, **168**
  interaction with Latina lesbians, 167, 171
  Latina lesbian writers' web, 167
  national editorial advisory board, 166–167
  second edition, 169
  third edition, 169–171, **170**
Connell, R. W., 119
Constitutionalist forces, 84
Contacto (TV show), 158
Contreras, Frances, 20
corridos
  and Chicano resistance, 25
  contrast with Anglos, Cubanos, 26
  In Miami, 26
corridos
  Gabino Barrera y 11 Exitos Más (album cover), **27**
Council of the Indies, 66
country and western music, 28
creativity, connection with spirituality, 7
Cruz, Vanessa
  and *esto no tiene nombre: revista de lesbianas latinas en Miami*, 150, 151, 154–155
  Hurricane Andrew effects on, 164–165
  nutritionist in Miami, 174
  as a writer, 155
Cuba, cockfighting in, 113–114
Cubans
  members of Las Salamandras de Ambiente, 143
  in U.S. Hispanic marketing industry, 220
Cuéntame, una charla anónima (de la tierra), 147, 148, 163–164
cultural authenticity, 50
cultural continuity in Mexican American cultural identity, 65
cultural dislocation, 6
cultural identity. *see also* identity
  under Anglo American sociocultural domination, 59, 60, 90
  art and establishment of, 3
  Bali shadow puppet show and, 10
  cockfighting and, 121, 134
  establishment of, 2–3

in *Hunger of Memory: The Education of Richard Rodriguez* (Rivera), 10, 90
Mexican Americans, 2
Mexican autobiography in creation of, 10, 90
nostalgic recuperation of, 65, 83
specific sense of self, 3
cultural production, 216, 221. *see also* U.S. Hispanic marketing
Puerto Rico's marketing industry, 216
culture, meaning of, 128
culture industries, 212, 213, 214, 224
Cyber Arte: Tradition Meets Technology (exhibition), 178–179

D
Dávila, Arlene, 213–214, 217, 219, 222
Davis, Mike, 205, 206
TheDay of the Locust, The (West), 116–117
deculturalization, Mexican American cockfighting as resistance to, 110
Deep Play: Notes on the Balinese Cockfight (Geertz), 115
de la Cruz, Sor Juana Inez, 178, 185 n2
de la tierra, tatiana
alienation from Anglo lesbian groups, 144
alliance with women of color, 144
Colombian consulate demonstration, in 158–159
in Colombian media, 158–159
Coral Gables, 158
conflict with Las Salamandres de Ambiente, 147–152
on *Contacto* (TV show), 158
distribution, 172–173
esto no tiene nombre: revista de lesbianas latinas en Miami, incorporation of, 154
esto no tiene nombre: revista de lesbianas latinas en Miami, marketing, 157–159
experience with conmocíon, 174
growth as writer, 155
Hurricane Andrew, 164–165
librarian at the University of Buffalo, 174, 175 n5
as pornographer, 175 n2
relationship with Margarita Castilla, 164–165
Delaware, misconceptions about, 201–203
del Castillo, Adelaida, 120
de Lourdes, Maria, 29
demons, 10
De Ordine (Augustine, Saint), 111
Depression-era conditions, 60–61

descalzo, 57–58
in *Memorias,* 56–57, 59
Róbles Pérez, Francisco as, 57–59
dialectical analysis in Mexican American autobiographies, 97 n2
Díaz de Castillo, Bernardo, 70
discrimination, "resistance masculinity" as response to, 133
diversity, 203–209
Divine Comedy (Dante), 6
Doctorow, E.L., 84
dominant ideology and popular culture, 205, 206, 209 n1
Don Quixote (Cervantes), 2–3
"double consciousness," 59
double "self," concept of (DuBois), 59
duality
in Chicano art, 8
of female selves, 21
Dueling Machos: Masculinity and Sport in Mexican Baseball (Klein), 118
Durango (Benavidez), 2

E
East Coast, misconceptions about, 201–203
East Los Angeles, 195
Ehecatl-Quetzalcoatl, 20
Einfulung, Theory of, 3
El luto humano (Revueltas), 51
El Rancho de Agua Fresca, 123
El regalo (Restrepo), 163
emigration, Mexican to U.S., 59, 71, 73
England, introduction of cockfighting from, 110–112
English language
as assimilation tool, 134
contrasted with Spanish, 6
in *esto no tiene nombre,* 160–161
used at home, 6
Escondido Center for the Arts Museum, 196
esto no tiene nombre: revista de lesbianas latinas en Miami
Castellanos, Mari, 153
censorship concerns, 148
Chicana feminist writing in, 160
core group, 148–149, 150
covers, **146,** 161, **162**
decline of, 164–167
distribution, 172–173
editorial committee, 150
editorial conflict, 145, 147, 148, 150–151
editorial policies, 150–151, 155
English language in, 160–161, 161

en nuestras mentes (on our minds), 153
fear of lesbophobia, 147
first issue, 144
funding, 156
general observations, 160–164
incorporation, 154–155
Lambda Community Center of Greater
   Miami, Inc., 154
Latina lesbians, 150
lesbian sexuality, 148
marketing, 157–158, 157–159
morality conflict, 150
as national lesbian publication, 152
Newsletter Committee Document, 150
Puerto Ricans, 160–161
Las Salamandras de Ambiente, conflict
   with, 147–154
second issue, 147–148
sexual vocabulary in, 153
Spanglish in, 161
third edition, 152
ethnicity, 211–229
ethnic Mexican, definition of, 136 n1
ethnography
   ethnicity in culture industries, 213, 224
   fieldwork, 211–212
   globalization challenges to, 211
   problems of access, 212, 214
   researcher self in, 213, 224
   "situated knowledges," 212
   women scholars in, 212
Exposito, Daisy, 217

F
family secrets, role in autobiographical
   impulse, 91
Faulkner, William, 52, 53, 54
The Feathered Warrior (cockfighting
   magazine), 123
female selves, duality of, 21
Fernandes, Castor, 217
field, as space of ethnographic work, 211–
   212, 225 n2
fieldwork, 211–212
fighting cocks. *see also* gamecocks
   Mexican male devotion to, 109
   physical interaction between men and,
   116
   as political symbol, 114
   psychological identification with, 109
   treatment of, 113, 122–123
film
   as attempt to return home, 35

Los Angeles, 202
   minority access to, 25
   nature of, 34
foundational narratives, 41, 47–48. *see also*
   Mexican American autobiographies
*Framing Blackness: The African American
   Image in Film* (Guerrero), 203–204
Frankenstein (Shelley), 9, 10
Fuentes, Carlos, 51, 52
The Funding Exchange's Out, A Fund for
   Lesbian and Gay Liberation, 166

G
gachupin, 56, 57
gaff in cockfights, 115
   American, 127
   British origin of, 113, 115
   used by R. Garcia (uncle of Jerry), 125
galleros, 128, 131, 132. *see also* gamecock
   handlers
gallo, 116. *see also* fighting cocks; gamecocks
gamecock handlers
   attitudes of, 117, 128
   description of, 136 n3
   Garcia, R (father of Jerry Garcia), 132
   Garcia, R (uncle of Jerry Garcia), 125–
   126, 132
   as male roles, 117
   relationship with gamecocks, 132–133
gamecocks, 116, 123, 132–133. *see also*
   fighting cocks
Garcia, Jerry
   as Chicano, 135
   childhood exposure to cockfighting, 128–
   129
   as cockfight observer, 122–123
García Márquez, Gabriel, 52
García, Rebecca, 163
Garcia, R. (father of Jerry Garcia)
   as active cockfighter, 136 n4
   childhood in Mexico, 123, 125
   cockfighting life, 122–125, 129
   in cockfighting world, 124
   contrast of cockfighting to working life,
   123, 124
   as handler, 123–124, 132
   and his first car, **122**
   introduction to cockfighting, 126
   life in Texas, 123
   migration to Northwest, 124
   racial discrimination in Texas, 124
   recognition as cockfighter, 123, 124

status derived from cockfighting, 122–123, 127, 129, 134
transition from gaffs to knives in cockfights, 127
Garcia, R. (uncle of Jerry Garcia)
as active cockfighter, 136 n4
childhood in Mexico, 125
as cock breeder and handler, 125–126
cockfighting life, 122, 123, 125
contrast of cockfighting to working life, 123, 124
Monterrey, Mexico, 125
status in cockfighting world, 122–123, 127, 134
transition from gaffs to knives in cockfights, 125
Geenty, Brian, 154, 172
gender
conflicts in *Memorias* (Róbles Pérez), 89
contradictions in Mexican hacienda society, 45
discourses in California testimonios, 48
disparity, 221
displays, 128, 132, 134
in domination, 120
ethnography, 212
male identities, 119
Mexican hacienda society, 42, 83, 89
genealogy
ideological content in, 50
self-invention in, 70
as tool of continuity, 65
geographical biases, 202–203
global culture industries, 212, 214, 224
globalization, x, 211
global marketing, hierarchical organization of, 224–225
Gómez, José Míguel, 114
Gómez-Quiñones, Juan, 128
"Great Migration" of 1900-1930, 50
Grit and Steel (cockfighting magazine), 123
Guerrero, Ed, 203–204
Gutiérrez, David G., 59–60
Gutiérrez, Ramón, 98 n12–99 n12

H
Haas, Lisabeth, 61
hacendados, 55
hacienda. *see* Mexican hacienda society; Mexican hacienda system; Porfirian hacienda economy
hacienda (rancho) system in Southwest, 51, 57

"hacienda syndrome," 47, 90, 97 n6
hacienda system, land displacement, 59–60
Haciendo Caras (Anzaldúa), 207–208
Hall, Stuart, 209 n2
hallucinatory expression, 15–18
Herrera family, 99 n15–100 n15
Herrera Pérez, Concepción, 54–55, 100 n15
Herrera Pérez, María, 80
herstory, 141, 144, 175 n3
Hispanic-Anglo dichotomy in U.S. Hispanic Marketing, 223
Hispanics
anglo marketer attitudes towards, 217–218
description, 217–218
as market, 217
as marketers, 217
Hispano-centric mores, 56
historical literary scholarship and oral narratives, 48
historical memory, 52
history, Faulkner's concept of, 54
hogar, maguey as symbol of, 20
Hombres y Machos (Mirandé), 118
home
cinema as attempt to return, 35, 37
maguey as symbol of, 20
problem of, 34–35
women and, 35, 37
Homeless Diaries (1995), 33, 35
homelessness, 35
homoeroticism, in cockfighting, 116
homophobia among Mexican men, 117
homosexuals in Puerto Rico, 35
homosociality in cockfighting, 116
"hoodrats," 178
Hopi culture, 7–8
Hotel Senator (exhibition), 9–10
house of the national, 37
huérfanos, early autobiographers as, 91–92. *see also* orphanhood
Huerta, Dolores, 178
Huerta, Victoriano, 85
Hunger of Memory: The Education of Richard Rodgriguez (Rodriguez), 52
Hurricane Andrew, 164–165

I
identity. *see also* cultural identity; Latino/a identity; Mexican American cultural identity; Mexican identity
background, 53
bicultural, 101
black racism in Anglo concepts of, 209

and cockfighting, 114, 120, 134
in *conmoción*, 169, 171
construction of U.S. Latino/a, 216
deconstructing, 224
disruption of, 45
in the face of orphanhood, 60
knowledge of, 10
maguey as symbol of, 20
marketing construction of Latino/a, 226
negotiating in lesbian spaces, 144
and orphanhood, 10
Puerto Rican *vs.* Latina, 222
racism in, 209 n2
ideological contradictions
in Chicana/feminist writing, 98
Róbles family, 42
Ideologies of the Self: Chicano Autobiography
(Saldívar), 96 n1
immigrant community, 64
immigrant narrative, *Memorias as,* 59
immigration
from 1900 to 1930, 59–60
during Mexican Revolution, 59–60
as origin of "double consciousness," 59
radio dialogue about, 14
impulse to self-invention, 74
Indians
as "Other" in California testimonios, 104
n32
in Zacatecas hacienda system, 66–67
indígenas, 21, 66–67
indigenous peoples of Mexico, Positivism´s
effect on, 100 n19
Infante, Pedro, 27
'I Yam What I Yam': *Cooking, Culture and*
Colonialism (Goldman), 96 n1

J
Jerez de la Frontera, Spain, 56, 100 n18
Jerez, Zacatecas, Mexico, 65, 93
Lira Pérez, Juan in, 68, 71, 76
Madero Revolution and, 86
in *Memorias,* 49, 56
during Revolution, 84, 87
Róbles Pérez in, Francisco, 68
Joyce, James, 6

K
Katz Radio Group memo, 218
Kingsville, Texas, 19, 21
knife (in cockfighting)
Mexican, 127
Spanish, 113, 115

L
La Adelita (Hernandez), 178, 185 n3
labor activism, Róbles Pérez, Francisco, 61–62
labor unions, 60–61
labor unrest, 1930s, 62
La Bufa (mountain), 65, 66, 68, 85, 104
Labyrinth of Solitude (Paz), 118
L.A.: Capital of the Third World (Reiff), 198,
204
L.A.: City of the Angels (course), 203–208
La Esquina de Erotiza Memaz (column in *esto*
no tiene nombre), 169
la estupenda esto-peña (the stupendous *esto-*
club), 153
la familia, 5
La Liberación de la Teta (Titty Liberation),
167
Lambda Community Center of Greater
Miami, Inc., 154, 172
land displacement, Porfirian modernization,
59–60
La niña, la puta y la Santa María (Libre de
Marulanda), 161
Lanza, Mario, 70
La Relación, 100 n18
Las Four (Lopez), 178
Las Salamandras de Ambiente
Cuban members of, 143
description of, 142–143
dissent with *esto no tiene nombre,* 147–152
dissolution of, 174
identification with Miami, 143–144
Latina lesbian members of, 153
membership of, 143
as publicly recognized Latina lesbian
organization, 143
rupture with *esto no tiene nombre,* 153–154
L.A. Story (film), 205, 206
Latina as native anthropologist, 213–214
Latina identity, 178
Latina lesbian community, in *esto no tiene*
nombre, 161
Latina lesbian groups, Las Salamandras de
Ambiente, 142–143
Latina lesbian magazines, national, 141–142,
152, 153, 156–157, 166–174
Latina lesbians in Miami, 141–176
Latina lesbian writers' web, 167
Latin American lesbians, 144
Latin American professionals in U.S.
Hispanic marketing industry, 220
Latinas, Miami lesbian
Castilla, Margarita, 143, 148, 149

coming out, 148
compared to Anglo gay community, 143
cultural identification of, 143
Pereira-Pujol, Patricia, 143, 148
"Latin Boom" in U.S. culture, 218
latinidad, 216, 218, 219
Latino/a identity
and ethnographic fieldwork, 213–214
homogenization of, 216, 218
"one and one-half generation," 220–221
Latino culture, stereotypes of, 119
Leal, Luis, 41–42
Lesbian and Gay Community Center, Miami Beach, 143
Lesbian community, Boston, 149
lesbian magazines, Latina. *see* Latina lesbian magazines, national
lesbian relationship with home, 35
lesbian sexuality, 148
lesbians, in Puerto Rico, 35
lesbophobia, 147
Libre de Marulanda, Rosita, 167
linguistic dislocation, 6
Lira Pérez, Juan
alleged rape of Dominga Róbles, 75–76, 89
attitudes toward Mexican Revolution, 56, 78
claims of Spanish ancestry, 56
death of as rupture, 58, 73, 77, 79
Dominga's rape, 47, 76, 80
father of Róbles Pérez, Francisco, 68, 71
in foundational narrative, 73
genealogy, **44**
and ideal of patriarchal society in Mexico, 89
in Jerez, 68, 71
Last Will and Testament, 103 n28
later life, 72
during Mexican Revolution, 78, 81, 84–87, 85, 86–87, 87–88
nostalgic version of, 76, 80, 83, 94
and patriarchal authority, 88–89
in Pérez Róbles family narratives, 47–48
Róbles family view of, 75–77, 79–80, 81, 89
with sons in Jerez, **73**
Lopez, Alma, 177–193
childhood, 177
focus on female images, 178
Las Four, 178
Our Lady at Museum of International Folk Art, 178–179

López de Santa Ana, Antonio (General), and cockfighting, 113
Lord, Audre, 34
Los Angeles
Community Arts Movement, 207
experiences of, 11–13, 204
in film, 202
"imagined community," 203–204
L.A. Rebellion (1992), 206–207
multicultural, 204
myths, 9, 202
rappers, 207
stereotypical assumptions, 201–204
Sunshine/Noir opposition, 205, 206
U.S. Mexicans in, 1, 195
violence against Mexican Americans, 195
Los Angeles freeways, 11
Los de abajo (Azuela), 50
Los Tres Ases, 27
Loving in the War Years (Moraga), 144
lower class
cockfighting, 123, 126
homophobia, 117
los de abajo, 50, 58
in *Memorias* (Róbles Pérez), 72
mestizos, 67
protest masculinity, 118, 120, 128, 132, 135

M
machismo
definitions, 118, 119
dominance over women, 119, 120
in Mexican American cockfighting, 109, 117–118, 121, 127–128
in Mexican family structure in U.S., 128
Paz, Octavio, 118
as resistance to dominant culture, 118–120, 128, 133
machismo/*marianismo* model, 119
Maderistas, 84, 85
Madero, Francisco, 50, 56, 78–79, 80, 84–85
Madero Revolution
end of *cacicazgo,* 85, 86
rural grievances and, 86
and silver mines, 86
in Zacatecas (city of), 84–85
maguey
as icon, 20
in Mexican Revolution, 20
mythology of, 20–21
symbol of home, 20
male dominance, in ethnography, 212

Mama Cash, 166
Manifest Destiny, 203
marginalized status of Mexican Americans, 120
marital decision making, *machismo* and, 119
Martinez, Marion, 178–179
masculine expression, black, 120
masculinity. *see also machismo*
    "butch," 161–162
    as form of domination of women, 120
    Mexican American cockfighting and, 109, 115–120, 121, 127–128, 131–132
    in prehispanic Mexico, 110
    working class as protest, 118–119
Mayahuel, 20
Memorias (Róbles Pérez)
    author's family, 69
    as autobiography, 99 n14
    depression-era conditions, 60–61
    descalzo in, 56–57, 59
    as example of Genaro Padilla's autobiographical model, 42, 56–57, 57–57
    as immigrant narrative, 59, 73
    mediated by author's involvement, 99 n14
    mythologizing, 49, 67
    nostalgia, 47, 56, 92
    racial segregation, 60–61
    as representation of family history, 83
    resistance to cultural evisceration in U.S., 47
    social rupture, 47, 56–57, 78
    transitions, 56–57, 58
    utopian aspects of, 47
Menchú, Rigoberta, 178
Mesoamerica
    ballgame, 112
    blood sport, 110–111, 112
    gladiatorial sacrifice, 112
    introduction of cockfighting to, 110–111, 112
mestizas, 21
mestizo heritage, 56
mestizos, in Zacatecas hacienda system, 67
Metropolitan Community Church, Miami, 143, 150
Mexican albums (recordings), 26, 29
Mexican American, definition of, 135 n1–136 n1
Mexican American autobiographies
    archaeological efforts to recover, 42–43
    as Chicano foundational narratives, 42
    in Chicano literary canon, 45

    contradictions in, 48
    as cultural legacy, 45
    dialectical analysis in, 97 n2
    as distinct genre, 42
    "double consciousness" in early, 59
    fictionality in, 74–75
    as foundational narratives, 41
    "hacienda syndrome" in, 90
    interactions with American identity, 45–47
    and Mexican-American social elites, 45
    as narrative of social rupture, 45
    narrative strategy in, 60
    overview of, 41
    Padilla, Genaro's treatment of, 45, 47, 60, 74
    as products of Mexican-American social elite, 45
    for restoration of integrity, dignity, 45
    and social disruption, 45
    United States Hispanic Autobiography (1988), 41
    unpublished, 41–42
Mexican American cockfighters, socioeconomics of, 126
Mexican American cockfighting. *see also* cockfighting in the Pacific Northwest; cockfighting in the United States
    Chicanos and, 114, 126
    as culturally important tradition, 110
    description, 128–130
    disputes, 131–132
    family attitudes towards, 122–123
    form of liberation, 128–129
    gaffs *vs.* knives, 127
    gambling, 113, 114, 129–131
    history, 111, 112
    homoeroticism, 116
    homosociality, 116
    and identity, 114
    influence of Mexican immigration, 126
    influence of Spanish, 110, 112–113
    knife, transition from gaff to, 127
    legal ramifications, 115, 129
    machismo, 117–118, 121, 127–128
    male-to-male gaze, 116
    masculinity, 109–110, 115–120, 121, 127–128, 131–132
    as men's activity, 113, 116, 117
    as metaphor, 114
    and Mexican culture in U.S., 121, 134
    promotional magazines, 123

as resistance to Anglo dominance, 110, 119, 120
The Rites of Men (Burstyn), 116
rules of engagement, 131
women, 117
Mexican American cultural identity. *see also* cultural identity; identity
  cockfighting as connection to, 120
  cultural continuity in, 65, 134–135
  "resistance masculinity," 120
Mexican American historical consciousness, 52–53, 54
Mexican American history
  genealogical inquiry into, 52
  "Great Migration" of 1900-1930 in, 50
  investigation of early, 52, 98 n11
  Mexican period in Southwest, 51
  military defeat of Mexico in 1848, 50–51
  mythologizing early, 52
  Porfirian hacienda system, 51
  views about inception of, 50
Mexican American literature, nineteenth century, 90
Mexican Americans and "otherness," 120
Mexican Americans in the Pacific Northwest, relation to U.S.-Mexico border region, 120
Mexican American society, in foundational narratives, 47–48
Mexican braceros, 125
Mexican cockfighting, 110, 115. *see also* cockfighting in the Pacific Northwest; cockfighting in the United States; Mexican American cockfighting
Mexican Constitutional convention, 1856, 85
Mexican Consulate, Los Angeles, 60–61
Mexican *corrido* albums (recordings)
  album cover, Gabino Barrera y 11 éxitos más, 27
  post revolutionary masculine ideals in, 27
Mexican creatives, in U.S. Hispanic marketing industry, 220
Mexican cultural identification, criteria of, 133–134
Mexican culture in U.S.
  cockfighting, 121, 128
  masculinity in, 121, 133
  traditional family structure, 128
Mexican emigrants to U.S., socioeconomic origins of early 20th century, 97 n9–98 n9
Mexican hacienda past as myth
  descalzo as prince in disguise, 58

nostalgia, 47, 56, 92
Rulfo, Juan version *vs.* Francisco Róbles Pérez version, 67–68
social empowerment of, 57, 65
suppression of reality, 52, 57, 65
Mexican hacienda society
  class conflict, 42, 83, 88–89
  class contradictions in, 45
  conflictive power relations in, 48
  feudalistic nature, 67, 77, 83, 89
  gender conflicts, 42, 45, 48–49, 83, 88–89
  Lira Pérez, Juan, 56–57, 57–58, 71, 72, 82, 88, 94
  in *Memorias* (Pérez), 42, 45, 55, 58, 65, 67, 93
  in Mexican-American autobiographies, 45, 47
  nostalgic portrayals, 45, 47, 56–57, 65, 67–68, 70–71
Mexican hacienda system. *see also* Porfirian hacienda economy
  caciquismo, identification with, 51
  foundational socioeconomic institution, 50–51
  in *Pedro Páramo* (Rulfo), 89
  in Zacatecas (state of), 66–67
Mexican history
  Porfirista regime, 71, 85, 101 n23–102 n23
  Revolution, 20, 51, 78, 81–82, 84, 87, 97 n9–97 n9, 98 n10, 99 n15
Mexican homeland
  in Chicana feminist writing, 97 n7
  deconstructing, 67–68
  mythologized, 51, 65, 67, 70
  utopian vision of, 48
Mexican homeland mythologized, 51, 67, 70
Mexican identity
  and Chicanos, 52
  cockfighting and, 121
  definition of post-Revolution, 28
Mexican identity in U.S., machismo in, 121
Mexican manliness, compared to roosters', 117
Mexican masculinity and, cockfighting, 117–118, 127–128
Mexican mining, economics of, 66. *see also under* silver mining; Zacatecas (state of)
Mexican patriarchal authority, 88–89, 97 n7
Mexican Revolution
  in 1913, 84
  as cause of emigration, 97 n9–98 n9
  hacienda system as determinant of, 51

impact on Southwest U.S., 99 n15
in Jerez, 78, 81–82
maguey and soldiers, 20
in *Memorias,* 98 n10
in Pérez family accounts, 77, 98 n10
political dissolution (1913–1914), 87
romantic representation of ancestors' role
in, 50
in Torreón, Coahuila, 98 n10
Mexicans
ethnic
marginalization, resistance to, 132
masculinity, forms of, 132
"narratives of dispossession," 45
Mexican (Spanish) colonial mythos, 70
Mexica-Tejanas, 21
Mexico's borders with United States, 53
Mexico, U.S. annexation of Northern, 1848,
48, 59
Miami
corridos in, 26
cultural dislocation in, 27–28
Latina lesbians in, 142
rancheras in, 26
middle class. *see also* class; lower class; upper
class
assimilationist ethos, 53
compared to working class, 119
representatives, 36
U.S. Hispanic marketing to, 219
migrants, relationship with home, 35
minority access to, 25
modernization, during Porfirista regime, 71
Moraga, Cherríe, 167
Morales, Alejandro, 48
Mora, Pat, 21
Moya, José Luis, 84
muerto, 5
Museum of International Folk Art (Santa Fe,
New Mexico), 178–179
museums, 196
My History, Not Yours (Padilla)
as discursive framework for Perez,
Vincent, 90, 96 n1
"hacienda syndrome," 90
nostalgic impulse in, 42, 49
reification in Mexican American
autobiographies, 45, 49
"retrospective narrative habit" discussed
in, 45
rupture in social self-consciousness, 60
as study of Mexican American
autobiographies, 45, 90

transformation of group experience, 50
mythico-religious concepts and maguey
imagery, 20–21
myth of Juan Lira Perez destroyed, 78, 79
mythologizing early Mexican American
history, 51, 52, 57
mythologizing Mexican homeland, 51, 67, 70
myths of Los Angeles, 9, 202

N
Nabakov, Vladimir, 3
narratives of dispossession, 45, 47
narratives of origin critiqued, 51
narrative strategy in Mexican American
autobiographies, 60
Natera, Pánfilo, 84, 85, 87
National Lesbian Action Foundation
(Astraea), 156–157
nativas, duality of, 21
Negrete, Jorge, 27
Negrón-Muntaner, Frances
AIDS in the Barrio (1989), 33
*Brincando el charco: Portrait of a Puerto
Rican (film),* 33, 34
Homeless Diaries (1995), 33
Puerto Rican ID (video), 34
Nepantla, 21
New Ethnicities (Hall), 209 n2
New Yorker Magazine, California Issue
(1998), 209 n1
niña, la puta y la Santa María, La (Libre de
Marulanda), 161
Noriega, Chon
with father, Saturnino, 32
niece and nephew of, 31
with sister, Reni, 30
Noriega, Gavino, 26
Noriega, Saturnino, newspaper article, 28
nostalgia
in narratives of dispossession, 45, 47
in narratives of origin, 50
in nineteenth century texts, 48
and resistance, 49
Róbles family counter to, 42
nostalgic desire, 56–57, 57
nostalgic impulse
in Mexican American autobiographies, 75
Padilla, Genaro's treatment of, 60
nostalgic vision of hacienda society, 64, 70
Nunn, Tey Marianna, curator, *Cyber Arte:
Tradition Meets Technology,* 179–180

O
Oak Park, Illinois, 29
Obejas, Achy, 167
Ochoa, Ruben, with Joey Azul, **196**
off our backs (magazine), 153
"Okie" agricultural workers, 63
Olmec civilization, 112
"one and one-half generation," 220–221
One Hundred Years of Solitude (Márquez), 48, 51
On Our Backs (magazine), 153
Open Meadows Foundation, 157
oral narratives in historical literary
    scholarship, 48
origins in *Pedro Páramo* (Rulfo), 104 n30
orphanhood
    as break with past, 91–92
    and cultural fragmentation, 65
    of early autobiographers, 91–92
    identity in the face of, 60
    in *Memorias* (Róbles Pérez), 56–57
    of Mexican Americans in Mexico, 90
    in *Pedro Páramo* (Rulfo), 104 n30
    Róbles Pérez, Francisco, 70, 82
    as signifier of alienation from Mexico,
        91–92
    as signifier of alienation in U.S., 59
The Other Side/El Otro Lado (Martinez, R),
    205, 206
Our Lady (Lopez)
    Catholic support, 183
    digital print, **179**
    first appearance, 177
    intended meaning vs viewer experience,
        180
    at Museum of International Folk Art,
        178–179
    protests against, 180
    reaction to, 179–180
    Trujillo, Anthony (Deacon), 180
    Villegas, Jose, 180

P
Pachuco a la Vidrio (Ochoa)
    Azul, Joey, **196,** 198
    details, **197**
    guerrilla performance, 196–197
pachucos, 195, 196
Pacific Northwest, racism in, 124. *see also*
    cockfighting in the Pacific Northwest
Padilla, Genaro, 57
    critical, interpretive activity, 42, 45
    and *Memorias*, 42, 96 n1

Mexican-American autobiographies, 45,
    47, 60, 74, 90–91
    and narratives of dispossession, 45, 47
    paradigm, 42, 45, 47, 59
    recovery of Mexican-American narrative,
        42, 45
Pancho Villa, 87
Paredes, Américo, 25–26
Pat Mora: Interview (Rebolledo), 96 n1
patriarchal authority
    in Mexican family structure in U.S., 128
    in Mexico, 88–89, 97 n7
patriarchal myth, 55
Paz, Octavio equation of machismo and
    Mexican masculinity, 118
Pedro Páramo (Rulfo), 5, 51, 53
    deconstructing Mexican homeland, 67–
        68
    hacienda system in, 89
    mythologizing Mexican homeland, 67
    origins as central theme in, 104 n30
    orphanhood as central theme, 104 n30
peleas de gallos. see cockfighting in the United
    States, Mexican American cockfighting,
    cockfighting in the Pacific Northwest
Pereira-Pujol, Patricia
    at *conmoción,* 167
    at Florida International University, 174
    graphic artist, 155–156
    Hurricane Andrew effects on, 164–165
    publisher of *esto no tiene nombre,* 155
Pérez, Casimiro, 103 n29–104 n29
Pérez Doran, Esther, 61–62, 63–64, 93–94,
    94, 96 n1
Pérez family history
    Memorias as representation of, 83
    Róbles version, 42
Pérez family narrative, Lira Pérez, Juan in,
    47–48
Pérez Family Tree, **44**
Pérez, Marcos, 103 n29–104 n29
Pérez Róbles, Dominga, 79–80
Pérez Róbles, Dominga, rape of
    charges against Lira Pérez, Juan, 76–77,
        80, 81, 104 n31
    compared to rapes in *Pedro Páramo*
        (Rulfo), 89
    in context of social class, 52, 89
    metaphor in Róbles family narrative, 77
    suppression of in Pérez Róblez family
        narrative, 52, 76
performance art, 9

Personal and historical memories of alta
  California (Vallejo), 45, 91
Philip II of Spain, King, 65
Pídeme tu hambre…en español (Cristina), 161
Pierre Menard (Borges), 3
popular culture relationship to dominant
  ideology, 205, 206, 209 n1
population growth, Mexican, 60
Porfirian hacienda economy. *see also* Mexican
  hacienda system, Mexican hacienda
  society
  feudalistic structure of, 89
  foreign investment in, 101 n23–102 n23
  land displacement, 59–60
  in Pérez journal, 55
  in Róbles family narrative, 47
Porfirista regime
  emigration during, 71
  hacienda society and, 71, 85
  Lira Pérez during, 71
  Zacatecas (state of) during, 71
Positivism, effect on indigenous Mexicans,
  100 n19
pre-Columbian America. *see* Mesoamerica
prejudice, 5, 9
prerevolutionary Mexico
  hacienda life, 45
  in Mexican American memory, 54
  mythologies of, 51
prerevolutionary social conflict, 70
psychoanalytic elements, wedded with
  history, 118
Puerto Rican cinema of the Other, 36, 37
Puerto Rican filmmakers, 33
Puerto Ricans
  in *esto no tiene nombre, revista de lesbianas
    latinas en Miami*, 160–161
  in service industry, 215
  in the United States, 35, 36
  U.S.-born in Puerto Rico, 35
Puerto Rico, excluded groups in, 35–36
Puerto Rico's marketing industry, 216
  access, 215
  characteristics, 214–215
  compared to Mainland, 214–215, 215,
    216
  compared to U.S. Hispanic marketing
    industry, 219
  cultural distinctiveness, 215
  cultural formation, 215
  local cultural production, 216

Q
Quintana, Alvina E., 201–203, 208–209

R
race, Anglo American representation of,
  203–204
race conflict in labor unrest, 1930s, 62
racism
  experiences of, 29, 101 n21
  internalized dominance, 207–208
  in Pacific Northwest, 124
  and segregation, 60–61
  self-hatred induced by, 145
  in Texas, 124
  towards blacks, 209 n2
  U.S. Hispanic Marketing, 223
Ramirez sisters, 49
Ramona (Subcomandante), 178
rancheras, in Miami, 26
ranchers, American, in *Memorias* (Róbles
  Pérez), 60–61
rancho, in Mexican American memory, 54
Rancho Sespe, 55, 62–64, 93, 104 n33. *see
  also* Sespe Village; Spalding, Keith
Recovering the United States Hispanic
  Literary Heritage project, 97 n3
*Recuerdos históricos y personales tocante a la alta
  California* (Vallejo), 45, 91
Reed, John, 98 n10
Reiff, David, 198
Relación, La, 100 n18
relationship with home, 35
RESIST, 157
"resistance masculinity"
  and patriarchal notion of masculinity,
    128–129
  as response to discrimination, 133
  and women, 120
"retrospective narrative habit," 45
Revolution in 1913, 84
Revueltas, José, 51, 52
*Richard Rodriguez's Hunger of Memory: The
  Poetics of Experience* (Márquez, A), 96 n1
The Rites of Men, The (Burstyn), 116
Rivera, Tomás, 52–53
Róbles, "Aunt" Isabel "Chavela"
  geneology, **46**, 97 n5
  Pérez-Róbles family conflict at funeral of,
    42, 73, 75, 77, 82
Róbles, Berta, 76, 79, 88, 91, 103 n27
Róbles de Pérez, Juliana
  in Róbles family narrative, 79, 81, 82,
    100 n15, 102 n24

in Róbles Pérez family narratives, 56, 57,
79–80, 100 n15, 102 n24
Róbles Doran, Esther, 79–80
Róbles family narrative
attitudes toward in *Memorias* (Róbles
Pérez), 102 n24
as contradiction to notion of
orphanhood, 59
as contradiction to notion of Porfirian
hacienda society, 59
as contradiction to Pérez narrative, 47,
83, 88
Lira Pérez, Juan in, 47–48
narrative, 42
Porfirian hacienda economy in, 47
social contradictions in, 83
women's narratives in, 47
Róbles family tree, 46
Róbles Macías, Hipólita, 46, 69, 93
Róbles Pérez family tree, 46
Róbles Pérez, Francisco
and Anglo American sociocultural
regime, 70–71
attitudes toward Róbles forbears, 102 n24
attitude towards Díaz, Porfirio, 102 n24,
102 n25
awareness of Róbles complaints, 104 n31
as bicultural, 100 n19
childhood, 42, 55
childhood home of, 68
with children Esther and Juan (1931), **43**
disappearance of, 92–93
emigration document, **43**
emigration to the United States, 42, 55
family of, 69
Herrera family importance to, 99 n15–
100 n15
on his autobiography, 54
as labor activist, 61–62
as Mexican immigrant laborer, 42, 47, 55,
56, 58–59, 60, 61–62, 63
mythologizing early Mexican American
history, 64
mythologizing Mexican homeland, 65,
66, 67
parallels to Juan Rulfo's life, 104 n30
relationship with father, 68, 71
use of nostalgia, 47
rock 'n roll, 28
Rodriguez, Richard, 52–53
Romano, Octavio, 180
Rulfo, Juan
critique of hacienda myths, 51

exploration of historical memory, 51, 52
mythic hacienda portrait compared to
Francisco Róbles Perez's, 67–68
parallels to life of Róbles Pérez, Francisco,
104 n30
rupture, sociocultural. *see* sociocultural
rupture

S
sabung (cock) as metaphor, 117
salamander as lesbian symbol, 143
Saldivar, José David, 97 n2
Saldivar, Ramón, 73, 97 n2
Sánchez, Robert F. (Archbishop), 185 n4–
186 n4
Sánchez, Rosaura, 48, 90, 91, 99 n14
San Juan CinemaFest (1995), 33
San Juan de las Calabasas (Mexico), 68, 93
San Louis Potosí (State of), 86
San Luis Capistrano, California, 61
Santa Ana, California, 61
Santa Ana Pérez, 56
Santa Paula, California, labor strife at, 63
Sedeño, Pedro Romero, 180
The Self as Cultural Metaphor (Padilla), 96 n1
self in ethnographic research, 213
self-invention
in foundational Mexican American
narratives, 91
in genealogy, 70
impulse to, 74
self-loathing, 9
Sespe Ranch, 55, 62–64, 93, 104 n33. *see also*
Spalding, Keith
Sespe Village, 55, 63. *see also* Spalding, Keith
setter (setter-to), 136 n3
Sheehan, Michael J. (Archbishop), 180, 182,
185–186
She (Mendoza), 161–162
*Shot in America: Television, the State, and the
Rise of Chicano Cinema* (Noriega), 25–26
Siete Partidas, 88–89
silver aristocracy, 66
silver mines, Madero Revolution and, 86
silver mining, 65
social transformation and introduction of
cockfighting, 112–113
sociocultural rupture
autobiographical expression of, 45
border crossing as symbol, 59, 70
death of Lira Pérez as moment of, 58, 79
in *Memorias*, 78
nostalgia as response to, 45, 48, 70, 75

United States-Mexican War of 1846–1848 as cause, 45
Solis, Javier, 27
Southern California, racism in, 195
South Texas, 19–21, 21
Southwest. *see* American Southwest
Spain, introduction of cockfighting by, 110–111, 112
Spalding family, 55, 93. *see also* Rancho Sespe; Spalding, Keith
Spalding, Keith, 55, 63, 64, 101 n22. *see also* Rancho Sespe; Sespe Village
Spanglish, in *esto no tiene nombre, revista de latinas lesbianas en Miami,* 161
Spanish-American War, 38
Spanish ancestry, 56
Spanish Colonial history, 65, 70
Spanish Colonial mythos, 70
Spanish Conquest, 57
and introduction of cockfighting, 110–112
Spanish language
as basis of *latinidad,* 216, 218
contrasted with English, 6
as cultural criterion, 133
Latino/a identity, 222
use at home, 2, 6
as used by immigrants, 134
U.S. Hispanic marketing industry, 220
spirituality, connection with creativity, 7
The Splendid Little War (film), 38
Sunshine/Noir opposition, 205, 206

T
Tarascans, 57
Tejas. see Texas
television, minority access to, 25
Telling Identities: The California *Testimonios* (Sánchez), 90–91, 96 n1
testimonios
California, 91
compared to autobiography, 98 n14
Texas
as home, 19–20, 20, 98 n11
Mexican hacienda society in, 98
Mexican immigrant experience in, 123
Mexican period in, 98 n11
Texas, South, 19–21
Third Lesbian-Feminist Latin American and Caribbean Encuentro, 164–165
This Bridge Called My Back (Moraga and Anzaldúa), 144
Tlaxcalctecan Indians, 57
Tolusa, Juan, 65

Torreón, Coahuila, 87, 98 n10
Tres Ases, Los, 27
Triana, Martín, 84
Tzitzimime, 20

U
Umpierre, Luzmaría, 167
United Farm Workers, 62
United States, boundaries with Mexico, 53
United States, cockfighting in the. *see* cockfighting in the United States
United States cultural hegemony, impact on Mexican cultural legacy, 48
United States-Mexican War of 1846–1848, 45
University of Delaware, 202, 209 n3
upper class
in California *testimonios,* 48
Lira Pérez as member of Mexican, 58–59
in *Memorias* (Róbles Pérez), 47, 56, 69, 79, 89
Mexican Californian hacienda past, 58
pre-1848 California (Mexico), 47
in Puerto Rico, 215
urban renewal, 203
U.S. annexation of Mexico's northern region, 45
U.S. annexation of Northern Mexico, 1848, as origin of "double consciousness," 59
U.S. defeat of Mexico, 1848, as rupture, 59
U.S. Hispanic marketing
agencies in New York City, 214
agencies in Puerto Rico, 214
Anglo firms in, 219
anglo presence, 220–223
Anglo-Protestant ideal, 223
in corporate America, 219
Cubans, 220
ethnicity and culture as variables in, 213–214, 220
ethnography as validation, 218
gender disparity, 221
Latinos born/raised in U.S. in, 220–221
links with Latin America, 214
marketers as cultural brokers, 222
market segmentation, 211
networking, 220–221
"one and one-half generation," 220–221
Puerto Rico's marketing industry, 214
Puerto Rico's marketing industry compared to U.S. marketing industry, 219
racism, 223
Spanish language in, 220
status in, 221

U.S. Hispanic marketing on mainland
 agencies, 217
 compared to Puerto Rico, 217
U.S. *latinidad*, 214–215
U.S. Latino culture, commodification of,
 213–214
U.S.-Mexican border, "rupture" and, 70
U.S.-Mexicans in Los Angeles, 1
U.S.-Mexico border region, Mexican
 Americans in Pacific Northwest, relation
 to, 120
U.S. Puerto Ricans in Puerto Rico, 35

V
Vallejo family, 45
Vallejo, J.M.S., as orphan, 91–92
Vazquez, Carmen, 167
Venezuela, cockfighting in, 113
Vidal, Gore, 84
Villa, Francisco "Pancho," 56, 98 n10
 as romantic legend, 50
Villegas, Jose, 180
Virgen de Guadalupe
 as contemporary Latina, 180, 181
 male reaction to, 183
 perceptions of, 182
 portrayed by Chicana artists, 181, 182
 in public art, 181
 ubiquity of, 177, 180, 181
Virgin of Guadalupe, 20

W
warrior class in preshispanic Mexico, 112
wayang kulit, 10
"The White Cube," 196
white flight, 203
whiteness, simulation of, 9
whites, attitudes towards, 8
Why Cocks Fight (Wucker), 114
Williams, Hank, 28
witchcraft and maguey, 20
women
 attitudes of young men towards, 178
 ethnographers, 212
 and masculine domination, 120, 128–129
 status in 19th Century Mexico, 88–89
Women's Community Center, Boston, 149
women's narratives, in Róbles family
 narrative, 47

X
Xipe Totec, 195, 198

Z
Zacatecas (city of)
 history, 65, 66
 mythic version, 66
 siege of, 87
 silver mines, 57, 65, 66, 84–85
Zacatecas (state of), 56–57
 as embodiment of Mexican national
 character, 65
 Madero Revolution in, 84–86
 as mythic homeland, 64
 during Porfirista regime, 71
 silver mining in, 57, 65, 66
Zoot Suit Riots, 195

UCLA Chicano Studies Research Center Press

The First and Only Press Devoted Exclusively to Chicano Studies

TITLE	PRICE	COPIES	TOTAL
I Am Aztlán: The Personal Essay in Chicano Studies	$19.95		
The Chicano Studies Reader: An Anthology of Aztlán 1970-2000	$19.95		
Las Obreras: Chicana Politics of Work and Family	$19.95		
Shipping	$4 for first book, $1 for each after		
Sales Tax for California Residents	8.25 %		

Name _____

University _____

Address _____

City _____

State _____ Zip _____ Country _____

Enclosed is a check for $ _____ made payable to "UC Regents." Checks must be in U.S. funds drawn on a U.S. bank.

Please charge my   ☐ Mastercard   ☐ Visa   ☐ Discover

Account number: _____ – _____ – _____

Exp. Date: _____ – _____

Name on card: _____

Telephone: _____

Signature: _____

Inquiries should be directed to
Tel: 310-825-2642
Fax: 310-206-1784
E-mail: press@chicano.ucla.edu
Web: www.chicano.ucla.edu

SEND ALL ORDERS TO:
Lisa Liang, Business Manager
UCLA Chicano Studies Research Center Press
193 Haines Hall
Los Angeles, CA 90095-1544